On Humour

For Lucy with love

On Humour

Its Nature and Its Place in Modern Society

Michael Mulkay

Polity Press

First published 1988 by Polity Press
in association with Basil Blackwell.

Editorial Office:
Polity Press, Dales Brewery, Gwydir Street,
Cambridge CB1 2LJ, UK

Basil Blackwell Ltd
108 Cowley Road, Oxford OX4 1JF, UK

Basil Blackwell Inc.
432 Park Avenue South, Suite 1503,
New York, NY 10016, USA

British Library Cataloguing in Publication Data

Mulkay, Michael, 1936–
On humour: its nature and its place in modern society.
1. Man. Humour – Sociological perspectives
I. Title
302.5

ISBN 0–7456–0543–5

Library of Congress Cataloging in Publication Data

Mulkay, M. J. (Michael Joseph), 1936–
On humor/Michael Mulkay.
p. cm.
Includes index.
ISBN 0–7456–0543–5 (B. Blackwell)
1. Wit and humor — Social aspects. 2. Laughter (Psychology)
I. Title
PN6149.S62M85 1988
302.2 — dc 19

Typeset in 10 on 12 pt Plantin
by Opus, Oxford
Printed in Great Britain by T. J. Press Ltd, Padstow, Cornwall

Perhaps the mission of those who love mankind is to make people laugh at truth, *to make truth laugh*, because the only truth lies in learning to free ourselves from insane passion for the truth.

Umberto Eco, *The Name of the Rose*

Contents

Acknowledgements

I offer thanks to Brian Berriman, Anna Cornhill, Madeleine Walker and Jo Riding and her daughters for helping me to collect examples of humour as it occurs in natural settings; to Jonathan Potter and Steve Yearley for reading and commenting helpfully on the first draft of chapters 1 to 6 of this book; and to all (well, almost all) of the students at the University of York who have taken my course 'Analysing Humour' for their enthusiasm, their bright ideas and their stimulating project work. Most of all I thank my wife, Lucy, not only for typing the manuscript, and then retyping it without complaint, but also for her continued companionship and support.

I am grateful to Nick Garland for allowing me to reproduce his cartoon 'Whoops' (p. 200), which appeared in the *Independent* of Thursday 15 January 1987; to Christine Roche for permission to reproduce two untitled cartoons (pp. 140, 151) from her collection *I'm not a Feminist but . . .*, published by Virago Press, 1985; to Gerald Scarfe for permission to reproduce his cartoon 'Reagun, 1980' (p. 199) from his collection *Gerald Scarfe* published by Thames & Hudson, 1982; to Emanuel Schegloff for permission to quote at length from, and to use the transcription of the joke from, the late Harvey Sacks's 'Some technical considerations of a dirty joke', published in J. Schenkein (ed.), *Studies in the Organization of Conversational Interaction*, Academic Press, 1978; and to Jonathan Lynn and Antony Jay for permission to quote at length from *The Complete Yes Minister*, BBC Publications, 1984.

Introduction

In this book, I offer a sociological view of humour. Although there is a diverse secondary literature on humour, produced in particular by philosophers, psychologists and anthropologists, the subject has received little systematic attention from sociologists. The founding fathers of the discipline, for example, ignore it entirely. This widespread lack of concern on the part of sociologists is surprising. For humour is one of the few basic social phenomena which occur in all groups throughout the course of human history. One possible reason for this neglect is that sociologists have confused the 'non-serious' with the 'trivial'. They may have assumed that humour, because it is by definition outside the domain of the serious, is not worthy of serious investigation. The central theme of my analysis, in contrast, is that the exact opposite is the case. I will show that it is precisely the symbolic separation of humour from the realm of serious action that enables social actors to use humour for serious purposes, and that makes humour an essential area for sociological inquiry. Humour is of interest, not only in its own right, but also because its study helps us better to understand our serious social world.

For several centuries, at least since the time of Thomas Hobbes's *Leviathan* (1651), Western scholars have tried hard to make sense of the phenomenon of humour. In our own century, the writings of Sigmund Freud (1905) and Henri Bergson (1911) have been regarded as particularly noteworthy. Even today, their venerable accounts of the mechanisms of jokes and laughter are regularly used as the starting point for further study. This is not to say, however, that their ideas have been generally accepted – far from it. In fact, there is remarkably little acknowledged agreement about the nature of humour. Consequently, it has come to be almost customary for each new contributor to the literature to review the major theories of bygone days before presenting his own.

I have not adopted that approach in this book. (For an excellent review of this kind, see Paulos, 1980.) I have tried to avoid discussion of disembodied 'theories of humour' and to concentrate instead on careful examination, in depth, of people's actual humorous conduct. I do not mean to imply by this that my analysis is free of theoretical preconception or that the empirical material I shall consider can in any way speak for itself. I take for granted that the analytical meaning of the data employed in the following chapters is being actively created in the present text and recreated in your reading of it (Mulkay, 1985). Thus, I do not claim that my approach to the study of humour is necessarily better than other approaches that might be, or that have been, adopted. The justification for my strategy is simply that I prefer to formulate my sociology of humour whilst immersing my reader and myself as deeply as possible in the recorded traces of humorous interaction.

My aim has been to present a systematic analysis of the part played by humour in the social life of advanced industrial societies. In so doing, I have looked in some detail at spoken jokes, written jokes, 'dirty jokes', innocent jokes, adolescent humour, feminist cartoons, political cartoons, dinner table wit, joking relationships, bar room humour, ceremonial humour, graffiti, situation comedies, teasing and laughter. Despite my best efforts, however, it has proved impossible, in one comparatively short volume, to cover this broad subject in full. Consequently, certain important topics have been excluded or have been considered only in passing. For example, I have not examined ethnic humour at all (see Davies, 1988); nor have I dealt with practical jokes (see Fry, 1963), nor, apart from situation comedy, with the various forms of comic drama. Although I have included and discussed cartoons in two chapters, the main emphasis of the text is upon verbal, rather than visual, humour. Furthermore, I have based my discussion almost exclusively on humour occurring in the United States and Britain within the last two decades or so. The data used in subsequent chapters have been chosen to represent these two countries more or less equally. I have assumed that the social organization of humour is likely to be fundamentally the same in the other industrial nations as it is in these two societies. (For an excellent cross-cultural review of the anthropological literature on humour in preliterate societies, see Apte, 1985.)

I do not imagine that what I have to say here will be the last sociological word on humour. Indeed, I will be disappointed if this book does not help to stimulate a more active interest in humour among sociologists and others. For I have tried to provide a coherent and wide-ranging analysis that will furnish an organized frame of reference for further research into, and further informed speculation about, the social dynamics of humour and the interplay of humorous and serious conduct in every field of social activity. There have, of course, been occasional attempts in the past to develop a broad sociological overview of humour (see Fry, 1963; Hertzler, 1970). But these texts have not given rise to a cumulative tradition of sociological research. As a result, the various empirical studies of humour that have been carried out by sociologists have remained fragmentary and uncoordinated. In the chapters which follow, I examine a number of the most successful of these studies and try to reveal their analytical significance more fully by weaving their authors' observations into my own overall design. In so doing, I do not hesitate, wherever necessary, to reject or modify the original researchers' conclusions. But revisions of this kind are always based upon a careful re-examination of the evidence and are often linked to consideration of additional material of my own.

This book, then, offers a general, empirically based sociology of humour. But such a description of its content is deceptively simple. For, as most readers will know, there are many available sociologies; and some readers may be inclined to ask: 'What *kind* of sociology are we to expect?' The only answer I can give to this question is that it is not any kind of sociology that I can name. To put this more positively, my policy is to draw freely upon, and to incorporate into my argument, any study that seems to convey something interesting about the social character of humour, whether it employs the framework of functional analysis, the assumptions of symbolic interactionism, the methods of conversation analysis, or the resources of any other sociological perspective. Humour, it seems to me, is too rich, too varied and too complex to be confined within the narrow limits of any single sociological school. Indeed, no single discipline can cope adequately with humour. Consequently, I also try to integrate parts of the non-sociological literature into my analysis. In other words, I assume that we have more to gain than to lose by approaching this largely uncharted territory in a spirit of tolerant, yet rigorous, eclecticism.

The first half of the book provides a close examination of the dynamics of humorous interchange in small-scale social settings and an account of the basic features of humorous conduct. The second half deals with the part played by humour in society at large. Chapter 1 presents a detailed analysis of humorous exchange among a group of American adolescent males. This analysis enables me to convey directly how humour is organized in fine detail and to establish that humorous and serious conduct differ in certain fundamental respects. In the second chapter, the organizing principles of the serious mode and the humorous mode are discussed more fully. I argue that in the serious realm we normally employ a unitary mode of discourse which takes for granted the existence of one real world, and within which ambiguity, inconsistency, contradiction and interpretative diversity are potential problems. In contrast, humour depends on the active creation and display of interpretative multiplicity. When people engage in humour, they are obliged to collaborate in the production of a kind of 'controlled nonsense'. They temporarily inhabit, not a single, coherent world, but a world in which whatever is said and done necessarily has more than one meaning.

In chapters 2 to 5, various implications of this distinction between the serious and the humorous modes are explored, and some of the complexities of humorous interchange in face-to-face settings are examined in depth. In the latter part of the second chapter, psychologists' accounts of the 'mental processing' of humour are discussed and amended in order to allow for the interpretative duality built into humorous discourse. Chapter 3 deals with the semantics of humour and with the ways in which the linguistic resources of the serious domain can be redeployed to create a world of multiple meanings. It also describes how participants signal their adoption of the humorous mode, explains why they may respond seriously in situations where others have signalled their humorous intent, and shows how unintended humour can occur.

In chapter 4 I consider how standardized jokes and informal humour are connected to the surrounding serious discourse, and how informal exchange may generate the kind of transferable humorous packages that we call 'jokes'. Detailed attention is also given to the varied ways in which people employ humour in informal settings. It is shown that participants themselves distinguish between what we may call 'pure humour' and the 'applied humour' that occurs when social actors are taken to be making use of the humorous mode for serious purposes. In chapter 5 several kinds of applied humour are described, and the use of the humorous mode as a resource for accomplishing certain types of difficult interaction is documented in detail. The first half of the book concludes with a discussion of how far laughter should be regarded as part of the sign-language of the humorous mode.

In chapters 7 to 11 I examine how humour is moulded by the larger structures of modern society, and I assess the contribution made by humour both to changing and to maintaining those structures. Chapters 7 and 8 focus upon sexual humour and provide an explanation for the prominence of sexual themes and obscenity within humorous discourse. Chapter 7 deals with the particular interest in sexual humour shown by adolescents of both sexes, and describes how dirty jokes furnish them with an appropriate vehicle for the transmission of useful sexual information. In chapter 8 I turn to adult sexual humour. I argue here that the underlying assumptions of men's sexual humour, and the representation embedded in that humour of the relationships between women and men, give expression to men's domination of women in our society and operate to support and strengthen that domination. I show that, at the structural level, as at the level of direct interaction, the persistent use of particular forms of humour is likely to have serious consequences.

In chapter 9, the relationship between humour and social structure is examined in completely general terms. A major conclusion of this chapter is that humour which occurs within relatively formalized structures is closely linked to contradictions built into those structures, but that in such settings humour is employed in accordance with the requirements of those who occupy the positions of formal control. It appears that humour can be used to challenge existing social patterns, but only in so far as it is given serious meaning by means of criticism and confrontation that is already operative within the serious domain.

This conclusion is confirmed in chapters 10 and 11, which combine an examination of the mass production of humour with an assessment of the contribution made by humour to the sphere of politics. In chapter 10 it is shown that the formal properties of situation comedy require a static rather than a dynamic representation of the political system, that the political sitcom depends on, and nourishes, established political stereotypes, and that, even when sitcom is used to convey a critical political message, this message will be weakened, if not swamped, by the repeated signals of humorous intent that are essential to television comedy. Unlike the political sitcom, political cartoons are clearly sited within the sphere of real political action and their critical connotations are fairly obvious. It may be, therefore, that they do sometimes have a genuine political impact. But political cartoons operate within a wider realm of political language that is organized around the conflict between antagonistic social groupings. Political cartoons are a subordinate part of the oppositional language of politics. They appear overwhelmingly to reflect the existing forms of political life and to reinforce existing divisions within the political community. Thus one broad, overall conclusion of the second half of the book is that, although humour may often appear on the surface to challenge, condemn and disrupt existing social patterns, at a more fundamental level it works to maintain the social structures which give it birth.

The main body of the book, then, consists of a systematic, detailed and empirically documented account of the social character of humour and of its place in society. In the final chapter, however, some of the constraints of empirically based analysis are put aside and I allow myself greater freedom to speculate about certain fundamental aspects of humour and the human condition. I will not summarize these speculations here, except to say that they are as much concerned with serious conduct and serious discourse as with humour. Given the dominant position in our culture of that mode of discourse which we use to create the serious world, it is inevitable that the final significance of humour lies in what it tells us about the serious mode and about the recurrent failure of that unitary form of discourse to cope with the multiple realities which are generated by the basic processes of social life.

1

The Humorous Mode

Humour is an ordinary, everyday activity. There are a few people who claim to have no sense of humour. But the great majority of us have taken an active part in creating humour on countless occasions. We are intimately familiar with its processes and, to varying degrees, we have acquired the craft skills that this form of social intercourse demands. This does not mean, however, that it is easy to provide or to obtain an accurate account of the nature of humour. For example, when comedians or skilled raconteurs are asked how they make people laugh, they tend to reply, not with a serious analysis, but with another joke. The essential problem, I suggest, in talking or writing seriously about humour is that humorous and serious discourse operate according to fundamentally different principles. The attempt to make serious sense of humour is analogous to that of using words to describe pictures. It is without doubt possible, and the enterprise can have important benefits. But there are inherent difficulties and there is a constant danger of misrepresentation.

In the following passage, we can see how the incompatibility of the humorous and the serious modes can create practical problems for the serious analyst.

> As part of research activity, I set myself the assignment of discovering the number of smiles and laughs that came to me during the course of an eight-hour period. The experiment lasted only six of the proposed eight hours . . . I found that I became too self-conscious. I would become aware of an impending smile and prepare to record it. But in my anticipating it, it would fail to appear. I had entered a different mood. The intention of recording the smile contributed to the moment in such a manner as to alter its nature and puncture the humor.
>
> During the six hours of the experiment, I made several attempts to manipulate this self-awareness so that it would no longer present such an operational difficulty. These attempts were, by and large, unsuccessful. (Fry, 1963, pp. 4–5)

Fry's experience suggests that it is extremely difficult, if not impossible, to observe or to analyse humour from the inside; and that thoughtful reflection about humour employs a perspective which is markedly alien to the social practice under investigation. It also confirms my suggestion above that there are problems in using our ability to take part in humour as the basis for an analysis of humour that satisfies the criteria of serious discourse.

In the light of these considerations, I have chosen to begin my own serious exposition with a discussion of an empirical study of humour carried out by Harvey Sacks (1978) which appears to resolve, or at least avoid, Fry's dilemma, by the simple device of first recording humorous interaction as it occurs in a natural setting and then subjecting the transcript of this interaction to systematic and detailed examination. I will show that this approach to the analysis of humour, in which the analyst remains firmly within the serious mode, can be highly informative, and that Sacks succeeds in revealing various features of the social world of humour which are not normally visible 'from the outside'. Sacks's analysis is important because it shows clearly that, although humour is strikingly different from serious conduct, it seems, when seriously observed, very far from being a random, disorderly form of social activity. By starting this book with a discussion of Sacks's 'Some technical considerations of a dirty joke' (1978), I will be able to establish at the outset that the strange world of humour appears to be organized in fine detail and that its internal processes are open, to some degree, to description and analysis in serious terms.

Sacks's study deals with the delivery and reception of a specific, standardized joke on one particular occasion. The phrase 'standardized joke' refers to a linguistic package with more or less stable content which can be passed from person to person for retelling at some other time. The analysis is divided into two main sections. In the first, Sacks attempts to identify the joke's basic structure. The second section deals with the joke's 'dirtiness', with its dissemination and with its place in the wider American culture. In this chapter I will concentrate on Sacks's analysis of the joke's structure. Consideration of its obscene content and its social transmission will be delayed until chapter 7. Sacks's structural analysis of this joke furnishes a series of important observations that apply to standardized jokes in general, whether or not they happen to be dirty. His systematic attention to the detailed organization of a particular joke forces us to look carefully, and seriously, at what actually happens when a joke is told. It thereby helps us to begin to make sense of the special world of humour and to discern its distinctive features. As the chapter proceeds, however, I will use additional material to show that Sacks's analysis, like that of many other observers and theorists of humour, is seriously weakened by his failure to recognize that he is involved in reformulating the events of the humorous realm from the divergent perspective of the serious world.

The transcription which follows is a slightly simplified version of that published by Sacks (1978). This joke was tape- recorded in the 1960s during a conversation among a group of American males in their late teens. The passage begins with the teller inviting his friends to listen to a joke that has been told to him by his twelve-year-old sister.

Sacks's joke

Ken: You wanna hear – My sister told me a story last night.

Roger: I don't wanna hear it. But if you must.

Al: What's purple and an island. Grape Britain. That's what his sister told him.

Ken: *No.* To *stun* me she says uh
There was these three girls and they just got married?

Roger: hhhh-hhh

Al: heh heh heh

Ken: And uh

Roger: Hey waita second. Drag that by again heh.

Ken: There was these three girls. And they were all sisters. And they'd just got married to three *bro*thers.

Roger: You better have a long talk with your sister.

Al: Waita second heh!

Roger: *Oh.* Three *bro*thers.

Ken: And uh, so

Al: The brothers of these sisters.

Ken: No they're *diff*erent you know *diff*erent families.

Roger: That's closer than be*fore* (I think).

Ken: So

Al: hhhh*hah*

Ken: *Qui*et.

Al: [unclear]

Ken: So, first of all, that night they're on their honeymoon the mother-in-law says well why don't you all spend the night here and then you can go on your honeymoon in the morning. The *first* night, the mother walks up to the first door and she hears this '*uu*ooo-ooo-ooo,' the second door is '*HHHOHH*hhh,' third door there's *NO*thin. She stands there for about twenty-five minutes waitin for somethin to happen. *N*othin.

(1.0 second's pause)

Next morning she talks to the first daughter and she says 'How come you – how come you went *YAAAaaa* last night' and the daughter says 'Well it *tick*led, Mommy.' Second girl, 'How come you *screamed*.' '*Oh, Mo*mmy it *hu*rts.' Third girl, walks up to her. 'Why didn't you *say* anything last night.' 'Well *you* told me it was always impolite to talk with my mouth full.'

(1.3 seconds' pause)

Ken: hhhhyok hyok. Hyok.

(2.5 seconds' pause)

Al: *HA-A-A-A!*

Ken: heh-heh-huh-huh

Roger: Delayed reaction.

Al: I had to think about it awhile you know?

Roger: Sure.

hih heh You mean the *deep* hidden *m*eaning there doesn't *hit* you right away heh

Al: hhih

Dan: It's pretty interesting.

Al: What he *m*eant to say is that – that um

Roger: Kinda got psychological overtones.

Ken: Little sister's gettin older.

Al: eh-hih-hih

Ken: yihh hih-hih That's what I *m*ean to say.

Dan: *Sounds* like it.

Ken: For twelve years old tellin me – *I* didn't even know

Roger: How do you know she's just not repeating what she heard and doesn't know what it means.

Al: Did she have to explain it to you Ken?

Ken: Yeah she had to explain it in detail to me

Al: Okay Ken, glad you got a sister that knows somethin.

Ken: She told me she was eatin a hot dog

(3.0 seconds' pause)

Roger: What does *th*at mean.

Al: Yeah come on. Explain it to us. Explain

Ken: *I DON'T KNOW* I just said that.

Al: Explain everything you know, Ken.
        Explain everything.

The structure of Sacks's joke

This joke, Sacks suggests, has an elaborate and detailed structure, without which it could not operate effectively upon its recipients. This structure, it is said, involves and depends on a series of implausibilities. Sacks proposes that, if participants are to respond properly to the joke, to collaborate in its telling, the joke must be organized to draw attention away from these implausibilities. He points out that, traditionally, analysts have dealt with the apparent implausibility of much humour by proposing that recipients 'suspend disbelief'. But this view, according to Sacks, is 'nonsense'. It is nonsense because, he argues, when one examines the structure of standard jokes carefully and in detail, one can see that it is not left to recipients to decide to ignore their implausibilities (Sacks, 1978, p. 259). Sacks maintains that his joke, and by implication all effective jokes, are designed in a way which conceals their implausibilities.

Having read the joke, you may feel that my exposition so far of Sacks's analysis is rather odd. 'What implausibilities?', you may think. 'I didn't notice any.' That, however, is one of the points that Sacks wishes to make. I have used this joke often in teaching and it is the case that nobody, on a first hearing or reading, appears to notice the implausibilities that Sacks proceeds to identify. Our failure to do so, he insists, is not due to a voluntary inhibition of our critical faculties; it is not due to our suspending disbelief. It is, rather, a consequence of the textual arrangement or structure of the joke itself.

One example of the kind of implausibility or 'implausible consistency' noted by Sacks is the mother's 'nonchalantly received luck of encountering the sounds' in which she is manifestly interested at exactly the moment when she arrives at the first two doors (1978, p. 255). Somehow or other we, as recipients, become surprised only by the absence of instantaneous and comparable sounds at the third door, without noticing the equally, if not more, surprising production of appropriate sounds at just the right moment at the two preceding doors. Similarly, few recipients are likely to wonder about the fact that all the sounds were produced by the daughters, even though we know that there were two people in each room and that any of the sounds could in principle have been made by a son-in-law. In addition, there are the implausible questions addressed by the mother to the daughters during the next-morning sequence. Each of these questions is odd, but particularly that directed to daughter number three: 'Why didn't you *say* anything last night.' The only possible answer from a daughter as yet unaware of her mother's nocturnal perambulations might seem to be something like: 'But Mommy, I said a great many things last night. Whatever do you mean?' However, not only does such a 'literal response' not normally occur to us as recipients, but most of us, like the young men on the tape-recording, seem to treat the third daughter's actual response as entirely appropriate and entirely understandable. Recipients seem to find this improbable exchange between mother and third daughter to be no more puzzling than the string of coincidences that make up the story line of the joke. Sack's argument is that, behind the joke's surface content, there are a series of related features which direct attention away from the 'implausible concatenation of events' (1978, p. 259) and bring into focus instead only those elements required to establish the joke's humorous meaning.

The first structural feature that Sacks identifies is that of sequential organization. His central point here is that the joke is organized in terms of several sequences in such a way that the first parts of each sequence provide instructions for the recipients' interpretation of what comes later. For example, in relation to the first-night sequence:

> First of all this looks like simply an ordering of the mother's behavior relative to a series of doors behind which we know are the newly married couples, where this just happens to be the order in which she approaches the doors. But on close inspection we find that the sequence's components are 'sequentially organized in fine detail.' And by that I mean, e.g., the mother 'walks up to' the first door, 'and she hears this' sound. She doesn't 'walk up to' the second door, and she doesn't 'hear this' sound; it's just reported as 'second door is *HHHOHHhhh.*' We employ the description of events at the first door to understand that object, and find that there was a second event which was identical to the first, except for a difference in the sound itself. We don't get, or need, the whole description repeated for the second event, nor for the third. (Sacks, 1978, p. 253)

The sequence of events which occurs the next morning closely resembles the sequence of the night before. The first sequence provides a guide for what is to come in the second sequence, and is essential if we are to be able to understand what happens during the second. Thus the daughters' replies, 'Well it *ti*cked, Mommy' and 'Oh, *Mo*mmy it *hu*rts', are only understandable, and only understandable in sexual terms, as a result of earlier references to their being on their honeymoon and to prior recognition of the sexual significance of the sequence of sounds the previous night. Similarly, and critically for the success of the joke, we can only take the third daughter's literally inoffensive remark about not speaking with her mouth full as concealing a reference to oral sex if we have already given a sexual meaning to the two other daughters' references to 'it' tickling and 'it' hurting.

The effectiveness of Sacks's joke, then, depends crucially on the sequential ordering of its components and on the interpretative work made possible by that ordering. Within each of the two main sections of the joke, these components are arranged as a three-part sequence. Because so many standard jokes make use of three-part sequences, it is important to take note of Sacks's observations on this feature. He draws attention to the fact that, by the end of the first-night sequence, we have been furnished with a puzzle, namely: Why is there no sound at the third door?

This array of events provides the mother with a puzzle: Why no sound at the third door? Now there is a constructional element to the puzzle sequence (which appears as well in the solution sequence) and that is the use of three components in a particular order: two sounds followed by one silence. This is an ideal construction; a perfect economical use of a number of components to get a puzzle; i.e., it turns out that you need *at least* three to get the silence as a puzzle, and you also need *no more than* three to get the silence as a puzzle. Suppose there were two daughters; at the first door sound, at the second door silence. So? One was sound and one was silence. There's no particular issue as to why there was silence; we could equally well wonder why there was sound. But the two sounds suffice to make the silence noticeable. And you don't need four, five, or eleven doors . . . Three suffice. Three is the minimal but sufficient number for making the minority event peculiar and therefore focusable-on as a puzzle. And the arrangement which has the silence occurring last works to build up an appreciation of the expectable, normal, majority character of the sounds. (1978, p. 254)

In this passage, Sacks shows how the three-part sequence in the joke creates a contrast between sound and silence, and how the placing of the two sounds establishes the immediate production of sound as normal and the absence of sound as unexpected, as puzzling and as requiring explanation. Whenever the three-part sequence occurs in a standard joke – for example, in 'Englishman, Scotsman, Irishman' jokes – it operates in this way, focusing attention on the third item and obliging recipients to try to understand how that item's pecularities can be accounted for. In Sacks's joke, the three-part sequence is used again in the second section to provide an answer to the puzzle. The first two items are sufficient to establish a pattern of 'normal sexual activity' in the course of which women can freely vocalize, in contrast with which the silence of daughter number three can be interpreted as due to her engaging in oral sex.

Sacks emphasizes that the three-part sequence is 'a perfect economical use of a number of components', and he suggests that this economy of structure is generally characteristic of the joke. In other words, the joke is highly condensed. There are very few redundant words and no deviations from the central focus. For example, we do not find the first daughter saying: 'Well it *tick*led, Mommy. He was trying to be so kind and gentle, but that really didn't help.' Nor does daughter number two enlarge on her experiences, with such explanatory comment as: '*Oh, Mo*mmy it *hu*rts. I suppose that's because I was still a virgin.' Unlike a story or dramatic narrative, which would require embellishment along these lines, the standardized joke normally depends on the elimination of all material which is not strictly necessary in order to 'see the point' of the joke.[1] Thus Sacks's joke is pared down to a few basic components: Mommy, three sisters, honeymoon, three rooms, two sounds, one silence, hurting, tickling, not talking with one's mouth full. These are the essential elements of the joke which, when arranged in the proper sequence, enable us to understand the joke's meaning as we interpret the punch line.

Of course, although most of us do succeed in making sense of that punch line, Sacks points out that the third daughter's closing remark is far from explicit.

> And it is characteristic for jokes, and present in this one, that while the puzzle is solvable from the punch line, the solution isn't asserted in the punch line but will have to be interpreted out of it. That is, the third daughter's answer is not itself a solution to the puzzle. It's what does the answer *mean* that's a solution to the puzzle. (1978, p. 258)

Whereas in a story it is *possible* to have an explicit ending – for example, 'They married and lived happily ever after' – in a joke, if Sacks is right, the ending or resolution *must* be implicit; it must be available from the ordered arrangement of components without being openly expressed. Indeed the implicit nature of the punch line is typical of the way the joke conveys its sexual content; that is, the joke's sexual focus and the sexual referents of its terms are never allowed fully into the open. The point of the joke is recognizable only through the interpretative work that we are made to carry out as recipients.

So far we have seen that Sacks emphasizes the detailed sequential arrangement of the joke, its use of two parallel three-part sub-sequences, its formulation as a puzzle and solution, the economy of the joke's components and its provision of a covert meaning that is made available through its organization without being made explicit. The final element to which Sacks refers in his discussion of the joke's structure is the textual contribution of the 'Mommy'. The Mommy figure, he suggests, operates as a guide. The Mommy directs recipients' attention towards certain features and interpretative possibilities, and away from others. The Mommy initiates all the activity reported in the joke. By her actions, she indicates to us which events are to be expected and which are not. And she formulates the questions in the next-morning sequence through which the meaning of these events is finally revealed.

> Plainly one could have a story where she goes to the first door and hears a sound, and then stands there listening for some extended period of time, and a whole range of happenings could be reported. By the fact that at each door where she hears a sound she moves promptly on, we know that she's interested in hearing some sound.

And her nonchalantly received luck of encountering the sounds at the moment she arrives at the first two doors sets up a consistency under which, at the third door, she (and a recipient) can become puzzled immediately. And that immediacy, for one, provides that the extended wait at the third door becomes an observable additional event and thus underscores the oddness of the silence. So, from the way the story reports on the mother's movements, and on what seems adequate to have her move on or stop, we get the puzzle she has. Further, we get *only* the puzzle she has, and not other possible puzzles; for example, it could be quite puzzling, could seem quite implausible, that at the first two doors we get a sound then and there. But since there is no issue for 'the mother' e.g., she doesn't wonder if each couple is waiting for her arrival at the door, whereupon they issue a sound, then there is no issue for us recipients of the story. And by the end of the first sequence we know that the puzzle is, and is exclusively, why no sound at the third door. (Sacks, 1978, pp. 254–5)

Humour and implausibility

We can now begin to see how the implausibilities that Sacks identifies are created. They arise directly out of the ordered sequencing of events combined with their highly condensed portrayal. For instance, the immediate production of sounds at the first two doors, and of nothing else, is required to establish unambiguously the puzzle of the silence at the third door and to focus attention exclusively on the presence and absence of sounds. As Sacks puts it: 'The joke employs a series of co-occurrent coincidences which turn out to be organizationally crucial; i.e., without them we wouldn't have the joke' (1978, p. 257). If we so wished, we could change the order and character of events in Sacks's joke as follows: first door – long silence whilst Mommy ruminates on the pains of motherhood; second door – immediate sound; third door – Mommy talks to Daddy until, after a while, a sound is heard. Such a story could be developed in various ways to make it interesting and to avoid any untoward coincidences. But it would no longer be a standard joke. Some of the implausibilities would have disappeared. So, however, would the clear focus on the puzzling silence at door three and the possibility of resolving that puzzle with a single remark. Thus, it is the very structure of the joke, in particular, its streamlined, economical presentation, its three-part patterning of events, and its need covertly to convey both a puzzle and its solution, that creates the implausibilities to which Sacks draws attention.

At the same time, Sacks suggests, the joke's structure tends to cover

over these implausibilities. Recipients do not need to suspend disbelief, he claims, partly because the joke is organized so that it does not occur to them that suspension of disbelief is necessary: 'The thing to see is that while, for the story to come off, we may need to accept its events, the story is in the first place built in such a way as to have it not occur to us that "this is implausible but we shall suspend disbelief"' (1978, p. 257). Sacks's reference to the way in which the joke is 'built' seems to suggest that we do not notice its implausibilities because of the way in which the joke is constructed by the teller. Sacks maintains that the sequential organization of the joke focuses attention on the dynamic unravelling of its events and away from the series of implausible coincidences. At the same time, the unquestioning acceptance of these coincidences by the 'Mommy' and by the joke's other characters diverts attention from their improbability. As his argument develops, however, it becomes clear that Sacks attributes at least as much significance to recipients' tendency to respond to jokes in a rather special way.

> In the course of the joke, one is not ever in a position to assess the complex of its components, but is fully occupied in understanding it, piece by piece, so that, arriving at its end, one can solve the punch line as fast as possible. This is a critical task posed for a joke's recipient . . . And recipient's task is to 'get' what the answer means. It is not only a task provided by the array of events, but, since failing to 'get' the joke can be treated as, e.g., a sign of one's lack of sophistication, then the social circumstances, as well, urge a recipient to be working to find what the punch line means. And from the joke's beginning, that will be the test of him. Recipients will be working to come up with an interpretation of the punch line which they can exhibit by, e.g., laughing, and laughing as soon as possible. And the whole thing is over as soon as they've laughed.
>   Thus, while the joke needs a total concatenation of events which can thereby have an extraordinary implausibility, it need not be left to whether people will or will not grant their plausibility. Recipients can have their minds directed in ways that will involve them in not at all seeing an implausibility. There can be no room in the story to engage in assessing its plausibility when it emerges sequentially, piece by piece; one is hearing it as it's being told, going through it and understanding it, and seeing that its characters are understanding it as one is understanding it. In these ways a recipient will not see that the joke which is testing him is crucially implausible; i.e., that without this implausible concatenation of events, the joke collapses. (1978, pp. 258–9)

Sacks is arguing, then, that the sequential organization of the joke, its puzzle-solution format and its dependence on covert meaning place special interpretative demands on recipients, and also that recipients are required by the very nature of joking exchanges to indicate quickly and clearly that they have satisfied these demands – that is, that they have seen the point of the joke. This view of standard jokes as, in part, an interpretative test appears to be supported by the exploration of the joke's meaning by the boys and by their probing of each other's level of comprehension at the end of Sacks's transcription. Thus Sacks supplements his analysis of the joke's structure with the suggestion that recipients are so intent on solving the puzzle in order to exhibit the correct response as soon as the joke is finished that they simply fail to notice its implausibilities. As a result, any suspension of disbelief is quite unnecessary.

Although Sacks's analysis of the structure of the dirty joke is a considerable advance upon the traditional notion of the suspension of disbelief, the difference between Sacks and the traditional view is not perhaps as dramatic as Sacks seems to imply when he dismisses that view as nonsensical. For instance, Sacks emphasizes that the recipient of a standardized joke is required to adopt a distinctive interpretative stance. He stresses that the recipient's 'critical task', from the joke's beginning, is to see the point of the joke. That point, as he emphasizes, may well be missed by recipients who attend unduly to implausible coincidences or to actions which would seem distinctly peculiar in other contexts. It seems to me that Sacks's position here comes very close to accepting that recipients do suspend disbelief, in the sense that, once the joke is underway, they ignore implausibilities and unlikely coincidences in order to pursue the goal of solving the joke's puzzle *within the framework provided by its own portrayal of events.*

I suggest, therefore, that although Sacks appears to dismiss the idea that recipients suspend disbelief when they listen to standardized jokes, he does seem to accept, and is right to accept, that they attend to humorous discourse in a rather special way. Let me build upon this part of Sacks's analysis by proposing that, as participants, we approach humour with an interpretative procedure which differs significantly from that applied to serious discourse. When we listen to a joke, we do not expect or require that the events depicted should exhibit the same kind of interpretative consistency as that to be found in serious conversation. I suggest that we distinguish humorous from serious discourse and that we employ what we may call different 'plausibility requirements' within these two discursive modes. We can see this most clearly when we consider jokes that have a simpler structure than Sacks's joke and where the 'implausibilities' are so obvious that they can hardly escape our attention. Take the following highly standardized two-liner:

What do you get if you cross an elephant with a fish?
Swimming trunks.

This joke is utterly implausible and the structure is too simple to hide this implausibility. Yet recipients seldom object or complain that they had difficulty with the idea of interbreeding elephants with fish. The reason is presumably that this is not the discourse of a biology seminar, where such an unlikely notion would be quickly noted and corrected, but the discourse of humour, where quite different conceptions of consistency and coherence seem to apply. Sacks may be right to maintain that some 'implausibilities' are not noticed in complex jokes because the joke structure and the obligation to respond quickly to the punch line draw recipients' attention elsewhere. But the last example surely demonstrates that this is not always the case; that on some occasions obvious implausibilities are simply ignored because they are characteristic of humour and to be expected in the humorous domain. Let us consider another instance where we are required to accept, and where we do accept, an evidently absurd representation.

'The dapper man'

On the first evening after moving house, Bob went down to the local pub and started talking to the barman. After a while, their talk was interrupted by the arrival of a dapper little man, evidently a regular, who greeted the barman, ordered a glass of sherry, drank it, said goodnight, walked up the wall, across the ceiling, down the opposite wall, and out through the door. There was a short silence before Bob said, quaveringly:
'Wow! *That* was strange'.
'Yes', mused the barman. 'That *was* strange.
He usually drinks whisky'. (Nash, 1985, p. 107)

Although this joke is more complex than the swimming trunks joke, and although we have a textual guide like the 'Mommy' in Sacks's joke, it is unconvincing to maintain that this joke is composed in a way which draws our attention away from its implausibilities. For the dapper man joke seems designed to *emphasize* the remarkable and utterly implausible event witnessed by our guide. The sequencing in this joke first creates a sense of normality in which Bob chats to the barman and a perfectly ordinary customer enters, greets the barman, orders and consumes a drink, and says goodnight. These everyday actions provide the background against which the dapper man's defiance of the force of gravity stands out unambiguously. No attempt is made to divert our attention from these events, to persuade us that Bob merely *thought* he saw the man walk across the ceiling or to indicate in any way that some alternative interpretation may be possible. Rather, we are given a completely 'objective description' of the dapper man's remarkable physical actions. Only after this description is Bob allowed to comment; his remarks at this point confirm both the strangeness and the 'reality' of what we have been told.

In this case, then, we are required to accept, for the purposes of the joke, that the impossible has happened. Indeed, the joke turns upon the revelation in the punch line that this 'impossibility' is not only a 'possibility' for the barman and the dapper man, but is a perfectly normal part of their everyday world. Although the joke depends on our sharing in some sense Bob's conception of normality and strangeness, this in no way prevents us from entering and appreciating at the same time the world of the dapper man (Koestler, 1964). For this character exists within the interpretative world of humour, where the range of possibilities has been greatly extended; where, it seems, anything is possible.

> From Bob's point of view, the wall-walking episode is more than out of the ordinary; his quavering comment means 'It's impossible', or 'I wouldn't believe it if I hadn't seen it'. For the purposes of the story, he is *committed* to a view of likelihood; his astonishment (contrasted with the low-key response of the barman) arises out of that commitment. He *must* believe – his role in the narrative demands it – that this is a preternatural event. In this, the character-within-the-tale possibly differs from the listener/reader, the audience of the story. Our perception of reality is the same as Bob's, but we are not committed to it in the same way; if we were, we would not be so ready to stand back and laugh. We accept that the outrageous thing *does* happen, and by that acceptance we have access to the humour of the barman's response. Unlikelihood does not provoke in us an astonishment from which we cannot free our minds. We accept the impossible as a theoretical postulate, the necessary condition of the joke. (Nash, 1985, p. 108)

In the case of the dapper man, we are required to accept the impossible in order to allow the joke to proceed to its denouement. Our willing assent to the feasibility of the dapper man's utterly implausible behaviour is essential to the joke. Consequently, this example illustrates that standardized jokes can operate outside the assumptions and expectations of ordinary, serious discourse. Such jokes create their own framework of expectation in relation to which humorous incongruity is fashioned. In this respect, the implausible coincidences in Sacks's joke correspond to the dapper man's astonishing capacities. Their implausibility in terms of the discourse of 'the real world' is irrelevant for participants and therefore goes unremarked. Participants are surely aware that the events depicted in a joke occur within the special world of humour where, in principle, as long as the speaker sustains the humorous mode, *almost anything can happen*.

It appears, then, that when speakers move from the serious mode of discourse to the humorous mode, they are allowed much greater freedom in what they can say. In the realm of humour, we can tell of men who walk upside down, of elephants that breed with fish, and of other marvels too numerous to list. These impossibilities are possible because humour is marked off from serious discourse; and because the requirements of acceptable discourse vary from one mode to the other. Thus Sacks appears to be wrong if he is suggesting that the structures of standardized jokes are neccesarily designed to hide away the implausibilities which they generate. For humour operates according to plausibility requirements that are quite different from, and much less stringent than, those operative in serious discourse.

It is worth noting that, at the outset, the recipients of Sacks's joke do actually notice and attend to some of the joke's possible implausibilities. Roger and Al, in particular, playfully interrupt the teller several times in order to 'object' to what they treat as incongruities. But these objections appear themselves to be humorous. For instance, it is unlikely that Roger really interprets the opening of the joke as implying that the three sisters had married each other or that Al really takes the joke to imply that the sisters had married their own brothers. In other words, Roger and Al seem to be pretending to be disturbed by implausibilities which they are actually formulating for humorous effect. As we see here, adoption of the humorous mode appears to depend, not upon participants' ability to conceal implausibility, but on the contrary upon their active involvement in its production. As participants, we do not need to have our attention drawn away from the implausibilities of humour, because in this discursive mode they are an expected feature of the discourse.

It is clear from this discussion that analysts *of* humour operate within a different discursive mode from participants *in* humour. In trying to understand humour seriously, we are necessarily transporting it into a different interpretative realm. This is perhaps why professional humorists are often resistant to detailed academic study of humour. It may be that they are right to protest that serious analysis can never properly grasp the nature of their creative endeavours and to insist that they should be left to pursue their craft undisturbed. The British comedian Ken Dodd gave expression to this view, when he summed up his reservations about the psychoanalytic theory of humour. 'The trouble with Freud,' he quipped, 'is that he never played the Glasgow Empire on a Saturday night' (Wilson, 1979, p. 189).

Analysts of humour are, of course, unavoidably committed to assessing humour according to the requirements of the serious mode. But, in so doing, we must be alert to the dangers involved. Like Alice in Wonderland, we will run into trouble if we do not remember at all times that what we see in the land of humour operates according to quite alien principles. Thus Sacks, despite the accuracy of his detailed observations, was led astray because he failed to keep in mind that, in the domain of humour, discourse is organized with a fundamentally different objective in view. As a result, in pursuit of serious 'technical considerations', Sacks thought that he saw various implausibilities which simply *had* to be hidden away if recipients were to give credence to the joke. It seems likely, however, that these implausibilities are only evident when one looks into the world of humour from outside.

If one enters into that world, as we all do when we act as participants rather than as analysts, a different conception of plausibility comes into effect. Within the realm of humour, almost anything is allowed and implausibilities do not have to be camouflaged. Nevertheless, this does not mean that, in any particular joke, nothing will be taken to be remarkable, unexpected or incongruous (Nash, 1985, p. 108). Indeed, in every joke and in every humorous remark, structure and content are in fact designed to produce the incongruity essential to humour. It is a paradoxical feature of the humorous mode that, although its standards of feasibility, consistency and coherence are much less restrictive than in the serious mode, it must continually generate incongruity and contradiction. In the discussion above of Sacks's transcript, we have seen some of the methods used for this purpose in standardized jokes. Let us now turn to a consideration of the basic characteristics of serious discourse in order to be able to appreciate more clearly what is distinctive about the operation of the humorous mode.

Note

1 Humour is sometimes created by departure from the kind of economical, condensed discourse characteristic of most standardized jokes. For example, there is a type of joke, which is called in Britain a 'shaggy dog story', that involves continual digression from, and elaborate ornamentation around, the main story line, culminating in a weak climax. The humour depends on the contrast between the slow, complex build-up and the banal, often somewhat irrelevant, punch line; and on the implied contrast with, and reversal of, the customary structure of the standardized joke. The proper response to such a story is a groan. This enables recipients to register their recognition that the joke does not conform to the normal pattern. Douglas (1968) suggests that the shaggy dog story is only told in a society which has been satiated with jokes.

2

Serious Discourse and the Duality
of Humour

The phrase 'serious discourse' clearly covers an enormous range of social situations and discursive phenomena. It can equally well refer to a squabble between neighbours as to a debate among physicists; it includes professions of love as well as of hate; and even academic analyses of humour come within its scope. These variations within the realm of serious discourse are undeniable, and are undeniably significant in other analytical contexts. I will, however, ignore this diversity and concentrate on a few basic features that are built into most, if not quite all, forms of serious discourse, and particularly into ordinary, everyday reasoning about the world. Systematic deviation from the basic presuppositions and procedures of ordinary serious discourse is most likely to occur within the arts. (For a discussion of poetry as a special kind of discourse, see Ward, 1979.) But in everyday interaction, as well as in such specialized language-communities as law, science and politics, these presuppositions and procedures are pervasive.

The basic, taken-for-granted assumptions and practices of serious discourse are the proper focus of attention here because it is their absence that makes humour possible. In the following discussion of serious discourse, I will draw heavily on work by Melvin Pollner concerning 'mundane reasoning' (1974; 1975) and, through Pollner's analysis, on ideas derived from Alfred Schutz (1967) and William James (1950).

Some basic features of serious discourse

The starting point of Pollner's analysis is the claim that all of us almost all of the time, when engaged in the mundane activities of our everyday lives, presuppose that we inhabit a social world in common with the people around us. This assumption is implicit in the very structure of the language that we customarily use when speaking and writing seriously. Consequently, in our reasoning about the world, we take for granted that we are dealing with objective phenomena which exist independently of our actions and discourse and which are experienced in much the same way by other human beings. Each actor supposes that he inhabits a real social world, where people act in predictable ways for reasons which are commonly understood. As mundane reasoners and speakers, we work on the assumption that there is but one reality, which is, under normal circumstances, as accessible to other people as it is to ourselves.

Divergent accounts of particular parts of the everyday world are, of course, regularly produced. But such discrepancies are treated as unwelcome and, usually, as indicating that some error has been made. Participants are very seldom willing to give equal credence to contradictory accounts. Rather, they choose those accounts which they take to be the most reliable and to represent most accurately the real state of affairs. Although different speakers repeatedly advance incompatible claims, and although particular individuals' claims vary considerably from one occasion to another, each speaker talks on behalf of a world which is taken to exist outside his speech and to be available to others if they approach it in the proper manner (Mulkay, 1985). By selecting from the changing welter of observation and interpretation that surrounds us and by explaining away others' errors, we each sustain a sense of referring to a unitary realm that lies behind the interpretative flux and multiplicity of the social world in which we live (Heritage, 1984; Gilbert and Mulkay, 1984; Potter and Wetherell, 1987).

Because serious speech presupposes the existence of a single, organized, independent world, serious speakers are obliged to avoid speaking in two contradictory ways at once (James, 1950, p. 290). Thus, in endorsing certain versions of the world and thereby disregarding others, we each create in our own discourse a boundary between the real and the unreal which we take to be characteristic of the world itself.

> The subjects adhered to become real subjects, the attributes adhered to real attributes, the existence adhered to real existence; whilst the subjects disregarded become imaginary subjects, the attributes disregarded erroneous attributes, and the existence disregarded an existence in no man's land, in the limbo 'where footless fancies dwell'. (James, 1950, p. 290; cited in Pollner, 1975)

In the realm of serious discourse, it is assumed not only that each speaker will maintain a firm boundary between the real and the unreal, but also that the boundaries of different speakers will coincide. This expectation follows from the assumption that speakers are representing in their speech one and the same, knowable-in-common world. Consequently, disagreement about the events of that world tends to be avoided or minimized (Pomerantz, 1984; Mulkay, 1985). When disagreement becomes noticeable, further interpretative work is routinely carried out to explain how it has occurred. Pollner refers to instances where there are discrepant claims about 'what really happened/is happening' as 'reality disjunctures'. He emphasizes that reality disjunctures appear regularly and in every area of social life; and that this could, in principle, be taken to suggest that there is not one coherent world, but a multiplicity of contradictory worlds.

> matters adjudicated in the courts, disputations in science, disagree-ments in everyday affairs, and so on can be conceived of as an ever-growing compendium of instances testifying to the fact that there is no 'same world'. The very conflicts which are mundanely regarded as a 'failure' in the perceptual process through which the world is observed and its features brought to formulation *may alternatively be regarded as 'evidence' of the absurd and radical subjectivity of the world*. (Pollner, 1974, p. 46; my italics)

Pollner stresses, however, that mundane reasoners, or in my terms producers of serious discourse, very seldom come to this latter conclusion. The reason for this is that their discourse about reality disjunctures takes utterly for granted that discrepant formulations of the world cannot originate in 'the world itself', but must arise out of human failure to observe or report that world accurately. Because this assumption and the related presuppositions outlined above pervade people's thinking, talking and writing, because they are essential to our use of the serious mode of discourse, our culture provides a wide variety of well established interpretative techniques for explaining how such failure may have taken place. In Pollner's analysis these procedures for attributing and account-ing for error are documented in detail. In general terms, such practices can be seen as convenient devices which enable speakers to explain away reality disjunctures by reference to participants', usually some *other* participant's, perceptual, intellectual or linguistic incompetence. Through the regular use of such interpretative practices, disjunctures are routinely handled in a manner which constantly reaffirms the underlying existence of a unitary world and which constantly reinforces our reliance on a unitary form of serious discourse. In John Heritage's words:

> the intersubjective availability of 'real world' events is assured in no other way than through the practices with which discrepant accounts are reconciled. It is a *presupposition* of these practices in that, from the entire range of possible explanations of discrepancy, only those predicted on the original assumption of a known-in-common world are invoked and used. Each one of this restricted range of explanations respects the availability of a known-in-common world and each 'explains away' discrepancies by reference to conditions which leave that availability intact. (1984, p. 216)

Pollner's analysis focuses on disagreements about the nature of the world, and he describes in detail how participants cope with disagreement within the interpretative framework of serious discourse. There are, however, numerous other phenomena which cause difficulties within this framework of assumptions: for example, inconsistency, ambiguity and paradox. When the latter occur during serious discourse, attempts are often made, as with disagreement, to remove them or to reduce their impact (Raskin, 1985a). Thus, when a speaker's or writer's claims are taken to give rise to paradox, this is virtually never regarded as following from the paradoxical character of the world, but from some fault in the reasoning (Ashmore, 1985). Paradox is routinely used in serious discourse, along with ambiguity and inconsistency, as sufficient grounds for questioning or rejecting the assertions to which it is attributed. In this way, discourse is constantly corrected and revised to make it appear to embody and display the one meaning required by the basic assumptions of serious discourse.

There can be no doubt that disagreement, contradiction, ambiguity and paradox occur regularly in serious discourse. Indeed, it is probably the case that life in the everyday social world would be impossible without a certain degree of linguistic imprecision and ambiguity (Stubbs, 1983). But within the serious mode, such features have to be treated as problematic in so far as they threaten to undermine the basic presupposition that, despite the diversity of conflicting views, opinions and interpretations current within the social world, there exists one real world which is in principle the same for all participants and which is independent of participants' discourse about that world.

These basic features of the serious mode are necessarily characteristic of analytical work dealing with humour. Victor Raskin for example, whose ideas will be examined in the next chapter, insists that his book on the semantic theory of humour is not, and is not intended to be, funny (1985a, p. 7). He quotes with approval Leacock's claim that 'people who sit down to write books on humour are scientific people, philosophical analysers who feel that they must make something serious, something real of it' (1937, p. 15). Discourse about humour is serious discourse about one of the realities of the world. Raskin states clearly how a serious analysis of humour must cope with these realities. It must:

(i) provide complete and non-contradictory descriptions of the data and thus distinguish any such description from a non- description;

(ii) provide a procedure and an evaluation measure for comparing two alternative descriptions of the data and for preferring one of them over the other;

(iii) provide a procedure for the corroboration of the description by other competent persons. (1985a, p. 48)

These requirements for a satisfactory theory about humour encapsulate all the basic features of serious discourse discussed above..Criterion (i) stipulates the need to eliminate contradiction and ambiguity. Criterion (ii) requires the formulation of the one true version. Criterion (iii) provides for the absorption of that version into the body of commonly accepted knowledge. It seeks to ensure that our analysis of humour can become part of the known-in-common world. Moreover, these criteria are to be put into practice by means of clear-cut, consistent, explicit procedures, about which there can be no disagreement. The end-product of Raskin's exercise in serious analysis is intended to be a coherent, unitary account of the semantic mechanisms of the humorous mode. However, as we will now see, this mode operates according to fundamentally different assumptions, employs distinctly different discursive forms and generates radically different interpretative outcomes from the serious mode examined in this section.[1]

Bisociation

The basic principles and practices of the humorous mode are the reverse of those operative within serious discourse. Whereas ambiguity, inconsistency, contradiction and interpretative diversity are often treated as problems during serious discourse, and attempts are regularly made to remove them or to reduce their impact, they are necessary features of the humorous mode. In contrast to the unitary character of serious discourse, humour depends on the discursive display of opposing interpretative possibilities. In the realm of humour, not only are our everyday assumptions about the one, known-in-common world constantly confounded, but the interpretative expectations generated in the course of humorous discourse itself are undermined as that discourse proceeds. This does not mean that the discourse of humour makes no sense. Rather, humour involves a kind of controlled nonsense. Judged by the criteria of *serious* discourse, humour *is* nonsensical. Nevertheless, the assertions of humorous discourse are always understandable in terms of the special requirements and expectations of the humorous realm.

The central process whereby the interpretative disjunctures characteristic of humour are created has been termed 'bisociation' by Arthur Koestler (1964). Variants of this concept are employed by many of the leading analysts of humour (e.g. Fry, 1963; Douglas, 1968; Suls, 1972; Paulos, 1980; Raskin, 1985a). The basic idea is that humour occurs when there is a sudden movement between, or unexpected combination of, distinct interpretative frames. In Koestler's words, the production of humour necessarily involves 'the perceiving of a situation or idea in two self-consistent but habitually incompatible frames of reference' (1964, p. 35). As Paulos puts it: 'a necessary ingredient of humour is that two (or more) incongruous ways of viewing something (a person, a sentence, a situation) be juxtaposed' (1980, p. 9). Let us look at one of Koestler's jokes with this in mind.

Koestler's joke

In the happy days of *La Ronde*, a dashing but penniless Austrian officer tried to obtain the favours of a fashionable courtesan. To shake off this unwanted suitor, she explained to him that her heart was, alas, no longer free. He replied politely: 'Mademoiselle, I never aimed as high as that'. (1964, p. 36)

In Koestler's joke, the courtesan addresses the Austrian officer in the metaphorical language of a bygone age. In this form of discourse, 'heart' stands for 'affection', which is itself an indirect way of referring to 'sexual congress'. In other words, the courtesan is using the conventional terminology of polite society to reject the attentions of a young man who cannot afford her favours. Although her phrasing is indirect, her meaning is quite clear to those who belong to, or are familiar with, this culture. Thus the first two sentences of the joke remain within a single discursive code, as they report the actions of both parties in straightforward, serious terms. The officer's response, however, is noticeably different. The young man seems to adopt a recognizably jocular tone and to be 'making fun of the courtesan'. We receive this impression, I suggest, even though the officer's reply is described as being politely delivered – that is, as remaining within the serious mode – and even though in the written version we are unable to tell whether he speaks in a humorous tone of voice.

This impression of humorous intent is conveyed by the final words of the passage, 'never aimed as high as that', and by the relationship between these words and what has gone before. Most readers are able to make sense of this phrase as a response to the courtesan's previous remark. But it becomes an understandable response only if we treat the officer as using a potential ambiguity in the courtesan's word 'heart' to change the frame of reference. More specifically, the officer disregards the conventional, metaphorical meaning of 'heart' and treats it as if it had been intended anatomically. By referring implicitly to the physical location of the lady's heart and by proposing that his interest lies in some lower part of the body, the officer chooses to take her metaphorical language literally. In so doing, he rejects the 'pretence' of sincere emotional attachment between the courtesan and her male partners which is sustained by her conventional phraseology, and replaces it with an 'admission' of his own frank sexuality.

We can agree with Koestler that his joke is created by means of a sudden movement from the metaphorical frame of reference to the topographical or literal frame of reference (Koestler, 1964, p. 36). Alternatively, we can describe the joke as involving a confrontation between the young man's frankness and the sexual hypocrisy of polite society. It is not necessary to identify these 'frames of reference' precisely in order to 'see' the joke; nor is it necessary for purposes of analysis. The joke depends simply on its capacity to convey, and on our ability to recognize, that one interpretation of the courtesan's remark has been unexpectedly replaced by another internally consistent and understandable, yet incongruous, interpretation.

This joke, like many others, is made possible by a verbal ambiguity (Redfern, 1984). We can see this clearly if we replace the word 'heart' with the word 'affection'. 'My affection, alas, is no longer free' conveys much the same meaning as the original phrase. But if this alternative wording is used, the officer's reply 'I never aimed as high as that' is not amusing, but meaningless. The word 'heart' is what Walter Nash calls the 'locus' of the joke (Nash, 1985, p. 7). It is the interpretative duality of this word which enables the young officer to respond to the courtesan with a reply which is unexpected, yet which makes perfectly good sense within a new frame of reference. It is the ambiguity or duality of this word which provides an interpretative bridge between the courtesan's statement and the officer's intentional 'misunderstanding' of her statement.

In relation to the earlier discussion of serious discourse, it is important to recognize that the word 'heart' is not inherently ambiguous. Under normal circumstances, the courtesan's conventional turn of phrase would have received a proper response formulated within the same frame of reference. It is not that there is a necessary ambiguity in the courtesan's discourse which creates misunderstanding and gives rise to the joke. Rather, the ambiguity on which the joke is built is created by the way in which the officer chooses to employ the semantic possibilities provided by the courtesan's utterance. It is not, one assumes, that the young man actually misunderstands the lady, but that he elects to appear to misunderstand her for humorous effect. Thus, unlike serious discourse, humour actively creates and fosters ambiguity, and uses it to generate incongruity and interpretative contrast. Whereas ambiguity is often treated as a problem in serious discourse, where interpretative work is routinely carried out to reduce it, in humour ambiguity is a basic feature of the discourse and interpretative work is geared to its production.

Although Koestler's joke, like humour in general, depends on ambiguity and the combination of discrepant frames of reference, these features are employed here, as always, in an orderly, understandable manner. In Koestler's joke, as in Sacks's and in standardized jokes generally, the specific content of the punch line must be unexpected in the light of what has gone before. Yet it must also be understandable in terms of a new reading of what has gone before. This new reading is made available in the punch line itself. The overall structure of the joke must be understandable because, otherwise, the joke would become fragmented into two separate segments of discourse. It would cease to be a joke. An effective punch line introduces a new perspective which deviates from the rest of the text, yet which retains some kind of interpretative coherence. However, the new meaning supplied by the punch line is never made fully explicit. In other words, the punch line of a standard joke is always allusive. This was true, as we saw earlier, in the case of Sacks's joke. It is also true of Koestler's joke. If the young officer had replied openly, 'Mademoiselle, I do not want your affection. I merely want the sexual use of your body, but unfortunately I cannot afford to pay for it', we would have not a joke, but an entirely serious interchange. Thus an essential feature of the standard joke is that the change of interpretative perspective accomplished in the punch line is brought about in a covert or implicit manner.

In the serious mode, allusive remarks can properly lead to requests for clarification. Implicit meanings can often be made more explicit without the discourse thereby breaking down. Participants can, in principle, say, 'I'm sorry, I didn't understand. Could you say that again?' This is much more difficult, however, within the realm of humour. Genuine requests for clarification are serious by their very nature. Even when they are jocular in tone, such requests almost unavoidably generate a serious response. As we saw at the beginning of Sacks's transcription in the previous chapter, when Al and Roger object humorously to supposed implausibilities in Ken's dirty joke, Ken does not continue with the joke but returns to the serious mode as he tries to provide the necessary clarification: 'No they're *differ*ent you know *differ*ent families,' he says emphatically. Whether or not these objections were meant seriously, it seems that Ken had to break off from his humorous presentation in order to deal with them. Similarly, if we were to respond to a teller of Koestler's joke by asking, 'What did the officer mean when he said "I never aimed as high as that"?', we would have abandoned the humorous mode by the very act of making that request. Attempts to explain the meaning of a joke spoil that joke because they seek to make it conform to the requirements of an alien mode of discourse; that is, they try to make it clear, explicit and unitary. As we all know, when you have to explain what a joke means, it has failed to work as a joke.

The allusiveness of humour is necessary because humour depends on bisociation, on the combination of divergent frameworks, on the maintenance of an interpretative duality. If the officer *had* replied openly to the courtesan in the words suggested in the last paragraph but one, the interpretative duality required by humour would have been lost. It is the allusive nature of his reply that enables the young officer to say several things at once and thereby to escape the restrictions of the serious mode. It is through allusion that he is able to combine the appearance of politeness with a covert rebuff; to combine the appearance of having misunderstood the lady, with the reality of having understood her all too well; to respond to what she has just said, whilst transforming the meaning of her remark through the introduction of a new interpretative framework. All of these interpretative dualities depend on the young man's use of allusion. They disappear, as we have seen, when we make his implied meaning explicit. This is characteristic of humour in general. Although serious discourse is by no means always clear and explicit, humour differs from serious discourse in *requiring* at least a duality of meaning, and often a multiplicity of opposing meanings. This requirement is accomplished in large measure by means of bisociation, which is in turn dependent on the creation of ambiguity, and on the use of allusive language.

Koestler's joke illustrates one further important point – namely, that adoption of the humorous mode does not necessarily mean that the utterance in question is without serious intent or devoid of serious implications. For us now, removed in time, place and culture from the original event, Koestler's joke may be told purely for humorous effect. For those involved, however, the humorous remark was barbed; there can be no doubt that it contained a serious message. The joke suggests that the very duality of humour can enable speakers, like the young officer, to convey serious meanings whilst appearing merely to jest. I will return to this issue in later chapters. For the moment I will put it aside in order to consider how we respond to the interpretative duality of standardized jokes.

'Getting' the joke

Standardized jokes are organized so as to create narrative expectations which are subsequently confounded and overthrown. Such jokes first establish a reality and then undermine it. It is for this reason that the sequencing of components and the three- part lists discussed by Sacks are so important to the structure of formalized humour. In the vast majority of jokes, the early parts of the sequence or the first two items in a three-part list construct a frame of reference which is unexpectedly altered in the concluding part or punch line. The punchline to a standardized joke is not, of course, *wholly* unexpected. The standard format of such jokes typically reveals them to be intended humorously quite early in the sequence. Thus, as a joke nears its culmination, recipients are normally aware that some kind of interpretative reversal is at hand. What they cannot usually specify in advance, however, is exactly how this reversal is to be accomplished. As we saw in chapter 1, the recipient's task is to show that she has grasped the meaning implied in the punch line and how that meaning follows from, yet also departs from and challenges, the initial frame of reference. Her task is to appreciate the bisociative structure of the joke: that is, the merging of two (or more) frames of reference which are incongruous yet which, when combined in the joke, nevertheless make some kind of sense. This, I suggest, is basically what happens when we 'get the joke'.

My description of 'getting the joke' emphasizes that it requires a recognition and acceptance by recipients of interpretative duality. To 'get' a joke is to see that the meaning implicit in the punch line both follows from, and at the same time contrasts with or contradicts, the initial frame of reference. However, psychologists who have examined the appreciation of humour have offered a somewhat different account of the process involved. Let us examine and appraise one of these psychological views and, in so doing, extend our understanding of the nature of humour.

Jerry Suls (1972) provides the model to be considered here, of how recipients process and appreciate verbal jokes and captioned cartoons. Suls proposes that jokes are found to be funny as a result of a two-stage mental process. In the first stage, the recipient uses the early parts of the joke to construct a story line or 'narrative schema' (1972, p. 86). The schema is formulated on the basis of the initial linguistic input, but it necessarily goes beyond this input and implies how the story will, or should, evolve. Although there may, in principle, be many possible lines of development for any particular opening, each recipient is assumed to opt for one specific schema. This is because human 'information-processing strategies and capabilities are such that initial information is usually processed with a single interpretation. Therefore, the recipient cannot maintain a set of multiple interpretations, [only] one of which may happen to be correct' (1972, p. 84).

Suls's basic assumption here is similar to William James's assertion, cited above in the discussion of the serious mode, that people are unable to sustain contradictory perspectives on the world (see also Raskin, 1985a, p. 64). But in my view, Suls has failed to make a critical distinction between our normal pattern of serious language-use, which does require coherence and consistency, and our basic psychological processes, which are quite capable of operating according to entirely different principles. Nevertheless, whether or not this is so, we have certainly seen in Sacks's analysis that a particular kind of 'expectation' can be created through a joke's detailed textual organization. In the case of Sacks's joke, one 'expectation' generated in the course of its telling was that sound should emerge from each daughter's door. In the case of the dapper man joke, the text 'suggests' that the barman will comment on the dapper man's wall-climbing capabilities. In Koestler's joke, we are led to 'expect' that the young officer's polite reply will be couched in terms similar to those used by the courtesan. It seems likely, therefore, that Suls is right in claiming that particular narrative expectations are generated in the course of a joke's telling and are recognized by recipients.

Suls continues with the proposal that this first stage of information-processing is disrupted and brought to an end, in the case of jokes, by a sudden incongruity. As he puts it, the recipient 'experiences an abrupt disconfirmation of his prediction' about the development of the story line (1972, p. 87). In other words, the 'joke's ending does not follow logically from its preceding text' (1972, p. 84). The recipient, it is suggested, is surprised at the appearance of incongruity, and a second stage of information-processing is set in motion. The recipient's aim during this second stage is to find out how the punch line can be made to follow from or to be congruent with what has gone before. This aim is pursued by means of a search for a set of 'cognitive rules' which will enable the recipient to remove the incongruity and to make sense of the entire joke within one coherent framework or story line. To summarize Suls's view of what happens when people find a joke funny, we can say that amusement arises when people experience 'a sudden incongruity which is then made congruous' (1972, p. 82). When what was thought to have been an incongruity has been satisfactorily explained, the information processing will cease and laughter will ensue (1972, p. 91).

Certain aspects of Suls's information-processing model are consistent with the analysis of humour that I have been developing. In other respects, however, the two lines of argument are incongruous. Because I am engaged in serious discourse, I am obliged to attend to these incongruities and, if possible, to remove them. I will do so by showing that Suls's analysis is internally inconsistent and therefore wrong; that is, it is unacceptable within the serious mode.

Suls's central mistake, as I hinted above, is to assume that information-processing within the humorous mode is identical to that underlying serious discourse. He takes it for granted that recipients of jokes are expecting a congruent outcome and are surprised – this is Suls's word – when incongruity appears during the course of a joke's telling. But surely we are not *surprised* to find that a joke ends with a punch line that we could not predict. I suggest that we would be surprised only if what is recognizably a joke did *not* end in this way. If this is so, it seems unlikely that recipients are mentally predicting that the joke will develop in a straightforward manner in accordance with the 'initial information input'. Such a prediction would only be appropriate in the serious mode.

If participants are not expecting and not predicting a congruent completion of the humorous narrative, why should analysts assume that recipients will necessarily seek to resolve those incongruities which do in fact occur? Why should we not assume that participants can, when they deem it appropriate, accept and even strive for inconsistency, incongruity and interpretative duality? Indeed, if we refuse to accept that this is possible, we are unable to cope with the distinction which both participants and analysts make between jokes and puzzles. In the following passage, Suls tries to deal with this issue.

> The two criteria for humour – incongruity and its resolution – may seem to be possessed by other kinds of stimuli which do not evoke humour, for example, mathematical dilemmas and puzzles. The problem is resolved when we realize that incongruity and unpredictability are different. The conclusions of mathematical dilemmas and puzzles are frequently unpredictable but are not incongruous; joke endings, on the other hand, are incongruous. This is so because a joke's ending does not follow logically from its preceding text. (1972, p. 84)

Suls argues here that jokes are distinct from puzzles because puzzles have a congruous ending, whereas jokes do not. However, as we have seen, he maintains elsewhere in his analysis that 'humour derives from experiencing a sudden incongruity *which is then made congruous*' (1972, p. 82). This latter claim seems to be essential to his model. Yet, if we accept it, his attempt to distinguish jokes from puzzles is undermined. According to Suls's main argument, jokes and puzzles seem to present recipients with the same cognitive task: namely, that of re-establishing one coherent, overall interpretation in a situation of apparent incoherence and ambiguity. We can agree that this is true of puzzles. But if we believe, as Suls himself does, that puzzles differ from jokes, we have to find some alternative account of the interpretative work carried out by recipients of jokes.

I suggest that jokes are designed to display congruity *and* incongruity at the same time; and that recipients presumably respond to them accordingly. Jokes do have to make sense. They have to furnish an understandable connection between the punch line and the rest of the text, and thereby between the divergent frames of reference juxtaposed within the joke. But the range of interpretative connections allowed in the realm of humour is much wider than that permissible in serious discourse. For example, the connection may depend on the dual meaning of a word such as 'heart' or upon the nebulous association of elephants and fish available in the phrase 'swimming trunks'. When recipients 'get' the meaning of interpretative connections such as these, they are not trying to establish the kind of congruity that would be required in serious talk or writing. They are, rather, registering that some kind of unexpected, unspecified, and perhaps unspecifiable, link is possible.

Recipients must also be registering, however, the contrast, contradiction and incongruity which persist in jokes, even though they do make sense. For example, we cannot process the information provided by the swimming trunks joke or the dapper man joke so as to eliminate incongruity. Yet we can still 'get the joke'. We can grasp the connection, for example, between elephants, fish and swimming trunks; but that connection is both understandable *and* ludicrous. Similarly, even in Sacks's or Koestler's jokes, where the humour stays closer to the known-in- common world, the remarks uttered by the third daughter and the young officer remain incongruous, even though we understand what they imply. The young officer's grossly sexual innuendo is easily understood. But this does not make it any the less incongruous a reply to the courtesan's polite utterance. Indeed, it is presumably the incongruity of the officer's remark that makes it necessary for him to convey his meaning behind the veil of humorous allusion (see chapter 5).

As a further illustration of this point, consider the following joke:

A supposed advertisement displayed in the carriages
of the London Underground:
WANT TO LEARN HOW TO READ?
PHONE 123 456
FOR FURTHER INFORMATION

Paulos gives this as an example of a modal joke, where 'the content of a statement is incongruous with its form or mode of expression. That is, the statement's mode of expression belies its content, and the resulting incongruity is often humorous' (1980, p. 42). We can, of course, construct an explanation which will plausibly explain how this peculiar advertisment came to appear. We can suppose, for instance, that those responsible for its being publicly displayed overlooked the fact that the audience in which they were interested could not read. In other words, we could assume that the people offering the advertisement were incompetent. Alternatively, we might decide that they could think of no cheap form of advertisement which did not need to be read. They may have hoped, therefore, that people who could read would pass on the message. Thus we can, if we so wish, formulate plausible accounts of how the humour came into existence. But no 'information-processing' of this kind can remove the incongruous relationship between the communicative medium and the specific message. The point of this joke is to create and display this incongruity for our appreciation. It is not a puzzle requiring us to think of some way in which the 'mistake' could have happened. To 'get' this joke does not, I suggest, mean that one can imagine how people may have produced an ineffective advertisement, but that one has registered and enjoyed the incongruity built into the advertisement.

Incongruity is an essential and persistent feature of humour. The basic bisociative structure of humour is designed to create and display this feature. Yet, as we have seen, despite incongruity, jokes nevertheless make sense. Their narrative lines and interpretative links are understandable. But the sense-making processes of humour are often quite unlike those of the serious realm; the congruity achieved in the humorous realm is frequently incongruous when judged by ordinary standards. Even where this is not so, jokes necessarily display congruity *and* incongruity within the one text; and the task of the recipient is to register both these elements. It is this interpretative duality which distinguishes jokes from puzzles, and humour from serious discourse. In the realm of humour, we strive to create and convey to others, not the one, unitary world, but many possible worlds, each characterized by interpretative duality and contradiction.

Humorous duality on display

In order to clarify the implications of this discussion of 'getting the joke', let me examine and revise Suls's account of how a specific joke may be processed by a recipient.

Suls's joke

O'Riley was on trial for armed robbery. The jury came out and announced, 'Not guilty'. 'Wonderful,' said O'Riley, 'does that mean I can keep the money?' (1972, p. 90)

Suls suggests that the first two sentences of this joke create an expectation or prediction on the part of the recipient that O'Riley will say something like 'Wonderful. Does that mean I can go now?' Consequently, his actual answer is unexpected. It departs from this expectation and, in implying O'Riley's guilt, contradicts the jury's verdict. The punch line, therefore, creates an incongruity which needs to be resolved. Moreover, Suls maintains, we must provide a coherent interpretation that enables us to offer a serious answer to O'Riley's question about whether or not he can keep the money and that removes the apparent clash between the jury's verdict and O'Riley's guilt.

Suls proposes that the recipient can re-establish congruity by formulating 'rules' to the effect that juries sometimes make mistakes, that legal innocence may differ from real innocence, and that O'Riley can in fact keep the money because he has been found legally innocent. According to Suls, laughter or amusement breaks out when the recipient has worked through these considerations and has come to realize that there is, after all, no incongruity. For Suls, amusement is akin to a feeling of relief which occurs when we manage to re-establish interpretative coherence and unity.

> O'Riley's question points out that the courts make mistakes, that legal truth and actual truth do not always correspond, and that the legal truth determines public consequences. In short, O'Riley can keep the money since, by law, he did not steal it. For successful solution of the problem, some routine like this is necessary. When the incongruity has been explained, the process should terminate and laughter ensue. (1972, p. 91)

My reading of this joke and my account of its processing are rather different. In my view, the joke is designed to create and display incongruity by juxtaposing and contrasting 'actual guilt' with 'legal innocence'. We are not expected or required to answer O'Riley's question in order to 'get the joke'. Rather, O'Riley's question is merely a means of revealing, implicitly, that he is actually guilty despite the jury's verdict. The joke does present recipients with a puzzle. But it is not the kind of puzzle which requires us to carry out interpretative work in order to re-establish congruity and to tie up loose ends. The joke is, instead, a vehicle by means of which 'understandable incongruity' is created and communicated to others.

In contrast to the modal joke about the advertisement in the London Underground, the humorous outcome of Suls's joke is made easily understandable. This is done by means of a feature which Suls entirely ignores. Unlike Suls, I would attribute some importance to the fact that the central figure in the joke is named 'O'Riley' and is therefore either Irish or of Irish descent. We know from common experience as well as from systematic study that stupidity is almost always the defining characteristic of Irishmen in jokes (Davies, 1982; 1987; 1988). O'Riley seems to be no exception. For it is presumably O'Riley's stupidity that leads him to disclose his guilt, without apparently realizing it. I suggest, therefore, that O'Riley is a textual device, akin to the Mommy in Sacks's joke, for constructing incongruity. Through his supposed stupidity, he displays to us what we already know, yet which is normally kept hidden: namely, that it is possible to be both guilty and not-guilty at the same time. But O'Riley does this in joke form, by means of a sudden bisociation accomplished allusively. O'Riley and O'Riley's stupidity are used to bring about a swift transition between, and combination of, innocence and guilt, through which incongruity is generated, displayed and communicated.

It seems to me that what Suls calls 'second-stage problem- solving' would be quite redundant here, and that recipients have no need to explain away this incongruity or to furnish an answer to O'Riley's punch line. For O'Riley's Irishness, which is established at the joke's outset, makes the affair immediately comprehensible. We know *from the start* that here is a joke, that O'Riley is Irish and that he will do something foolish. In the serious realm – for example, in a discussion between a solicitor and her client – participants would be careful to establish that two conceptions of 'guilt' are available and that there is no real contradiction in describing a person as legally innocent but actually guilty. Suls proposes that we go through this kind of reasoning in order to make sense of O'Riley's imaginary conduct. I suggest, in contrast, that jokes in general, and this one in particular, are designed to *generate* incongruity, and that mental processing takes the form of recognizing the incongruity offered by the joke. Our task as recipients is not to devise a rational explanation of the failure of our serious expectations; for we know in advance, from 'O'Riley' and the joke format, that incongruity is only to be expected. Rather, our task is to *grasp* that incongruity, and, in a face-to-face situation, to show our appreciation of it to the teller.

Suls's joke, then, provides the basis for a socially coordinated display of incongruity and interpretative duality. The joke is structured to bring sharply to recipients' attention that one can be simultaneously innocent and guilty. In the world of humour, unlike the so-called real world, we require people and things to be both A and non-A at the same time. In the humorous domain, the rules of logic, the expectations of common sense, the laws of science and the demands of propriety are all potentially in abeyance. Consequently, when recipients are faced with a joke, they do not apply the information-processing procedures appropriate to serious discourse. In the realm of humour, recipients are not expecting or seeking congruity. For they have temporarily abandoned the assumptions of the ordinary world and are responding to, registering and celebrating a world of discourse where interpretative duality is the basic principle and understandable incongruity the overriding aim.

Note

1 My discussion of the basic characteristics of serious discourse focuses on language as a set of symbols by means of which we represent or establish the meaning(s) of the world in which we live. Clearly, language is much more than

this. In particular, it is also a resource for acting upon the world and for interacting with other people. The meanings we accomplish are intimately linked to the social interaction in which we engage (Austin, 1962; Garfinkel, 1967; Grice, 1967; Atkinson and Heritage, 1984). My brief account of the presuppositions of serious discourse is not intended to deny this. Indeed, I will try to show in later chapters how the distinctive attributes of humour enable participants to put it to work for serious purposes. For discussions of how humour may contravene the guidelines for conduct that are appropriate in serious, bona fide communication, see Hancher, 1980, Martinich, 1981 and Raskin, 1985a.

3

Semantics and Signals

In the two previous chapters I have consciously adopted an interdisciplinary perspective on humour. Humour itself does not stay within disciplinary confines and, although my overall concern is with humour as a social phenomenon, much can be learned from consulting the work of linguists, psychologists and thinkers such as Koestler, who defy categorization. I will now examine a linguistic theory of humour in order to extend our understanding of bisociation and incongruity. This will lead to a discussion of how humour is signalled and how the humorous mode is established during the course of social interaction.

A semantic theory of humour

Koestler proposed that humour is created when two incompatible frameworks are brought suddenly together. He also referred to these 'frameworks' as associative contexts, types of logic, codes of behaviour, matrices of thought and as universes of discourse (1964, p. 38). As a result of this conceptual looseness, it is never entirely clear in Koestler's discussion of the mechanics of humour, whether he is describing psychological processes, social actions, cultural systems, behavioural responses or the properties of texts. Raskin's (1985a) theory of humour resembles Koestler's in that it also gives a central role to the combination, or bisociation, of divergent frames of reference. But Raskin is much more firmly committed than Koestler to conceptual clarity, in order to make it possible for him to provide complete, unambiguous and non-contradictory descriptions of the data of humour (Raskin, 1985a, p. 48). He therefore identifies the focus of his analysis clearly and explicitly as verbal humour and the linguistic properties of texts. He offers us a theory which is an attempt to state formally the necessary and sufficient conditions for a text to be funny (1985a, p. 47). His theory identifies the special characteristics that are possessed by texts which are recognized as humorous (1985b, p. 35).

What Raskin calls his 'main hypothesis' can be formulated quite simply. It is that a text is a single-joke-carrying text if it satisfies two conditions:

(i) the text is compatible, fully or in part, with two different scripts;
(ii) the two scripts with which the text is compatible are opposing scripts. (1985a, p. 99)

Raskin examines and lists several hundred recognizable jokes, every one of which, he suggests, satisfies the conditions specified by his theory. In order to understand this theory, we must have a clear idea of what he means by 'script' and what it means to say that two scripts are 'opposite' or 'opposing'. My comments on these terms will necessarily be rather simplified. Interested readers should consult Raskin, 1985a/b.

Raskin's theory is concerned with the semantic structure of humorous texts; that is, he assumes that the text's humour is embodied in the meaning of its words. He stresses, however, that particular words are used in many different ways as the social and interpretative context varies. We cannot, therefore, find the meaning of a joke simply by reading off from a dictionary the specific meanings of the words which make up that joke. Rather, each word, as it is read or heard, evokes a complex range of possible uses and implications. These constitute the script for that word.

The script is a large chunk of semantic information surrounding the word or evoked by it. The script is a cognitive structure internalized by the native speaker and it represents the native speaker's knowledge of a small part of the world. Every speaker has internalized rather a large repertoire of scripts of 'common sense' which represent his/her knowledge of certain routines, standard procedures, basic situations, etc.; for instance, the knowledge of what people do in certain situations, how they do it, in what order, etc. (Raskin, 1985a, p. 81)

As a joke proceeds, each new word and phrase adds another 'large chunk of semantic information'. Some of the interpretative possibilities opened up as the joke unfolds will be difficult to reconcile with what has gone before and will therefore be ignored or held in suspension. However: 'Every word of a sentence evokes a script, and the words of the same sentence frequently evoke the same script repeatedly' (1985b, p. 36). Consequently, as a result of overlap and interconnection between scripts, a consistent macroscript or scenario usually evolves fairly quickly (1985a, p. 126). This is similar to what the psychologist Suls terms the 'formation of a narrative line'; and, although Raskin claims to be dealing with the semantic features of texts, his definition of 'script' quoted above shows that he assumes a close correspondence between semantic structure and mental processes.

Raskin develops – but I will not describe them here – a series of procedures or rules for identifying the scripts and scenarios implicit in any humorous text.

The combinatorial rules of script-based semantic theory combine all the scripts evoked by individual words to calculate the meaning of an entire sentence. At the same time, on the basis of these scripts, they calculate and store all the extra- sentential information, contextual and situational, which will be used to interpret the following sentences. (1985b, p. 36)

With these combinatorial rules, Raskin has sought to devise a systematic set of linguistic procedures for identifying those aspects of the common-sense, known-in-common world that provide the semantic components for every joke. Raskin emphasizes, however, that joke texts are not designed to convey information about the world, but rather to use this information in order to create a special effect – namely, to make the hearer laugh (1985a, p. 101).

This special effect is produced by constructing a text which evokes and is fully or partly compatible with two opposing scripts or scenarios. Raskin points out that *any* ambiguous text will be compatible with more than one script. That is what we mean by 'ambiguity'. But not all ambiguous texts are amusing. Consequently, the critical and distinguishing characteristic of humour, in Raskin's view, is the opposition between the scripts involved. A joke is an ambiguous text which gives rise to a specific kind of semantic opposition. To claim that the scripts contained in jokes are 'opposite' is not merely to suggest that they generate some vague semantic divergence or incongruity. These scripts, Raskin insists, must be opposite in a very special sense (1985a, p. 107). In making this assertion, he attempts to be much more precise and rigorous than the many previous analysts, such as Suls, Paulos or Koestler, who have drawn attention to the incongruity of humorous discourse, but have accepted that humorous incongruity can be constructed in many different ways.

Raskin maintains that the basic semantic opposition employed in humour is that between real and unreal or between actual and non-actual. This basic contrast can be divided into three sub-categories. There can be a contrast between the actual situation occurring in a joke and some non-actual situation which is incompatible with the actual setting of the joke. There can be opposition between the normal state of affairs and some abnormal, unexpected state. There can also be a contrast between some possible or plausible situation and one much less plausible. These are the three basic types of textual opposition between the 'real' and the 'unreal' that are said to be essential to humour. In addition, the real/unreal opposition is often supplemented by additional binary contrasts. In the great majority of jokes:

One script refers to the real, normal or possible situation as reflected in the text and the other to an unreal, abnormal or impossible situation . . . The common actual/non- actual opposition is often reinforced by oppositions from a few binary categories that are essential to human life, such as true versus false, good versus bad, sex versus no sex, life versus death and money versus no money. (Raskin, 1985b, p. 37)

Despite these latter complications, Raskin's central claim is that a text is funny when it embodies two scripts or scenarios which express, within the semantic context created by that text, a contrast between the real and the unreal or between the actual and the non-actual. It 'is this oppositeness which creates the joke' (1985a, p. 100). It is this opposition between real and unreal that produces the special effect of humorous discourse and that distinguishes it from the serious mode. It is presumably this oppositeness which is recognized intuitively by ordinary speakers and which causes them to laugh (1985a, p. 101).

There is much to be said in favour of Raskin's theory. Jokes do often make use of basic binary contrasts: for example, the contrast between innocent and guilty in Suls's joke. It is also clear that, in various ways, humour does focus on the contrast between real and unreal (the dapper man joke), normal and abnormal (Sacks's joke), and possible and impossible (the swimming trunks joke). Moreover, Raskin's real/unreal contrast can be extended in line with the evolving argument of this text. For in the humorous mode it is the unreal, unexpected, abnormal and impossible that are interpretatively dominant. In the course of humour, the realities and expectations of serious discourse are opposed and undermined. Whereas the mechanisms of serious discourse are designed to maintain the sense that we live in a normal, predictable, real world, those of humorous discourse are designed to ensure that any apparent realities are contradicted and made to seem unreal.

There is, however, a certain element of paradox and incongruity about the humorous realm which, I believe, cannot be grasped by an analytical discourse such as Raskin's that is itself so emphatically realist. For instance, I am by no means convinced that Raskin's procedures for identifying scripts or his criteria for identifying the special kind of opposition characteristic of humour can be applied with as much rigour as he contends. To offer an illustration – it seems to me that the scripts associated with certain words in the course of serious discourse are different from the scripts for those same words when they appear in jokes. One example of this might be 'Irishman'. If I tell some new acquaintance about the etymology of the name 'Mulkay', explaining that it is a corruption of the Irish clan name 'Mulcahy', and so on, it is unlikely that the same script will be implied by the name or by the reference to Irishness as is occasioned by the use of 'O'Riley' in Suls's joke. I suggest that the connotations of 'Irishness' are different within the two modes. Similarly, references to clergymen and bishops evoke significantly different scripts when they appear in jokes – at least when they appear in British jokes – from when they are made in the course of serious discourse. British jokes about clergymen almost always depend on a high degree of sexual innuendo, which is entirely absent in the serious realm. Indeed, it is possible to suggest a sexual interpretation of the most innocent phrases, and to change from the serious to the humorous mode, simply by attributing them to a bishop speaking to an actress or vice versa.

1 I do like Victorian design – as the bishop said to the actress.
2 I wouldn't change it for anything larger – as the actress said to the bishop. (Nash, 1985, p. 42)

This humorous genre depends on a contrast between actresses and bishops. In texts of this kind, the former represent sexual licence, whilst the latter represent sexual innocence. To this extent, the customary serious script for the word 'bishop' is central to the contrast structure of the humorous text, and part of the humour may arise from the possibility that the bishop is utterly unaware of any lewd interpretation of the discourse in which he is engaged. Yet, at the same time, this type of joke necessarily represents bishops as having a pronounced interest in actresses. The regular combination of these two categories in the humorous mode suggests that they have something in common. Such jokes seem to imply that bishops may be less innocent than they appear. Thus part of the humour may arise, at a deeper level, from the possibility that, behind the mask of innocence, the bishop may be engaged in unbridled sexual activity and quite conscious of the alternative meaning that can be given to his words. The implicit character of humorous discourse means that we can never be sure whether innocence or sexual licence is the correct script.

Within the realm of humour, I suggest, both innocence *and* sexual promiscuity are part of the script for 'bishop'. In the course of humorous discourse the very meaning of words may become inherently contradictory. We have to recognize, therefore, that the humorous use of at least some words transforms the script with which they are associated. Moreover, the very nature of the humorous mode, and the way in which words are used within it, make it impossible to achieve the rigorous identification of the 'type of opposition' required by Raskin's theory. Consider the following clergyman joke.

The clergyman joke

The Archdeacon has got back from London, and confides to his friend the doctor, 'Like Saint Peter, I toiled all night. Let us hope that like Saint Peter I caught nothing'. (Raskin, 1985, p. 25, taken from Legman, 1975, p. 308)

Raskin identifies this as an opposition between the Archdeacon's actual debauchery and the non-actuality of honest toil. According to Raskin, 'the hero was involved in debauchery in real life . . . and he was not involved in honest toil as the comparison with Saint Peter suggests' (1985a, p. 111). This, however, seems an unduly literal reading and inappropriate to the humorous mode. In the first place, the 'real life' referred to by Raskin is the real life of the humorous world; that is, it may be nothing more than fantasy and, therefore, in one sense, quite unreal. Raskin's analysis, of course, requires us to take for granted the reality presented in the text of the joke. But when we try to do this, we experience difficulties arising from the character of humorous discourse. For instance, we know, from what seems to be an allusive reference to sexual activity, that the Archdeacon himself is not being entirely serious. Moreover, he certainly does not state openly that he was actually engaged in sexual frolics during the previous night. It may well be, therefore, that he is merely pretending to have done so. The sexual allusions may be nothing more than a joke (within a joke) and in no way a humorously disguised reference to actual debauchery. It may be, indeed, that the Archdeacon is doing no more than playing upon the sexual connotations of the 'clergyman script' in humorous discourse. Alternatively, the joke may be an instance of self-mockery by a clergyman seeking to avoid expressing pride in his genuine religious labours. None of these scenarios is, I think, debarred by the semantics of the text. Because the text is humorous and consequently ambiguous, indirect and allusive, we cannot know for certain what is the actuality and what the non-actuality whilst the speaker remains in the humorous mode. However we apply Raskin's categories and however we formulate the Archdeacon's actions, the components of the text resist clear categorization. Not only is the reality *of* the joke itself unreal, but the reality *within* the joke is impossible to specify.

Raskin treats the clergyman joke as if it unproblematically exemplifies the actual/non-actual contrast. It seems just as appropriate, however, to regard it as an example of the normal/abnormal contrast. Raskin himself admits that the three sub-types of humorous contrast overlap extensively. There is a considerable degree of 'mutual penetration and diffusion' (1985a, p. 112). We could, therefore, take the ordinary, serious script for 'clergyman', which would imply a devotion to godly things, a pursuit of

Christian objectives, and so on, and contrast these normal expectations with the abnormal behaviour implied in the punch line. However, the Archdeacon's so-called 'unexpected, abnormal' behaviour is, of course, exactly what *is* expected and normal in a joke. How we categorize his supposed behaviour will depend on whether and how we choose to employ the serious or the humorous script. Thus his inferred sexual misconduct can be either expected or unexpected. It can also be regarded as both unexpected *and* expected. In the humorous mode, the clergyman's script has an unavoidable duality which undermines any attempts at rigorous, formal categorization in terms of such contrasts as actual/non-actual, normal/abnormal or real/unreal.

This does not imply, in my view, that Raskin is wrong to stress the importance of the real/unreal contrast within humorous discourse. But it does imply that he is wrong to try to formulate this and related contrasts with undue rigour and precision. In the clergyman joke, as in humour generally, real life is unreal whilst the unreal is real; the expected is unexpected and the unexpected expected; and the main point of the discourse can only be hinted at. Humour differs from serious conduct in approaching reality and unreality playfully. It does not so much contrast one with the other as confuse the boundary between the two. Consequently, it is misleading of Raskin to suggest that the opposition between reality and unreality furnishes a clear, unambiguous feature around which humour is constructed. This cannot be so because the realm of humour, by its very nature, undermines that separation of reality and unreality which is central to serious discourse (Fry, 1963).

The underlying analytical error, which we have now encountered several times, is that of treating humour as if it were part of the serious mode. Raskin's mistake is to imagine that one can construct a rigorous, formal theory within the serious mode which can represent clearly, explicitly and with predictive accuracy the semantic processes of a realm which depends on ambiguity, allusion and interpretative duality, and which seems to operate, as far as we can judge, by undermining the very principles and practices presupposed in the serious realm.

This appraisal of Raskin's theoretical endeavours confirms that humour is an inherently paradoxical domain, where any apparent reality created by the text is destined to be contradicted or challenged by some alternative reality arising from the same text. Yet these alternative realities are always allusive and uncertain. They are realities which, paradoxically, are not to be taken seriously. This aspect of humour has been conveyed most effectively by William Fry:

> During the unfolding of humor, one is suddenly confronted by an explicit-implicit reversal when the punch line is delivered . . . the

reversal . . . has the unique effect of forcing upon the humor
participants an internal redefining of reality. Inescapably, the punch
line combines communication and metacommunication. One
receives the explicit communication of the punch line. Also, on a
higher level of abstraction, the punch line carries an implicit
metacommunication about itself and about reality as exemplified by
the joke . . . Content communicates the message 'This is unreal',
and in so doing makes reference to the whole of which it is a part . . .
Real is unreal, and unreal is real. (1963, p. 153)

We must conclude that there are no stable, unitary semantic structures
within the humorous mode. Humorous discourse is designed to make
impossible any firm distinction between real and unreal, between actual
and non-actual. Thus, whilst we remain wholly committed, like Raskin
and most other analysts, to the serious mode, humour will always repel
our advances. We cannot enter into the humorous mode in order to grasp
the principles by which it operates. For we can gain entry only by
abandoning the assumptions and procedures of the serious realm. As long
as we remain serious analysts, we are condemned to circle around the
humorous domain, occasionally venturing in to secure textual fragments
for analytical dissection, but viewing its products from an alien
perspective. Unlike analysts, however, participants seem to be able to
enter the humorous domain with relative ease. Let us examine how this is
done.

Entering the humorous mode

If social interaction is to work effectively, participants need to know and to
be able to inform each other which discursive mode is in operation. For
practical reasons, they have to be able to answer Erving Goffman's
question 'What is it that's going on here?' (1974, p. 8). Since, as we have
seen, the principles and practices of humorous and serious discourse are
radically different, failure by participants to realize that their partners
have switched from one mode to the other is likely to generate
misunderstanding, confusion and inappropriate responses. For example,
one distinctive feature of humorous interaction is that each humorous
contribution has to be marked by recipients in a rather special way: that is,
by laughter, smiling or some related token of appreciation. If this is not
done continually, humorous interaction lapses and participants return to
the serious mode (Fine, 1984, p. 85). In short, the humorous mode
requires participants to carry out particular kinds of interpretative work
and to deal with others' textual offerings in specific ways. How, then, do

participants gain entry to the humorous realm and how do they let each other know that humour is going on?

Participants display their departure from the serious mode by signalling that their speech, action and intentions are not those of the ordinary, mundane world. These signals may not necessarily be specific to humour, but may indicate more broadly that what is taking place should be regarded as occurring within a 'play frame', where events are 'not to be taken seriously'.

> First, humor is play. Cues are given that this, which is about to unfold, is not real. There is a 'play frame' . . . created around the episode. The frame can be indicated by a voice quality, a body movement or posture, a lifted eyebrow – any of the various things people do to indicate fantasy to one another . . . Usually these frames are established at the beginning of the humorous episode. A wink, a smile, a gurgle in the voice will set the stage before the joke begins its evolution . . . Although most cue-messages are non-verbal, humans are not limited to non-verbal cues . . . A canned joke may be prefaced by the statement 'Let me tell you a story', or 'Did you hear this one?' or 'I heard a good one last week', in addition to the non-verbal cues that are emitted. (Fry, 1963, pp. 138, 141–2)

Although, as Fry suggests, many of the signals used to indicate entry to the humorous mode or the 'play frame' are non- verbal, it seems likely from common experience that they often involve some change in the speaker's normal voice pattern. Fry points out that the adoption of a false dialect is often used as an indicator of humour, as is a 'mock-serious' form of vocal delivery (1963, pp. 144–5). Such changes in verbal style establish that what is being said is not 'real speech'. One important way into the humorous mode is for the speaker to use verbal inflection to make it clear that his speech differs from that employed in ordinary serious discourse. Although it is difficult to describe in detail exactly what vocal changes are used to signal the occurrence of humour, there is no doubt that we are able to recognize and to employ these changes effectively in the course of social interaction.

Consider the following transcription of a brief interaction during which humorous interchanges occur. There are three participants of roughly the same age: Mike (M) is a reasearch assistant, while Sara (S) and Boo (B) are secretaries. Each utterance is coded 'U' and each gesture, 'G'.

G1   The narrative begins when Mike enters the reception area, and walks to Boo's desk where he waits for her to notice him.

G2   Seeing Mike, Boo stops typing, and looks up at him inquisitively.

U1 M–B 'Do you have any of those stick-on tags for file folders?'
G3   Sara pauses in her typing as she listens to the dialogue between Mike and Boo.
G4   Boo pulls open a drawer in her desk, and she brings out several small boxes.
U2 B–M 'Yes, and you have your choice from a wide variety of colors. There's yellow, purple, red, green . . .' (Said archly)
G5   Mike and Sara grin.
U3 M–B 'I'll take the green; they go with my eyes.' (Said mischievously)
G6   Boo and Sara chuckle as Mike grins.
G7   Boo hands Mike the green tags.
G8   Mike takes the package, and he strolls out of the room.

(Flaherty, 1984, p. 78)

The humour in this passage is not standardized but informal. It is fashioned for the occasion and would be difficult to pass on to others in humorous form. Yet the humour was successful at the time in that all three persons are described as either grinning or chuckling; and the verbal sequence ends with proper public recognition by all parties that humour has been offered, accepted and understood as such (G6). The humorous interaction appears to start at U2, where Boo is described as signalling her change of mode by speaking 'archly'. It is unlikely that any of the participants could give a detailed account of how to speak 'archly'. Nevertheless, Mike recognizes from this cue, apparently correctly, that Boo has switched to the humorous mode and he responds in kind: that is, he begins to speak 'mischievously'. Thus this passage illustrates how entry into the humorous mode may be signalled by alterations in vocal inflection. It also suggests that the mode is sustained in part by the continual provision of suitable cues, as well as brought to an appropriate end by an exchange of 'terminal smiles' (Fry, 1963, p. 145).

This example also makes it clear that a humorous signal does not necessarily indicate that a *joke* is to follow. Rather, such signals mean 'interpret what is being said or is to be said as humorous discourse whether or not it is in joke form' (Nash, 1985, p. 36). They tell us that we are no longer operating within the serious realm and that we should no longer expect, or seek to maintain, the unitary discourse of the mundane world. Given what has been established above about the structure of humorous discourse, it follows that participants are required to sustain a form of interaction in which each contribution is open to two (or more) divergent interpretations. For example, one reading of Flaherty's transcript is that Mike accepts an invitation from Boo to enter the fantasy world of humour, and joins her in pretending that the stick-on labels are not merely functional objects but are also items to be playfully assessed and chosen according to aesthetic criteria. Alternatively, it may be that Boo's archly delivered reference to red (stop) and then green (go) is being taken as a sign that she is willing, whilst supplying the labels, to engage in a little light-hearted flirtation.

However these cues are understood by those involved, it is clear from the transcript that Mike follows Boo into the humorous mode and couches his reply in appropriately allusive terms. In other words, he responds in a manner which is entirely adequate at the level of serious interaction, yet which implies an additional level of meaning. Although this additional meaning is never openly declared by either party, it seems that the humorous duality of their discourse is evident to the second secretary as well as to the main participants. Thus this brief excursion into the realm of humour is accomplished partly by an exchange of cues which alerts participants to the need to speak and interpret in a manner appropriate to the humorous mode; and partly by an exchange of utterances which are designed to imply the existence of more than one framework of meaning (Flaherty, 1984).

Most intended humour, as in the exchange between Boo and Mike, is accomplished through a combination of humorous cues or signals and a verbal (or visual) text that encourages or at least allows some element of interpretative bisociation. It is possible, however, for written or spoken texts to be treated as humorous, even though they appear to contain no bisociation and no allusions to the alternative reality required by humorous discourse. In such cases, use of appropriate signals is particularly critical to recipients' awareness of entry into the humorous mode; various kinds of contextual or presentational cues are employed to suggest that the utterance is not to be taken literally, and that the recipient must formulate some counter-text of his own which contradicts the actual utterance and which will convey the speaker's real meaning. Such statements, of course, are called 'ironic'; and the implied counter-text is usually taken to be the opposite of what is actually spoken or written. In the case of irony the use of cues is all-important, because it is by their use alone that the speaker implies the need for an opposing script: 'the ironist insincerely states something he does not mean, but through the manner of his statement – whether through its formulation, or its delivery, or both – is able to encode a counter-proposition, his 'real meaning', which may be interpreted by the attentive listener or reader' (Nash, 1985, p. 152).

Thus, the statement 'There is a genius in the White House' (Wright, 1978) may be uttered in such a way (perhaps with peculiar emphasis on 'genius'), or in such a context (following a reference to a major political blunder) or by such a person (a political adversary of the President) that its insincerity, its implied duality and its deviation from the requirements of serious discourse are made manifest, even though the words of the text may seem to imply no script other than the straightforward expression of praise. In this kind of ironic humour, the recipient's recognition of interpretative duality is very heavily dependent on the speaker's providing appropriate cues and on the recipient's ability to recognize ironic inflection.

It might at first appear that slight physical movements, changes of tone and ironic inflections are somewhat intangible and uncertain ways of informing others of a change of discursive mode. But we must not forget that humorous discourse relies on subtle allusions and delicate nuances of meaning. It is perhaps not so surprising, therefore, that entry into the realm of humour is often accomplished by means of signals that are elusive as well as allusive. Particularly in the course of informal, spontaneous humour, which will often be interspersed among stretches of serious converse, it would be quite inappropriate to mark the transition into humour in any explicit fashion. Here the duality and allusiveness of the humour would be destroyed by attempts to furnish the kind of clear-cut interpretative instructions that might be suitable in certain serious contexts. Explicit, unambiguous signals would, by their very nature, anchor the discourse more firmly within the serious mode. Entry into humour has to be signalled in the kind of allusive manner that is dominant within this realm of discourse.

This is made particularly clear by Fry (1963), who has argued, following Gregory Bateson (1955), that humorous cues are essentially paradoxical in character. They are paradoxical, he maintains, because they convey that the discourse of which they form a part is not genuine, bona fide discourse (Raskin, 1985a, pp. 100–4) and should not be taken seriously. This implies, however, that the signals themselves cannot be taken seriously and therefore do not mean what they appear to mean. If this is so, it seems to follow that the discourse is serious after all and that the signals do mean what they appear to mean: namely, that the discourse is not serious. And so on. In the following passage, Fry formulates this paradox in terms of the real/unreal contrast emphasized by Raskin.

> Humor, then, is an episode set off from the rest of the world by a play frame: 'What is contained herein is not real' . . . The joke's play cues (which are part of the ongoing process and which appear at either the beginning or the end of the episode or repeatedly all the way through it – but which must be present) establish this process, which they are an integral part of, as unreal: 'This joke is not to be perceived in the same way as those instructions for feeding the chickens'. The cue sets up the situation as unreal, including, of course, itself as an integral part of the ongoing process. If the

situation is unreal, so is the cue-message, and the situation becomes real. If it becomes real, so does the cue-message, and the situation is unreal. A circular paradox is quickly apparent. (1963, p. 143)

Fry is making an important point here about entry into humour and about the nature of humorous discourse. Nevertheless, it is necessary to remember that what Fry calls 'paradox' appears as such only from the perspective of serious discourse. Fry's reasoning in the passage quoted above, and mine in the preceding comments, are both couched in the syllogistic, unitary terms of that form of discourse where things are either real or unreal, but never both at the same time. From this perspective, the interpretative duality of humour and its cues may seem circular, even logically vicious, and certainly difficult to accept. But viewed from within the humorous realm, semantic duality is not a problem. It is simply a taken-for-granted assumption. It is the aim and guiding principle of this form of social life. From within the realm of humour, it is Fry's (and my) reasoning which looks faulty and unconvincing. From the humorous point of view, the reaction to Fry's conclusion would take the form of the rhetorical question: How could the cues for humour be anything but real and unreal at the same time? Thus the 'paradox' of entry into the humorous domain involves a further interpretative duality in that the cues by which entry is achieved are paradoxical and problematic, yet also perfectly straightforward and normal. It is only by employing and responding to cues which embody these various kinds of duality that we are able to enter the realm of humour.

The cues and signals discussed so far are essential to all informal humour and to highly implicit humorous forms such as irony. Although these cues are necessarily ambiguous and implicit, they are indispensable, not only in establishing that the humorous mode is in operation, but also in making sure that the dominant mode of serious discourse does not reassert itself. As I mentioned earlier, the humorous mode can be sustained only by means of a continual production of appropriate cues, signals and responses. The humorous mode, like its serious counterpart, is kept in operation by its characteristic forms of interpretative work (Flaherty, 1984). When humorous interchange is maintained over a period of time, the interpretative work that it requires generates a distinctive group atmosphere which is quite different from that of serious discourse. As Fry puts it: 'You have only to walk into a group of such joking persons to be made to realize through the means of every possible communication mode – verbal and non-verbal ("We are telling a joke", eye winks, facial expression, posture, voice tones etc.) – how much involved in humor these participants are' (1963, p. 55).

One further way in which humour is signalled is through the use of verbal forms that have come to be restricted to the humorous realm. Standardized jokes, for example, often begin with a routine three-part list that would not be acceptable as part of serious discourse. The use of such a list, with or without additional cues, is sufficient to establish that one is speaking with humorous intent. There are also various kinds of humorous tag, puzzle formats, question and answer sequences, and standard introductions, which operate as fairly unambiguous indicators of humorous discourse.

> Many jokes are embedded in a fossil syntax, a received verbal structure that we recognize as belonging wholly or in the main to humorous practice. For example, the sentence frame *Come back . . . all is forgiven* is used only with the intention to joke, and never in the straightforward, unironic expression of a wish. I may say, without mischievous purport, *I wish Oscar Wilde were alive and writing today*, but if I exclaim *Come back, Oscar Wilde, all is forgiven*, it will be understood that I speak with some sort of humorous implication. (Nash, 1985, p. 35)

Standard jokes combine a conventional format with some kind of fairly obvious bisociative verbal allusion. This is true, for example, of Sacks's joke. But there are numerous other forms, such as the 'come back' form illustrated in the quotation from Nash, where the verbal content may be straightforward and unitary. In such cases, it is the humorous format in itself which implies that there is another level of meaning and that what is actually said is not what is really meant. In other words, the use of such uniquely humorous forms signals clearly that the humorous mode is in operation, and sets in motion the kind of play with reality and unreality that is characteristic of humour.

Natural humour

Humorous cues, standard formats, and so on, operate as signals of the *intention* to joke (Nash, 1985). These signals vary from one culture to another and from one group to another. However, within each culture or group they are widely shared, and when they are employed the texts or actions in question become 'recognizably humorous'. It does not follow, however, that participants in a recognizably humorous situation will be amused by that situation. Thus a person may watch a television programme which is presented as comedy and which is replete with humour of many kinds, yet never laugh and claim to have found none of it in the least funny. Or one may be told an ethnic, sexual or some other kind of joke which, although it is undeniably a joke, provokes anger rather than laughter.

These variations in individuals' responses to humour follow partly from differences in participants' knowledge of the physical and/or social worlds. For example, one could hardly be amused by Koestler's joke abut the courtesan and the Austrian officer if one had no familiarity at all with the conventional language of 'polite society'. Similarly, individuals will vary in their awareness of humorous forms, of the scripts implicit in the allusive punch lines of jokes, and so on (Nash, 1985). They may also vary in their willingness to treat certain topics in the playful manner required by humour. As Raskin puts it: 'Obviously, a seriously tabooed subject is hardly likely to amuse the person who maintains the taboo. Religious, ethical, and other norms can preclude the availability of the necessary second interpretation for the humorous text' (1985a, p. 129).

There are, then, innumerable reasons why particular recipients may not be amused by a text or action even though they recognize its humorous intent. Humorous signals indicate that recipients should look for a humorous interpretation of the speaker's discourse and that they should respond with appropriate indications of understanding and gratification. But humorous cues in no way guarantee that recipients will be able to accomplish a humorous interpretation or that they will be willing to respond in the expected manner. As we noted before, a social exchange can be recognized by all concerned as being humorous, or not entirely serious, without any of the participants actually professing to be amused.

It is also clear that participants can be amused by actions which are not signalled as humorous as well as by verbal formulations which appear to be intended as serious (Wilson, 1979). Sometimes things happen or words are uttered with no sign of humorous intent, yet which are found to be amusing, even hilarious. The classic example of unsignalled humour is that of the man who accidentally slips on a banana skin, thereby causing some person in the vicinity to break into spontaneous laughter at his mishap. Whereas the banana skin instance is undocumented and possibly apocryphal, the following quotation tells of a real-life 'banana skin joke' involving American military personnel on a helicopter trip during the Vietnam War:

> On the last part of the trip, flying into Dong Ha, the aluminum rod that held the seats broke, spilling us on the floor and making the exact sound that a .50-caliber round will make when it strikes a chopper, giving us all a bad scare and then a good, good laugh. (Flaherty, 1984, p. 75)

In this instance, no humorous cues were exchanged before the event which generated the laughter. We have to accept that there was something about that event which encouraged or at least allowed a humorous interpretation, without participants having any intention to joke and without their contriving entry into the humorous mode. The account quoted above suggests that the laughter followed from the recognition that what had at first seemed serious, was, in fact, a relatively trivial accident. Thus, we find here the kind of sudden movement between divergent interpretative frameworks, accompanied by a play upon the relationship between the real and the unreal, that is typical of humour. This example makes it clear that such an interpretative reversal can be sufficient in itself, without additional signals, to generate the terminal response required by humour – namely, laughter and smiles. It appears, therefore, that although signals, cues and the use of standardized forms are widely employed as means of entry into the humorous mode, they are not essential. Humour is possible wherever participants can accomplish an interpretation of events, actions or texts in accordance with the bisociative principle of humorous discourse.

The type of humour discussed so far in this section has been called 'natural humour' in contrast to 'contrived humour', and it has been argued: 'When such humour arises, reality is the joker; we do not have to account for the motives for these jokes, they simply happen, independently of a human intention to amuse. Frequently, natural jokes stem from unintentionally ambiguous or erratic speech, and from anomalous and unexpected events' (Wilson, 1979, p. 160). It is important to realize, however, that the humour of the event in the helicopter or of the banana skin joke is not intrinsic to the event in question. In this sense it is misleading to suggest that 'reality is the joker'. For it seems likely that the laughter which occurred in the helicopter grew out of interpretative work by participants similar to that contained in the retrospective account quoted above; and that the event could have been interpreted quite differently. Reality never speaks for itself. Whether we use its events as the basis for humour or for serious discourse depends on the interpretative procedures we bring to bear. Koestler makes this point emphatically in his discussion of a classic example of 'natural humour' which, he maintains:

> can be converted from a comic into a tragic or purely intellectual experience, based on the same logical pattern – i.e. on the same pair of bisociated matrices – by a simple change of emotional climate. The fat man slipping and crashing on the icy pavement will be either a comic or tragic figure according to whether the spectator's attitude is dominated by malice or pity: a callous schoolboy will laugh at the spectacle, a sentimental old lady may be inclined to weep. (1964, p. 46)

We do not have to follow Koestler's suggestion that the 'emotional climate' of humour is necessarily aggressive or malicious. Nor do we have to accept that the nature of the event changes for the two spectators simply in accordance with their differing emotional inclinations. Koestler is surely right, however, in maintaining that the one event can be given both a tragic and a comic, a serious and a humorous significance, depending on the kind of interpretative work carried out by different participants. Moreover, this variability is considerbly greater than Koestler suggests. It is not merely that a given event can be interpreted differently by different people as it occurs, but that the same person can formulate a given event as serious or humorous on different occasions and in different social situations (Mulkay and Gilbert, 1982). Whether the event reappears in the humorous or serious mode depends on the telling; and this will vary with the occasion and the participants involved. Humour is created out of 'real world' events through the interpretative work carried out by participants. Thus events which are entirely serious for some participants at a specific time may be humorous for other participants and even for those same participants at some later stage.

The boundary between the humorous and the serious domains is as ambiguous and uncertain as the discourse of humour itself. On some occasions, humour is clearly signalled and accepted unproblematically as humorous. On other occasions, it is signalled but deemed by some not to be amusing. In certain circumstances, usually when something unexpected occurs, some participants, but not necessarily all, find humour where it appears not to have been signalled or intended. Furthermore, events which were treated perfectly seriously at the time can often be reformulated as humorous in subsequent accounts. Even the most serious of texts, it seems, can be transformed into humour by means of appropriate interpretative work. Koestler draws attention to the way in which new ideas in science, that realm of ultra-realist discourse, have often been regarded as funny.

> Until the seventeenth century the Copernican hypothesis of the earth's motion was considered as obviously incompatible with commonsense experience; it was accordingly treated as a huge joke by the majority of Galileo's contemporaries. One of them, a famous wit, wrote: 'The disputes of Signor Galileo have dissolved into alchemical smoke. So here we are at last, safely back on a solid earth, and we do not have to fly with it as so many ants crawling round a balloon'. The history of science abounds with examples of discoveries greeted with howls of laughter because they seemed to be a marriage of incompatibles. (1964, p. 96)

The humorous reformulation of Galileo's scientific claims quoted by Koestler involves an obvious bisociation of opposing scripts or interpretative frameworks: namely, humans on earth and ants on a balloon. It illustrates how serious discourse is often reinterpreted, reformulated and transformed as it crosses the boundary into the humorous realm. As in the case of Galileo, quite radical reformulation can be required. In other instances, however, as in the following, the possibility of a bisociative reading is already easily available in the original serious text.

> (Woman poet, at a poetry festival, giving a lecture on women and poetry): There are things that only happen to women. Period.
> (Sherzer, 1978, p. 343)

This appears to be an example of 'natural humour' arising out of the ambiguity of language. Sherzer reports, however, that initially there was no response to the possible pun provided by the word 'period'. It was not until one isolated member of the audience had laughed that 'the entire audience broke into laughter' (1978, p. 343). We appear to have here an instance where one recipient spontaneously carried out the interpretative work needed to turn the poet's serious remark into a joke, and emitted the response appropriate to humour. This response then operated as a cue for the rest of the audience and drew their attention to the humorous possibilities of the discourse.

As Sherzer and others show clearly, serious discourse contains many ambiguities and potential dualities of meaning, which most participants ignore or simply fail to see (Wilson, 1979, p. 166). We would expect this to be the case, given our earlier analysis of the basic principles of serious discourse. However, the diversity of individual responses to discourse ensures that some at least of the humorous possibilities available within serious discourse will be recognized and will give rise to an unsignalled transfer from the serious to the humorous mode. Such spontaneous responses to 'natural humour' can themselves act as signals that the interpretative demands of serious discourse can properly be relaxed. Whether humorous cues are employed as signals of humorous intent or whether they arise out of participants' responses to the interpretative possibilities implicit in serious discourse or in natural events, they serve to make humour a collective phenomenon. Humorous cues and signals indicate to all involved that the dominant commitment to maintaining the appearance of a single reality can, at least momentarily, be relaxed, and that it is socially acceptable to enter that domain of meaning where the so-called certainties of the mundane world no longer hold and where the point of talking and listening and being alive is to enjoy the possibilities of uncertainty, ambiguity and interpretative multiplicity.

4

Informal Humour

The secondary literature on humour relies heavily on the analysis of 'cleaned up' written versions of standardized jokes. This analytical strategy tends to draw attention away from what has been called situational, or spontaneous or informal humour. Fry distinguishes between standardized jokes and situational humour as follows: 'Canned [standardized] jokes are defined as those which are *presented* with little obvious relationship to the ongoing human interaction. Situation jokes are indicated as those which are *spontaneous* and have, to a major extent, their origin in the ongoing interpersonal (or intrapersonal) process' (1963, p. 43; italics in the original).

Whereas a standardized humorous package (joke) can move from one setting to another and can retain its character as humour in each of these settings, spontaneous humour is created out of the discourse of a specific occasion and is not transferable as humour without considerable reformulation (Hall, 1974). Consequently, it is unlikely that the analysis of abstracted versions of standardized jokes will tell us all that we need to know about the spontaneous production of humour in the course of informal interaction. Moreover, situational humour is of particular importance because it is clear that much, if not most, humour occurring in the course of direct interaction is 'situational' or 'spontaneous' (Tannen, 1984, chapter 6). Accordingly, as this chapter develops, I will move from an examination of standardized jokes in informal settings to spontaneous, situational humour. This will lead to a discussion of the relationship betwen humorous and serious discourse in informal settings.

Standardized jokes in informal settings

When we examined Sacks's joke in chapter 1, we saw that the joke was preceded by an extended sequence of negotiations consisting of about twenty utterances before it finally got under way. In the course of this sequence, all those present participated in a joint preparation for the joke. It is clear from the transcript that it was the teller of the joke who initially signalled the possibility of a change from the serious to the humorous mode, when he said, 'You wanna hear – my sister told me a story last night.' But potential recipients did not wait passively for the joke. Rather, they proffered a series of playful remarks in which they 'made fun of' the proposal to enter the humorous mode by pretending, humorously, to be unwilling to do so or by appearing to take the opening lines of the joke seriously: 'I don't wanna hear it. But if you must.' . . . 'Hey waita second. Drag that by again heh.' . . . 'You better have a long talk with your sister.'

In this instance, therefore, we can observe that entry into the humorous mode was jointly accomplished. Before the standardized joke was actually delivered, recipients and teller worked together to cross the boundary from serious talk to humour. Although the recipients seemed, in one sense, to be resisting the transition to humour, this resistance was itself signalled as humorous and therefore, paradoxically, as endorsing that transition and as preparing the way for the standardized humour to come. Humorous resistance was used as an interpretative resource for marking a discursive boundary and for crossing that boundary into the domain of humour.

This sequence of 'boundary work' is undoubtedly exceptionally long. Somewhat shorter sequences, however, seem to occur quite frequently in informal contexts. Consider the opening section from a joke in my own collection. The participants are teenage girls who are talking together informally.

Madeleine's joke

A: Have you heard the one with the woman at the doctor's?
B: Might have. I dunno till you tell us.
C: Go on tell us anyway, it don't matter if we've heard it.
A: Right. At the doctor's
C: Don't tell me, there was this woman.
A: Oh shut up.
C: All right, all right.
A: At the doctor's was this woman with a baby . . .

In Madeleine's joke the three participants exchange seven conversational turns after the initial signal and before the joke is finally delivered. Participants' utterances are perhaps less obviously humorous here than in Sacks's joke. Nevertheless, recipients and teller clearly work together in Madeleine's joke to establish that what is to follow is not ordinary, serious talk: for example, C's 'Go on tell us anyway, it don't matter if we've heard it.' Furthermore, B's response 'I dunno till you tell us' can certainly be heard as being intended humorously; as can C's interruption 'Don't tell me, there was this woman', which follows A's clear announcement that the joke will be about a 'woman at the doctor's'. Indeed, C appears at this point to be making fun of the standardized form of the joke which she is about to hear. Thus, it seems that C, and possibly B as well, are responding playfully to A's indication that she is prepared to enter the humorous mode. As in Sacks's joke, recipients help the teller to cross the boundary into humour by displaying that this discursive change is acceptable and by reacting to the joke's opening words in a manner which carries them together into the humorous realm.

The next example of a standardized joke told in an informal setting is taken from Deborah Tannen's (1984) detailed study of conversation among friends during a Thanksgiving dinner party. In this passage, Peter tries to tell a joke as people gather around the dinner table and work out the seating arrangements. The kind of collaborative entry into humour that we have observed in previous instances is lacking here, and the teller has to try four times before he gains the others' attention.

'Smoking after sex'

(1)	Steve:	So should we do that? should we start
	Deborah:	sure
	Steve:	with the white?
(2)	Peter:	Didju hear about the – lady, who was asked,
(3)	Deborah:	I'm gonna get in there, right?
(4)	Chad:	Okay.
(5)	Peter:	Didju hear?
(6)	David:	We have to sit boy girl boy.
(7)	Chad:	Boy girl boy?
(8)	Peter:	Didju hear about the lady who was asked,
(9)	Chad:	There's only two girls.
(10)	Deborah:	What?
(11)	Peter:	Did you hear about the lady who was asked . . . Do you
	Chad:	Boy girl boy
	Peter:	smoke after sex?
(12)	David:	I don't know I never looked. (*nasal tone*)
(13)	Deborah:	And she said? What?
(14)	Peter:	I don't *know* I never *looked*
(15)	Deborah:	Oh (*chuckles*).

(Tannen, 1984, pp. 88–9)

In this sequence, Peter's humorous cue 'Did you hear about' is at first ignored by recipients as they deal with the serious task of arranging the seats for dinner. Without their collaboration, he is unable to continue with the joke, and on the first three occasions he stops after his humorous signal has received no appropriate response. By utterance 11, however, he seems to judge that his audience is at last prepared to accept the joke and he begins to deliver it with heavy emphasis. This example shows, therefore, that collaborative preparation for standardized jokes is not absolutely essential, although it may occur very frequently. In this case, no more than a minimal indication of acquiescence seems to have been required to enable Peter to adopt the humorous mode, apart from Deborah's 'What?' in line 10, which may have been an invitation for Peter to proceed. Once he succeeds in securing his friends' attention, however, they begin to participate actively in constructing the joke. David, for example, intervenes halfway through the joke and pronounces the punch line in a funny tone of voice, whilst Deborah first provides a response which allows Peter to restate the punch line and then supplies the terminal chuckles which are needed to complete the humorous exchange. Thus, although there is little collaborative preparation for this joke, it is taken over by the group in the course of its telling and becomes a joint accomplishment of the group's members.

Let us consider one more example from Tannen's Thanksgiving dinner party. This passage occurs immediately after Chad has referred to part of the turkey as 'the Pope's nose'.

'The Pope's nose'

(1) Peter: Oh, did you near? The new Po –
               the new Pope, performed his first miracle?
(2) Chad: What.
(3) David: What. Whatwhatwhat.
(4) Peter: He made a blind man lame.
(5) Deborah: *(laughter)*

(Tannen, 1984, p. 140)

Although this is apparently a preformulated, standardized joke which could easily be told elsewhere, it is not presented, as Fry's definition suggests, 'with little obvious relationship to the ongoing human interaction' (1963, p. 43). For the joke grows out of a prior serious topic and itself furnishes a topic for further conversation when participants continue by discussing its status as a possible 'Polish joke' (the new Pope was Polish). Nevertheless, not only is the joke clearly signalled by the teller as requiring a different kind of interaction from the previous discussion of the turkey, but other participants immediately respond in a special fashion: for example, David's 'whatwhatwhat'. In this case, as in previous instances, the humorous mode is created, maintained and finally terminated through recipients' active participation in a distinctive form of discourse. Although there is some degree of topic continuity as participants move from the serious to the humorous mode, they collaborate nonetheless in marking their humorous interchange as distinct from what has gone before and as involving interaction of a special kind. Thus Fry's point can be rephrased more accurately by stating that there can sometimes be obvious topical connections between formal jokes and the surrounding serious discourse, but that even when this is so, the transition to the humorous mode is accomplished in a way which creates a distinctive frame around the humorous interlude. It is in this sense that standardized jokes are separated from the ongoing interaction.

I have not examined the internal structure of 'smoking after sex' or 'the Pope's nose' in this section. These jokes seem to me to be straightforward illustrations of the principle of bisociation discussed in chapter 3. I have concentrated instead on the processes of cueing and on the relationship between standardized jokes and the surrounding discourse. I have shown that standardized jokes, although they are transferable from one situation to another, need not be entirely divorced from the ongoing discourse. They employ interpretative resources taken from the serious realm, and may be built upon and used to contribute indirectly to the serious talk in which they are often embedded. Standardized jokes are, however, separated from serious discourse in the sense that they are signalled and linguistically marked as a distinctive discursive mode. We have seen that adoption of this mode is not confined to the teller alone, but is undertaken collectively. The teller, in informal situations, does not deliver a pre-packaged unit of humour to a passive audience. Rather, the teller and her recipients work together to establish and sustain the operation of the humorous mode and to accomplish the proper performance and acknowledgement of the joke. It is presumably this active collaboration in the interpretative work required by humour that produces the unusually demonstrative kind of social involvement remarked by Fry among groups of joking people (see p. 51 and chapter 6).

The fine detail of collective involvement in humorous interchange that we have begun to glimpse in this section could not have been gleaned from the simplified, isolated fragments of standardized humour studied by so many analysts. Those written versions of standardized jokes, abstracted from their context of use, would never have revealed the truly social accomplishment of standardized humour which becomes visible when we examine transcriptions of naturally occurring discourse. This kind of material is even more essential if we are to understand situational humour. For such spontaneous humour can be observed only in the transient detail of informal discourse.

Pure, spontaneous humour

Let me begin my examination of situational humour with another example
from Tannen's dinner party. The passage starts with the guests remarking
on the presence of a tape recorder on the dinner table and on the fact that
it had been recording the prior stretch of conversation. Several comments
had been made earlier about the location of the tape recorder, particularly
by the host, Steve. For example, he had already proposed, in humorous
vein, that despite his efforts to keep the table attractive by putting the
recorder out of sight, 'It keeps coming back on the table. It must have a
will of its own. That's all I can say' (1984, p. 135). The following sequence
occurs later in the evening. In order to appreciate the final exchange
between Steve and Peter, one needs to know that Tannen had told her
friends that she wanted to record their talk in order to study misunderstandings.

(1) Steve: Be uh have we been . . . taping? This whole time?
(2) Deborah: I'm glad
                I didn't notice it until just now.
(3) Chad: She keeps that thing running.
(4) Steve: I keep I . . . I say, get that thing off the table. She says
                . . oh yeah okay I'll take it off the table and I look, . . .
                two minutes later and it's back. *(laughter)*
                . . . What's to analyze. There hasn't been *one* misunder-
                standing, we've all understood each other *per*fectly.
(5) Peter: What do you mean by that. *(loud laughter)*

                                                        (1984, p. 135)

There are two outbursts of laughter in this passage. The first is in response
to Steve's whimsical remarks about the tape recorder, and the second,
louder, outburst follows Peter's reply to Steve's statement that they had all
understood each other perfectly. I will concentrate initially on this second
item.

The exchange between Peter and Steve is an example of 'pure,
spontaneous humour'. One reason for calling this humour 'pure' is that
Peter's 'What do you mean by that', the locus of humour, meets with no
response other than laughter. Although Peter's words are formulated as a
request for clarification directed at Steve and as an indication that a
misunderstanding between Steve and Peter had just occurred, these
serious interpretative possibilities are completely ignored. His remark is
treated as an unambiguously humorous utterance intended solely to
produce amusement for the group as a whole. Steve, the apparent
addressee, does not take the remark seriously and makes no attempt to

remedy the supposed misunderstanding. Steve and his guests seem to take for granted Peter's exclusively humorous intention, and they respond unreservedly with a display of intense collective amusement.

Peter's remark is also a clear example of 'spontaneous' informal humour in the sense that it is created out of the ongoing discourse. It is true that 'What do you mean by that' is not a *unique* utterance. This formulation undoubtedly circulates like standardized jokes and can be inserted, like these jokes, into many different conversations. But whereas the standardized joke is a self-contained humorous unit, 'What do you mean by that' is not recognizably humorous in itself. Indeed, it is almost certainly used primarily in serious contexts. Thus it becomes humorous only if it is employed in a rather special way. Peter's reply to Steve is humorous only because it is fitted into the conversation in accordance with the structural requirements of the humorous mode. Unlike 'the Pope's nose' or 'smoking after sex' which do not *depend* for their humour on what has gone before, Peter's remark generates humour by combining with, and thereby transforming, the discourse in which it is placed.

In order to appreciate the humour of Peter's remark and to describe its humorous structure, we have to view it in relation to Steve's prior statement, 'There hasn't been *one* misunderstanding, we've all understood each other *perf*ectly.' The humour is created out of the relationship between this utterance and Peter's reply, 'What do you mean by that.' It is clear that this joint construction is organized in terms of the kind of binary contrast that Raskin drew to our attention in his analysis of standardized jokes. In this case, the contrast is between understanding and misunderstanding. It is also clear that the humour arises out of a sudden interpretative reversal which is implicitly created by Peter's reply. For Peter, in appearing not to have understood Steve's statement, turns the very claim that there have been no misunderstandings into a source of misunderstanding. Thus this informal interchange can be seen as involving the bisociation or merging of incongruous frameworks stressed by Koestler. Alternatively, we can describe it in terms of Raskin's incompatible scripts. In other words, the basic semantic structure of this spontaneous humour is the same as that characteristic of standardized jokes.

There are several other respects in which this example of situational humour fits the general analysis derived in previous chapters from the study of standardized jokes. For instance, the sequencing of semantic components is that found in such jokes; that is, a claim is first proposed (no misunderstandings) and then unexpectedly undermined ('I do not understand'). Secondly, the punch line is indirect or allusive. Peter does not actually say explicitly, 'No, you're wrong about there being no misunderstandings, because I didn't understand your last remark.'

Instead, he merely implies this response. Thirdly, the humour generates a multiplicity of possible and possibly conflicting interpretations of what is really being said. In other words, it generates ambiguity and confuses the distinction between reality and unreality.

For example, there is no real incongruity between Peter's humorous remark and Steve's prior statement, and therefore no humour, unless Peter has genuinely failed to understand. However, if he has failed to understand Steve's claim, he cannot intend to offer a humorous contradiction of that claim. Peter can only contradict Steve's assertion with humorous intent if he actually understands what Steve has said. Of course we, like the participants, know that Peter does intend to be funny and that he is not trying to express a genuine failure to understand. Consequently we are aware, as are Peter and his audience, that his apparent failure to understand does not really contradict Steve's claim and, therefore, is not funny. We must not forget, of course, that *Steve's* claim about there being no misunderstandings is itself uttered in the humorous mode and derives its humorous import from the implication that there certainly have been previous misunderstandings. However, if Steve is to be heard as implying that misunderstandings *have* occurred, then Peter's apparent failure to understand is entirely consistent with Steve's prior statement and is therefore once again shown not to be amusing. It seems to follow that participants should not really have laughed.

I have reached this patently foolish conclusion by deliberately perpetuating the error for which I have strongly admonished other analysts – namely, that of applying the interpretative procedures of serious discourse to the content of the humorous realm. My aim in devising this perfectly reasonable, yet self-defeating chain of reasoning, is to show that the interpretative relationships of informal humour are not unilinear. The discourse of spontaneous humour, like that of formal jokes, has a built-in semantic duality that persistently generates contradictions when approached from the perspective of the serious realm. It is clear, I think, that complicated interpretative possibilities, such as those sketched above, were not considered by Tannen or her friends during the dinner party. They were aware, I suggest, only of the kind of sudden semantic reversal typical of the humorous mode. They were operating collectively within that mode and were not expecting each other's remarks to make sense in the ordinary way. Nevertheless, my tortuous reasoning above does help to bring out the paradoxical character of this humorous interchange. In this respect, this example of situational humour closely resembles the standardized jokes examined in previous chapters. In so far as the exchange between Steve and Peter is representative of informal humour, and I suggest that it is, we can conclude that spontaneous and standardized humour share the same basic features of organized sequencing, semantic contrast, bisociation, allusion, interpretative duplicity and a blurring of the boundary between the real and the unreal.

Although standardized jokes and spontaneous humour are similar in these important respects, there are also certain points of difference. In the first place, we have seen that jokes can be slotted into a conversation without being linked to the surrounding talk. A good example of this was 'smoking after sex', where the semantic content of the joke was quite divorced from the ongoing conversation and required a marked change of focus on the part of recipients. In contrast, spontaneous humour *has* to be linked directly to the preceding discourse. This can sometimes be accomplished by a speaker's commenting humorously, often self-deprecatingly, on his own speech (Wilson, 1979, p. 220). More usually, however, the humour will be created by a second speaker taking up and in some way reversing the meaning of another speaker's prior utterance, as in the exchange between Peter and Steve. Thus spontaneous humour is necessarily fitted in an intricate fashion into the informal sequence of interaction and discourse. Although this need not be so with standardized jokes, the difference is one of degree. For, as we saw in the case of 'the Pope's nose', participants sometimes create interpretative links between a joke and the surrounding serious talk. Similarly, as we saw in 'smoking after sex', a standardized joke can be told by several speakers working together.

Another difference between spontaneous humour and standardized jokes is that the former is often built out of interpretative resources which are restricted to a specific context. A standardized joke like 'smoking after sex' can circulate from one group to another, and even from one country to another, because it depends on knowledge that is widely available about sexual habits and about guns smoking after being fired. Similarly, 'the Pope's nose' makes use of common knowledge about the nature of miracles and may also be interpreted in relation to a Polish stereotype that is a well established part of the American humorous tradition. Steve's situational humour about the tape recorder, however, and Peter's pretence of misunderstanding are humorous only within the social context of that particular party. Whereas the formal jokes told during the meal first imply, and then overturn, common-sense assumptions about phenomena which are widely known such as sex and miracles, the spontaneous humour plays with specific interpretative possibilities – for example, about tape recorders and misunderstandings – that had been generated earlier in the evening and that could not be assumed to operate in other social situations (see Hall, 1974).

There are two reasons, therefore, why spontaneous humour is not easily transferable from one situation to another. Firstly, it is difficult to use again elsewhere because it consists of direct speech involving, in most cases, more than one speaker. Consequently, it does not provide a self-contained interpretative reversal that can be repeated without modification on another occasion by a single speaker. Secondly, spontaneous humour often depends on knowledge that is short-lived and socially restricted. Spontaneous humour is typically produced by the bisociation of *local* frames of reference or the opposition of *local* scripts (Raskin, 1985a, p. 135). It would be misleading, however, to insist that spontaneous humour is not transferable at all. Fry actually goes so far as to suggest that standardized jokes are merely 'the situation jokes of yesterday. Something funny occurs during the process of living. We have a situation joke. That situation joke is told twenty minutes later. Voilà! We have a canned joke' (1963, p. 53). But this view of the relationship between situational humour and standardized (canned) jokes is, I think, much too simple. Situational humour may sometimes be open to reformulation as a standardized joke, but only if the background knowledge on which it depends is generally available or can be built economically (Sacks, 1978) into the semantic structure of the joke. Thus Raskin's joke about the clergyman having toiled all night could conceivably have originated in some actual clergyman's spontaneous, self-deprecating reply to an inquiry concerning his whereabouts the night before. But this spontaneous humour is transferable in standardized form only because it is created entirely out of semantic possibilities applicable to clergymen in general.

Standardized jokes, as Sacks pointed out, are not jokes about particular people on particular occasions; they deal instead with the stereotyped characteristics of anonymous stock figures, such as 'the clergyman', 'the Irishman' or 'the young officer'. (For a discussion of certain exceptions, see chapter 11.) Accordingly, spontaneous humour can be transformed into joke form only if it can be expressed in impersonal terms and only if it is based on knowledge and assumptions that are widely available. Most spontaneous humour cannot, I suggest, be easily reformulated in this way because it is intimately linked to the fleeting discourse of informal social life. Thus, such humour is normally as transient as the ephemeral social contacts out of which it is generated. Given this close connection between spontaneous humour and its context of production, let us begin to look more closely at how participants make use of humour in informal settings.

Hidden meanings and hidden motives

I began the last section by describing Peter's playful response to Steve at the dinner party as 'pure humour'. I meant by this that there was not the least trace of serious response to Peter's apparent failure to understand Steve's prior statement. The other participants made no attempt to explain the meaning of Steve's previous remark. They seemed to treat Peter's apparent failure to understand as mere pretence, to which the only appropriate response was laughter. They appeared to assume that the sole intention behind Peter's utterance was that of causing amusement. Undoubtedly, much informal humour is 'pure' in this sense. There are, however, good grounds for maintaining that informal humour is often 'impure' or 'applied' (Hall, 1974), in the sense that participants treat the discourse of humour as a vehicle for serious meanings and as a cover for serious motives. If this is so, the relationship between the serious and the humorous modes is more subtle and complex than I have so far suggested. Let us, therefore, examine this relationship in situations where the purity of the humour is more equivocal.

In the previous chapter, I quoted a transcription from Flaherty (1984) of a sequence of interaction during which a research assistant obtained from a secretary some stick-on tags for file folders (pp. 47–8). This is a good example of the way in which humorous interchange can be combined with what Flaherty calls 'reality work'. He points out that, although the interchange between Mike and Boo was clearly signalled by both parties as being playful, it was also used to convey serious information and to accomplish an actual exchange of tags.

> Note that the reality play [humorous interchange] does not curtail the reality work which encompasses the incident. Mike came for tags and he leaves with tags, but this achievement was much more enjoyable than it would have been had the participants only performed reality work. Pleasure is fostered by their jocular confederacy in driving a wedge of capriciousness between themselves and the tedium that would result from fastidious compliance with role obligations. (1984, p. 78)

Flaherty's example shows that adoption of the humorous mode does not necessarily imply that one's speech is completely devoid of serious meaning or serious intent. The humorous signals exchanged by Boo and Mike seem to imply that certain aspects of their speech are not to be taken seriously; but there is nevertheless a serious component. It seems that their words convey both serious and humorous messages at the same time. This observation provides a further illustration of the uncertain meaning of the signals for humorous discourse and of the indefinite boundary between the two discursive modes. Because it is in principle unclear what precise combination of humour and reality work is being offered in any humorously signalled utterance, recipients are always faced with a choice in deciding how to respond. On some occasions, as in Peter's reply to

Steve at the dinner party, recipients may treat a humorous remark as pure humour. On others, as in the case of Boo and Mike, a recipient may treat an utterance as both serious and amusing, and may respond in a like manner. It is also possible, as we will see later, for recipients to respond to humour with the utmost seriousness (Drew, 1986).

In Flaherty's example it is possible to interpret the humorous by-play between Boo and Mike as a mere embellishment to, a pleasant diversion from, the rather tedious reality work that is being accomplished. Flaherty himself adopts this view. He proposes that much informal humour is a harmless trifling with the assumptions and expectations of the supposedly 'real world', intended to relieve the tedium of the interactive work required to maintain that world. But, he suggests, this 'reality play' cannot be allowed to interfere with, or significantly influence, participants' serious 'reality work': 'For it to be amusing, an attempt at humour must have no grave consequences with respect to person, role or situation' (1984, p. 76).

I am sure that this claim is correct. But we must be careful not to misunderstand its implications. In so far as a humorously signalled act or remark is taken by participants to have had 'grave consequences', it will certainly not be regarded by them as 'pure humour'. For example, if I play a practical joke on a friend and inadvertently cause him serious physical injury, my action, despite any display of humorous intent, will undoubtedly be incorporated into the realm of serious discourse and will be treated as having been a serious act. We can agree with Flaherty, therefore, that some humour may be no more than a playful accompaniment to reality work, and that humour which is taken to have serious results will be deemed not to have been amusing. But we must not infer from these conclusions that those aspects of discourse which are recognized as humorous by participants can never be more than a frivolous addition to their reality work. Humour can undoubtedly be more than mere embellishment. It can be used to produce serious outcomes and it can be taken to be an expression of serious intent.

Let us reconsider, for example, Flaherty's own material on the interchange between Boo and Mike. I suggest that the ambiguous boundary between the serious and the playful elements in this discourse, as well as the interpretative duality of humour, make it *possible* for these actors to attribute serious, but unstated, intentions to each other. Thus Mike evidently recognizes Boo's reference to the colours red and green as being playful, and he responds appropriately. But we have noted before that the signals for humour are, in a sense, self- cancelling; they convey the paradoxical message that they themselves need not be taken seriously and therefore that the discourse to which they are attached may be, in some respects, genuine. Consequently, it is quite possible for Mike to be taking Boo's allusive remarks as referring seriously to more than the allocation of tags and to be proffering in return a humorously coded, yet potentially genuine, acceptance: "'I'll take the green; they go with my eyes." (Said mischievously)'.

I am not claiming that this is the correct interpretation of Flaherty's data. Indeed, there is no way of knowing what Mike's and Boo's intentions were. I am suggesting only that the allusive character of humorous discourse and its unavoidable interpretative uncertainty allow participants themselves to draw such inferences at the time or to seek to establish such an interpretation in the course of subsequent interaction. The indeterminate nature of the boundary between serious and humorous content leaves that boundary open to social negotiation. In the next chapter, we will examine examples where humorous interchange similar to that between Boo and Mike is a prelude to serious sexual conduct. However, the point that I wish to make here is that serious interpretations of humour were available in principle to these participants. More generally, I want to suggest that informal humour is frequently regarded by participants as a way of expressing serious intent and of conveying serious information without appearing to do so. Because, as we have seen, the boundary between serious and humorous discourse is unclear, and because humorous discourse is necessarily equivocal, participants often assume that humour is employed to hide the real intentions that lie behind others' speech.

Let me develop this point by returning once more to Tannen's dinner party. In a previous quotation we observed Steve, the party host and the person responsible for arranging the dinner table, complaining humorously about the tape recorder's being on the table. Tannen reports that he 'complained' in this fashion about the tape recorder three times during the dinner. On one occasion, a remark about the recorder is followed by a similar 'complaint' about a jar of commercial salad dressing called 'Marie's', for which David was responsible. I reproduce here just two short segments from a longer passage containing twelve conversational turns during which these 'complaints' were voiced.

(1) Steve: Do we have to have this here . . .
               Does this have to be here?
(2) Sally: [unclear]
(3) Deborah: No I mean
(4) Chad: She set it in the middle.
(5) Deborah: G'head. Spoil my dissertation . . .
(8) Steve: I mean *Marie's*.
(9) David: Well put it on the salad and then you can do whatever
               you want with it.

(Tannen, 1984, p. 113)

Tannen (Deborah) stresses that Steve's humorous intent is clearly signalled in these exchanges by means of an exaggerated tone of voice which he employed for this purpose on numerous occasions throughout the evening. The initial responses of Deborah and David, however, in (3) and (9) appear to be entirely serious. It is difficult, I suggest, to hear 'No I mean' and 'Well put it on the salad' as amused reactions to Steve's supposedly playful complaints. Deborah describes her own response as a *pretence* of annoyance at Steve's interfering with the research for her dissertation. But this version of her response is based solely on her utterance (5) and ignores her initial 'No I mean'. Moreover, she admits that, although she did not think that Steve's complaint was serious, she did feel some 'slight annoyance that Steve was drawing attention to the tape recorder' (1984, p. 134). Thus if we consider what she actually said at the time as well as her retrospective interpretation, it seems that although Deborah recognized Steve's apparent complaint as humorous, she first responded seriously (3) and only afterwards in humorous vein (5).

Tannen goes on to compare her interpretation of, and reaction to Steve's remarks with those of David. At the dinner table:

> He seems to take Steve's complaint seriously and explains that after the dressing is put on the salad, the bottle can be taken away. 'You can do whatever you want with it' sounds like a genuine expression of annoyance at Steve for complaining.
>
> During playback, David explained his understanding of what was going on. He believed that Steve was truly angry at me for having the tape recorder on the table, and then tried to cover his sincere anger by also saying something about the salad dressing bottle. (1984, p. 134)

David's account of what he thought was happening at the dinner table is consistent with what he said at the time. Unlike Deborah, David claims to have regarded Steve's humour as a cloak for more serious motives and, again unlike Deborah, he seems not to have adopted the humorous mode in replying to Steve's complaint. Steve, however, seems to have been outraged by the suggestion that his playful remarks had any serious intent.

> Steve, during his playback session, was speechless at my suggestion that he might have genuinely been angry with me for taping. He liked the idea of my taping, he insisted . . . He was just picking up on a fleeting impression he got and exaggerating it for comic effect [pure, spontaneous humour]. He felt the same way about the salad dressing bottle as he did about the recorder. (1984, p. 134)

Thus we have three radically different versions of this brief interchange from the main contributors, and three variant accounts of the relationship between humorous and serious discourse on this occasion. For Deborah, Steve's complaint was not intended seriously; yet she seems to have taken it seriously before switching to the humorous mode. For David, Steve's apparently humorous tone conveyed a serious message which David dealt with in a serious fashion; whilst for Steve, his genuinely humorous intent was clearly signalled and any serious response or serious interpretation was sadly inappropriate.

These observations suggest that we should not think in terms of there necessarily being a single boundary between humorous and serious discourse during any particular exchange. It seems that different participants can draw that line quite differently. What one participant claims to be mere playful embellishment or 'exaggeration for comic effect', another may take to be thinly disguised reality work. David's response to Peter shows that humour can have serious consequences, in that recipients can attribute to it serious motives, infer from it serious meanings and react to it in a serious manner. However, it is a critical characteristic of humorously signalled discourse that any serious intention and any serious meaning can always be denied.

Various analysts have noted this important point (Tannen, 1984, p. 132). As Gary Fine puts it, 'the implications of a humorous remark generally can be denied by its maker with little loss of face' (1984, p. 85). Or in Alice Roy's words, 'the speaker can mean what he says and at the same time disclaim what he says' (1978, p. 118) when operating in the humorous mode. This aspect of the interpretative duality of humour is, I suggest, as evident to participants as it is to analysts. Thus one would not expect David to be convinced by Steve's energetic denial of any serious intent behind his remarks at the dinner. For the whole point of formulating 'serious complaints' in humorous terms is to enable the speaker, if necessary, to furnish a plausible denial. By adopting the humorous mode to express what sounds like a complaint, the speaker can always deal with any negative response to that complaint, as did Steve, by saying in effect, 'Don't take me seriously. I was only joking.' Although such assertions of humorous intent will not always be accepted by others, the very nature of humorous discourse ensures that they cannot be easily overturned.

It is clear that participants can treat a speaker's adoption of the humorous mode as following from that speaker's wanting to avoid responsiblity for his speech. According to this view, use of the humorous mode is not playful, but part of a serious strategy. Humour is not being employed just to create amusement and pleasant diversion, but as a serious interactional ploy. Humour is being used to say something, whilst allowing the speaker to claim that it was never said. This, I suggest, is David's view of Peter's remarks about the tape recorder and the salad dressing. Furthermore, if recipients can interpret others' humour in this fashion, it seems reasonable to presume that they are themselves capable of the same humorous duplicity. It follows, I think, that not only do we all on occasion attribute serious intent to others' humour, but also that we all use humour as a critical resource for our own reality work. This is another of the paradoxes of humour, which I will explore further in the next chapter.

5

Putting Humour to Work

In this chapter I am going to examine some of the serious uses which people make of humour in the course of personal, and sometimes intimate, interaction. I will begin by discussing Drew's (1986) study, based on British and American data, of teasing among people who are friends, colleagues, members of the same family or who are generally familiar with one another. I will then turn to Emerson's (1973) study of the use of humour in dealings between staff and patients in an American hospital. This will lead to Walle's (1976) study of humour among customers and staff in an all-night diner in upstate New York. As we saw at the end of the previous chapter, we cannot *as analysts* easily attribute serious motives to participants who have adopted the humorous mode, because adoption of that mode necessarily implies that serious intent can be denied. We can clearly show, however, that certain kinds of humorous speech are regularly treated by *other participants* as if they are meant seriously. This is Drew's starting point in his investigation of serious receipts of teases.

Serious reactions to teasing

Teasing is necessarily an activity directed at someone else. To tease is to say or do something that is intended light-heartedly to make fun of somebody else's words or actions. Drew's study of teasing concentrates exclusively on verbal teasing, and is based on a collection of fifty teases extracted from a large corpus of natural conversation. In the course of his analysis, Drew shows how teases can be considered as part of, and as making a critical contribution to, conversational sequences involving both humorous and serious components. Although Drew does not formulate it as explicitly as this, the basic structure of teasing is as follows:

(1) First speaker: a serious remark or action.
(2) Second speaker: a tease directed at the prior remark or action.
(3) First speaker: a serious response to the tease.

Various modifications of this simple pattern do, of course, occur and are documented by Drew. Typically, however, teases are produced as humorously signalled responses to a serious conversational turn and are themselves then treated seriously by the initial speaker.

The following example is from a telephone conversation between a husband and wife. The husband has been complaining mildly about a function that they are supposed to attend at seven o'clock the same evening. The passage reproduced here was preceded by what Drew calls a 'little lecture' by the wife in which she emphasizes that they cannot avoid going. I have slightly simplified Drew's transcription and I have numbered the turns according to the basic schema above.

'Getting home on time'

(1) Alice: UH Hey *try* and get home at a
decent *hour* cz

(2) Larry: Ye *ah* be home by *nine*

(3) Alice: Noo *get* home pretty early okay?
Please.

(2) Larry: *Well I* can leave right *now* if you
want.

(3) Alice: Noo *(delay and breaths from both parties)*
Soo, okay?

(Drew, 1986, p. 12)

This is a useful example because Larry furnishes two teases, 'Ye *ah* be home by *nine*' and '*Well I* can leave right *now*', both of which follow serious utterances *from* Alice and both of which are received seriously *by* Alice. Thus the basic pattern occurs twice within this short passage.

We can reasonably ask at this point how Larry's remarks and the other items identified by Drew as teases are recognized as such, given that the actual recipient responds seriously. Drew's answer to this possible query is twofold. In the first place, he suggests, there is evidence that participants may recognize an utterance as humorous even though they do not display that recognition by, for example, laughing at the tease. Secondly, he maintains that teases have a distinctive structure which can be discerned by analysts as well as participants. Let us examine these two claims one at a time.

In order to appreciate the force of Drew's proposal that recipients may recognize a tease without necessarily revealing that they have recognized it, we need another example. Once again, I have simplified and condensed Drew's material, which is taken from Goodwin's videotape of a family dinner. This fragment begins with a tease in which one of the daughters questions an action performed by the mother.

'Goodwin's dinner'

(2) Dot: Do we have *two* *f*orks cuz we're on television?

(3) Mother: No we
(laughter from Angie, then Father and then Mother)

(2) Father: Right yeh probably the answer right there

(3) Mother: You have p*ie*, You have p*ie* tonight.

(Drew, 1986, p. 3)

This passage begins with Mother being teased by her daughter Dot. Mother starts to respond with a serious denial, 'No we', but this response is engulfed in laughter which clearly displays collective recognition of the humorous intent of Dot's remark. After a brief delay, Mother joins in the laughter, thereby showing that she knows that she is being teased. As the laughter subsides, however, the recipient of the tease is the first to return to the serious mode, which she employs to correct Dot's humorous suggestion that the table places were laid with two forks in order to give a good impression to viewers of the videotape. The extra fork, Mother explains seriously, was really for the pie.

The critical feature of this example in the present context is that, in her concluding utterance, Mother is replying seriously to Dot's remark and displaying no recognition at that moment of its humorous character. Yet she, along with the rest of the family, has just revealed that she knows that Dot's remark was a tease. We have in this instance a typical example of the collective production of humour, in which every member of the group furnishes signals of involvement in humorous interaction as well as evident recognition of others' humorous intent. Despite this, Mother insists on taking the initial tease seriously. In the light of this example and other cases where recipients spontaneously laugh at a tease before proceeding to reject or correct it in a serious manner, Drew concludes that the occurrence of a serious response does not necessarily imply that recipients have failed to perceive the prior tease.

Thus recognizing and displaying recognition are analytically separable activities. Although in practice the only research methodology for seeing that someone has recognized a tease is through their displaying that recognition (e.g. in laughing), it cannot be inferred from an absence of such a display that they did not recognize the tease. So in cases . . . of entirely serious responses to teases, it does not follow from the absence of an overt display of recognition of humour . . . that they have not recognized the tease. (1986, p. 10)

Teases are recognizable as humorous because they are constructed with certain distinctive features which serve as signals of the speaker's humorous intent and as cues that the apparent message should not be taken literally. Teases, Drew shows, are characterized by exaggerated or extreme reformulations of something that the recipient has said or done previously. These reformulations contrast with or contradict some statement, assumption or meaningful action uttered, implied or carried out by the recipient. They also, playfully, question the adequacy, reality or propriety of what the recipient has said or done, whilst simultaneously indicating that their own interpretative challenge is not to be taken seriously. In other words, teases resemble other forms of humorous discourse in that they depend on a sudden switch from an initial interpretative position to some opposing position. In accordance with the requirements of the humorous mode, such opposition is normally implied rather than stated explicitly. As in informal humour generally, the first speaker's script is disrupted and undermined by a script introduced by the second speaker. In the case of teases, the second speaker's script deviates from and thereby distorts that of the prior speaker. Moreover, although the second speaker threatens the reality proposed by the serious speaker, the teaser's own script is not presented as a genuine, serious alternative. In the act of teasing, the second speaker avoids any direct, serious criticism of his partner's speech or action, yet nevertheless undermines that speech or action by drawing it into the humorous domain through the reformulation contained in his own teasing remarks.

For example, in 'getting home on time', both speakers know that they are supposed to arrive at the function at seven o'clock and that Alice's request '*try* and get home at a decent *hour*' means 'get home in time to be there at seven.' Larry's tease begins as if it is an acceptance of that request. The 'acceptance', however, proceeds, as is appropriate for the humorous mode, to depart unexpectedly from the assumptions and implications of Alice's discourse. 'Ye *ah* be home by *ni*ne,' says Larry. Drew suggests that this kind of gross and clearly marked departure from what is clearly stated or obviously implied in the initial speaker's discourse is typical of teases and is what makes them easily recognizable as such by recipients.

> In summary, teases are designed to make it very apparent what they are up to – that they are not intended as real or sincere proposals – by being constructed as very obviously exaggerated versions of some action; and/or by being in direct contrast to something they both know or one has just told the other. So that speakers are not only proposing something which might constitute a tease, but are building these propositions in such a way as to signal – to leave recipients in no doubt – that they are not to be taken seriously as real versions of anything. (1986, pp. 18–19)

In 'getting home on time', Larry's lack of seriousness is emphasized by his second tease in which he swings to the other extreme and offers to come home much too early instead of much too late. There is no attempt here to maintain the consistency required of serious discourse. The internal incoherence of his own speech as well as the marked contrast with that of his wife clearly signals Larry's humorous intent. In appearing to take Alice's request seriously, whilst interpreting that request in such a ludicrous fashion, Larry makes Alice's request itself seem ludicrous. Generally, in constructing a tease, the speaker appears to formulate an implication of somebody else's speech or action which, if taken literally, would make that prior speech or action seem silly. For instance, if Alice can be shown to be implying that Larry should leave work in the middle of the day, then it is Alice, despite her seriousness, who deserves the laughter. Although it is the second speaker's tease which is signalled as being in the humorous mode and which generates the laughter, the amusement is directed at, and at the expense of, the serious initial speaker.

This facet of teasing cannot be observed distinctly where there are only two participants. But if we turn again to 'Goodwin's dinner', we can see it more clearly. For at the dinner, all those present join in laughing at a remark which makes fun of the mother's prior action; and the father openly supports the validity of his daughter's teasing remark with 'Right yeh probably the answer right there'. In other words, on this occasion all the participants, including the mother temporarily, endorse the humorous reformulation of the mother's prior action contained in the daughter's tease. At least for a while, the tease establishes the essentially amusing character of the mother's action in laying extra forks. This is typical of teases. They replace some prior, usually serious, version of events with an alternative reality. Moreover, although, as Drew demonstrates, this alternative reality is clearly signalled as being merely humorous, recipients are seldom content to leave the humorous reformulation uncorrected. For they respond overwhelmingly by returning to the serious mode and by reasserting the validity of their own serious speech. Although the alternative reality proposed in a tease is 'only a joke', it nevertheless requires serious attention from the recipient.

Drew identifies two characteristics of tease sequences that help us to account for recipients' pronounced tendency to respond seriously. The first is that, in many cases, the recipient's prior speech has been unusually emphatic. In 'getting home on time', for example, Alice has delivered a 'little lecture' about the need to be on time that evening. In other instances from Drew's collection, first speakers have been complaining vehemently, engaging in extreme self-deprecation, extolling someone's virtues, bragging and so on.

> Across these instances there appears to be something distinctive about the prior turn(s) just prior to the tease: in them, the person who is subsequently teased is *overdoing* something . . . In many cases the character of something being overdone is conveyed through specific, local features or components of the design of the turn(s). Often in conjunction with such components, however, is another very common way in which an activity may be overdone; which is the speaker's sheer persistence, over a number of turns, in telling, complaining, praising . . . it is a notable feature of their being overdone, of speaker *going on about* the matter, in the great majority of cases. (1986, p. 32–3)

It is the fact that teases are typically preceded by speech or action that can be taken to be immoderate or excessive in some way which gives rise to the ensuing tease. For, in the tease, the second speaker conveys an unwillingness to accept or cooperate with what the first speaker has said; or he may attribute by implication some kind of deviance to the first speaker. In 'getting home on time', for instance, Larry refuses to take Alice's repeated requests seriously. He responds to her emphatic and prolonged insistence with an absurd form of apparent acquiescence which, in effect, ignores Alice's speech and can therefore be taken as implying that it is in some unspecified way inadequate, unacceptable or defective. It is presumably for this reason that Alice continues to try to obtain genuine reassurance that Larry will be home on time. In 'Goodwin's dinner', not only does everyone adopt a non-serious reformulation of the mother's action, but that reformulation is clearly derogatory. It implies that her real motive for laying two forks was the improper one of wanting falsely to impress other people with her genteel family life. Thus the mother's serious reply is an attempt to negate the implied criticism.

In most cases, Drew suggests, the recipient of a tease has spoken or acted in an unusually emphatic or insistent manner and has displayed an evident commitment to or intense involvement in the speech or action which gives rise to the tease. It is this intensity, exaggeration or insistence which often generates the tease. For the tease is an attempt indirectly to reject, modify, question or bring into line the conduct of the recipient, whose frequently strong involvement in his own serious discourse is also, presumably, responsible to some degree for his unwillingness to remain within the humorous mode. Thus tease sequences typically end with a serious response from the first speaker because teases question, disrupt or undermine utterances or actions which have previously been strongly asserted or in some other way taken particularly seriously by that speaker. In returning quickly to the serious mode, recipients of teases are reasserting the reality or propriety of their own prior discourse.

In the light of Drew's analysis, it makes no sense to regard teasing as merely a form of play. Although teases are *signalled* as humour, and although participants may humorously react to and playfully embellish the initial tease, *recipients* time and again disregard or only briefly acknowledge the apparent advent of the humorous mode. In taking teases seriously, recipients seem to be making them equivalent to serious conversational turns. But a tease has major advantages over serious speech for the second speaker. For by adopting the humorous mode, the teaser can correct and reprove the other party without 'really' doing so. Whereas a serious condemnation or correction of the first speaker, or a refusal to cooperate, could well lead to open disagreement and antagonism, the allusive, self-denying discourse of the tease makes such interpretative confrontation less likely. In the last resort, the teaser can always insist that he is being wrongly accused of serious intent.

Drew suggests that 'teasing may be considered a mild and indirect form of reproof for a mild kind of transgression' (1986, p. 43). In other words, teasing may be used when a second speaker intends to challenge or correct a first speaker, but where the issue is judged by the second speaker to be too trivial to warrant open disagreement and dispute. In addition, teasing may be a form of mild reproof used particularly among friends and intimates in situations where open criticism and disagreement are deemed to be inappropriate. But whatever the precise contribution of teasing to social interaction, it is clear that it is intricately linked to the serious discourse in which it is embedded. It seems, paradoxically, that teasing is a form of humour which works to sustain one of the basic requisites of the serious mode: namely, that disagreement should be avoided as far as possible, particularly among persons who share the same social world (see p. 23). It appears that not only is teasing a form of amusing play, but it is regularly used as a way of formulating reproof, scepticism, correction and so on, in a manner which makes open disagreement about trivial matters less likely. Teasing is a device for reformulating others' speech and action, and thereby proposing an alternative reality, without seriously doing so. Teasing is a way of employing the humorous mode to sustain a sense of collective reality in situations where, to a minor degree, that shared reality is threatened by the message which is being conveyed. (For several cross-cultural studies of teasing, see Schieffelin and Ochs, 1986.)

Reassurance and forbidden topics

Teasing is necessarily directed at another actor's previous speech or action and occurs in second position in an interactional sequence. But informal humour can also be used in first position to initiate interaction, or at other points in a sequence in order to introduce new topics. Emerson's (1973) study of relationships among medical staff and between medical staff and patients in a hospital pays particular attention to the way in which humour is used to deal with the presentation of difficult conversational topics.

Emerson suggests that occasions regularly occur where hospital patients become concerned about, and want to talk about, sensitive issues such as staff competence, the maintenance of personal dignity, and the likelihood of death. In the hospital setting, however, informal discussion of such topics between patients and staff is prohibited unless the circumstances are exceptional (1973, p. 280). As a result, Emerson proposes, patients tend to refer to these topics obliquely, mainly in a humorous manner. In so doing, they seek to communicate about forbidden topics in a way which is effective, yet which does not count as a genuine contravention of the rules.

> Joking provides a useful channel for covert communication on taboo topics. Normally a person is not held responsible for what he does in jest to the same degree that he would be for a serious gesture. Humor, as an aside from the main discourse, need not be taken into account in subsequent interaction. It need not become part of the history of the encounter, or be used for the continuous reassessment of the nature and worth of each participant, or be built into the meaning of subsequent acts. For the very reason that humor officially does not 'count', persons are induced to risk messages that might be unacceptable if stated seriously. In a general hospital, for instance, where staff and patients take for granted that matters related to death, staff competence, and indignities to patients will be discussed circumspectly or avoided, many joking references to these topics are found. (Emerson, 1973, p. 269)

Emerson notes that humorous remarks about potentially serious topics often receive serious replies. It is this observation which leads her to treat such remarks as conveying in many cases a serious message, despite the first speaker's use of the humorous mode. Although the initiator of the forbidden topic normally provides signals of humorous intent, and although the second speaker usually acknowledges that intent, the latter typically responds as though the first speaker had spoken seriously. Thus the pattern reported by Emerson closely resembles that observed by Drew. Let us look at two examples of how patients introduce the forbidden topic of death into the discourse. In the first instance, an exceptionally obese terminal cancer patient is being helped to use the bedpan by four nurses. As is usual on such occasions with this patient, there is a general mood of hilarity in the ward as the nurses struggle to manipulate her heavy body.

On one occasion the patient abruptly stops her participation in the general merriment and pleads, 'Don't laugh at me'. The head nurse counters with 'You are laughing yourself'. The patient then resumes the mood of hilarity: 'If I'm going to die, I may as well die laughing'. After a second of awkward silence, the head nurse chides her. 'Who's going to die?' (Emerson, 1973, p. 273)

In the next example a former patient, scheduled for experimental surgery, calls into the ward to greet the nurses.

On discovering that Miss Northrup will be on vacation during the time he will be back on the ward, and learning the date of her return, the patient says, 'I'll be gone and buried by then'. Miss Northrup shakes her head and says gently with a smile, yet seriously, 'I don't think so'. The other nurses chime in with 'Oh, don't say that, Mr. Wales' and 'You're not going to die. We need you around. There are lots of things which have to be done'. The patient then apologetically claims, 'Oh, I was joking'. The nurses say, 'Oh' and the conversation goes on to something else. (Emerson, 1973, p. 277)

Emerson claims that in the course of exchanges such as these, participants are using humour to convey messages that might be unacceptable if stated seriously; and that they are negotiating private agreements to suspend the implicit rules forbidding certain topics. But if one examines carefully the typical examples quoted above, they may seem to suggest that patients' serious messages are persistently rejected by the staff despite their humorous format. In other words, use of the humorous mode does not appear to make these messages acceptable. Emerson does seem to be right in claiming that, in adopting the humorous mode, patients are attending to the prohibition against serious discussion of the likelihood of their dying in hospital. But at first sight there is no evidence that they succeed in suspending this prohibition as far as staff are concerned. Emerson provides no example where patients employ humour to raise a forbidden topic which is then taken up and elaborated. What seems to be accomplished by the use of humorous discourse, as the case of Mr Wales demonstrates, is that speakers can introduce a forbidden topic into the conversation whilst insisting that it was never 'really' mentioned.

Is there any sense, then, in which Emerson can be seen to be correct in maintaining that patients regularly succeed in making unacceptable messages acceptable by means of humour? I think that there is. If we look at the examples given above of patients' humorous remarks, we will see that they are not general statements about death, but concrete proposals that the speaker is going to die soon. In the context of the hospital, when uttered by a woman with advanced cancer or a man soon to undergo experimental surgery, such remarks can easily be taken to mean that the speaker is anxious about his or her imminent demise. On this reading, such humour is not only serious, but deadly serious; and it is in fact regularly taken to be so by the nursing staff. 'Who's going to die?' and 'You're not going to die' are typical of their responses. By seriously denying that the topic of death has any special relevance for the speaker, staff in one sense immediately reassert the implicit prohibition against this kind of talk. And, of course, patients may endorse this view, as we have seen, by making clear that they were 'only joking' and that the prohibition was not, therefore, genuinely infringed.

At the same time, however, the staff's refusal to accept that the topic of death has any immediate personal significance for the speaker operates as a form of reassurance. For nurses do not respond by bluntly refusing the patient the right to say such things. Rather, they assure him that the topic is inappropriate because, seriously, he *does* have a future. As they say to Mr Wales, 'We need you around. There are lots of things which have to be done.' In this way they establish interactionally the *unreality* of his humorous assertion about death (Raskin, 1985a). Thus the use of humour in such instances does more than enable patients to express major concerns without impropriety; it also enables staff to respond seriously by providing reassurance which would not otherwise have been forthcoming.

Emerson's study shows, then, that patients' use of humour has significant consequences in their dealings with medical staff. Not only does it allow patients to introduce prohibited topics, but it enables staff and patients to interact in relation to such topics. Emerson's documentation of the use of humour by staff is less extensive. Nevertheless, she does provide one example which deserves comment here.

> On a quiet evening a medical student wanders into the room of a twenty-six-year-old unmarried patient, much discussed on the ward because of an unexpected recovery from the consequences of an illegal abortion. The medical student remarks somewhat awkwardly but apparently in jest: 'You have a lot of teenage magazines around here. Are you a teenager?' The patient replies with a mild sardonic humor: 'Evidently in spirit'. When the medical student solemnly inquires, 'What do you mean by that?' the patient launches a confessional discussion about how adolescent she sees herself in believing she can get away with doing what she wants regardless of what adults say. (1973, p. 272)

In this passage, the medical student begins with a humorous remark. Unlike the previous examples of humorous initiation by patients, here the humorous mode is also adopted by the second speaker. This initial exchange is symmetrical, not only in the sense that both parties employ the humorous mode, but also in that the second speaker humorously accepts the somewhat personal topic proposed by the first speaker. Having obtained acceptance of a non-medical topic within the humorous mode, the medical student immediately reformulates this topic within the serious mode and once again his overture is accepted. As a result of these exploratory exchanges, an extended, serious discussion is set in motion dealing with issues that are not part of the medically focused inter-action that is customary between patient and medical student.

This instance is a good illustration of Emerson's claim that humour can be used to negotiate private agreements to suspend the general guidelines of the institutional setting (1973, pp. 269- 70). For we can observe clearly in this case how topics and interactional work outside the formal requirements of the hospital are first established humorously and only then pursued in a serious fashion. Emerson explains this kind of preliminary humorous exploration of difficult topics by suggesting that they involve the initiator in risk. Thus the medical student above, in claiming interactional rights to which he was 'not entitled within the conventional definition of the situation' (1973, p. 272), ran the risk of being rebuffed and treated by the patient as socially inept or personally intrusive. This risk is lessened, however, by the initial use of the humorous mode. For the topics of humorous discourse are signalled as not being real topics; as not being of interest to the speaker in themselves, but merely as sources of playful diversion. Thus if the second speaker responds in a negative manner, in whichever mode, the first speaker can sustain the appearance that this interactional failure is of no real consequence. If, on the other hand, second speaker adopts the humorous topic as well as the humorous mode, first speaker can have greater confidence that this topic, and its interactional implications, are accept-able to the recipient. Consequently we would expect, as happens in the case quoted above, that a symmetrical humorous exchange will be quickly followed by re-entry into the serious mode.

Emerson's study suggests, then, that humour can be used as a 'transitional device' to facilitate the introduction of awkward topics and the initiation of forms of interaction that may well meet with resistance. Adoption of the humorous mode gives participants a degree of protection against the negative consequences of their potentially deviant actions, and gives recipients a chance to indicate how far they are willing to cooperate before either party has become seriously involved.

There are, however, several limitations to Emerson's study. In the first place, the evidence furnished on this latter use of humour is rather limited. In addition, it is confined to one rather special social setting. We cannot ascertain from her study whether humour is employed as a transitional device only in formal, bureaucratic settings or whether it also operates in this manner in more informal contexts. Finally, we are given no indication whether standardized jokes as well as situational humour may be employed in a similar way. In the next section, we will examine a study which clarifies each of these points.

Humour in a sexual marketplace

Walle's (1976) study examines the use made of humour by customers and waitresses in an American all-night diner during the late 1960s. Walle looks at standardized jokes as well as spontaneous humour, and his study is particularly informative because it shows in detail how humour contributes to the social life of the diner.

A critical feature of the social organization of the diner was that the staff worked in shifts. Thus one group of waitresses began work at 5.00 p.m. and finished between 1.30 and 2.00 the next morning. The next shift began around 1.00 a.m. and finished at 8.00 a.m.. And so on. Walle noted that the period 12.45 to 2.00 a.m. was particularly busy, because at this time other bars and diners in the area closed and numerous extra customers came to the only all-night diner in the vicinity. This period during the early hours of the morning was known as 'the bar rush'. Walle makes two general observations about the effect of the bar rush. Firstly, the diner operated as a sexual marketplace during this period: that is, it became a place where people went expressly to find a sexual partner. In particular, during the bar rush waitresses and customers would arrange to meet immediately after the waitresses were released from work. Secondly, the nature of humorous performance and humorous interchange altered significantly during the bar rush. Walle suggests that participants' humour changed during this period because it was being employed as an interactional resource within the sexual marketplace.

Walle proposes that it is helpful to consider social action in the diner along a continuum ranging from the completely formal behaviour required to sustain interaction in a public dining area to the much more intimate pick-up attempt characteristic of the sexual marketplace. At the formal end of the continuum are actions such as giving and taking orders, serving, preparing and consuming food, giving and accepting payment, and so on. Although some participants, especially those who appear regularly at the diner, will inevitably develop more personal kinds of relationship, these relatively impersonal actions and interactions are sufficient for the operation of the dining room as such. The sexual marketplace, however, necessarily requires participants to act together in a more personal manner. For example, if participants are to succeed in arranging for sexual encounters to take place at the end of the waitresses' shift, participants must engage in relatively intimate inquiries, invitations and so on, during the bar rush. In so far as the diner is a genuine marketplace and the setting for the formation of entirely new sexual relationships, participants must move from the impersonal to the highly personal level of interaction within a matter of minutes – that is, roughly between 12.45 and 2.00 a.m.

Walle suggests that if participants in sexual negotiations at the diner moved too quickly from impersonal to intimate interaction, they ran the risks of causing offence to others and of bringing public humiliation upon themselves. It is possible, in principle, to minimize these risks by moving gradually from institutional behaviour to the exchange of common courtesies, and from there to more personal topics, leading eventually to sexual talk and finally to the pick-up attempt. But in the diner, time was short and waitresses were heavily engaged with numerous customers. Thus actors seeking to establish a sexual liaison had to act quickly. In the context of the bar rush, they could not avoid taking risks.

Different participants in the sexual marketplace employed different strategies to cope with this situation. Some, for example, simply 'propositioned' the other party without preliminaries. Most people, nevertheless, tried in one way or another to reduce the likelihood that their explorations or invitations would cause offence or meet with open rejection. Humour, Walle suggests, was widely used for this purpose.

> Various folklore performances [Walle discusses only humour in this study], since they implied a certain level of rapport between raconteur and audience, were often the first types of behaviour to appear during the transition from one level of interaction to another. If the performance was successful, the actor was encouraged to proceed to the more intimate level, while a rebuff would appear not as a rejection, but as a bungled folk performance. The actor, nevertheless, would be forewarned that a relationship at that level of interaction would probably not be possible. (1976, pp. 206–7)

Walle considers two aspects of participants' humour: its topic and its interactional form. As far as the topic is concerned, he distinguishes between general humour, topical humour and sexual humour. General humour is humour which deals with topics that have no personal or social implications and that would be unlikely to cause offence under normal circumstances. An example might be a typical elephant joke:

Question: How can you tell when an elephant has been in a refrigerator?
Answer: Footprints in the butter.

The topics of such jokes are socially and personally neutral. They can be told freely within the diner and in other social situations. 'Because general humor demands only that the joke teller and audience act in accordance with the most common denominators of social interaction', the performance of general humour is possible even among people whose social relationships are relatively impersonal (Walle, 1976, p. 208).

The next form or level of humour implies that participants are associated together more closely. 'Topical humor is not universally considered to be in good taste by all members of the society for it deals explicitly with certain beliefs held by only a portion of the society' (1976, p. 208). Thus topical humour deals with subjects that are less neutral than those of general humour, and this kind of humour is potentially more offensive. It is normally told, Walle suggests, among people who are reasonably familiar with each others' views and opinions, and who are on sufficiently friendly terms to allow each other, if necessary, a degree of humorous licence. As examples of topical humour, he cites racial and political jokes.

Finally, there is sexual humour, which is, of course, far from socially neutral. Walle suggests that the exchange of sexual humour between waitresses and customers in the diner implied the existence of a body of sexual knowledge shared in common and drew attention to the possibility of sexual relationships between raconteur and audience. Sexual humour implied that those involved could talk, and possibly act, together at the most personal and intimate level.

In addition to these differences in humorous topic, there were differences in the 'mode of presentation' or the 'interactional form' of the humour. Walle's categories here are similar to those I have used above. At the least personal level, there is what he calls 'spontaneous humour'.

> Puns and other spontaneous forms are a common means of starting or entering a conversation. On one occasion, two waitresses were talking about how the center fielder of the local minor-league basketball team (The Triple Cities' Triplets) had fallen down and missed a key play. A customer who was listening responded 'That's why they're called the *Trip*lets'. Spontaneous humour such as this is commonly [although not exclusively] performed among people who are not very intimate and often serves as an avenue or first step in interacting at a new and more intimate level of interaction. (1976, pp. 210–11)

Spontaneous humour can be interjected into the conversation by relative strangers and ignored or developed as participants choose. It can be used as the basis for further interaction, but it can equally well be treated as having no further interactional consequences. Pre-planned humour or standardized jokes, in contrast, make specific interactional demands.

They presuppose that recipients are willing to listen and respond appropriately to relatively extended conversational turns. Thus standardized jokes tend to foster a more definite social commitment between teller and recipient than does spontaneous humour. 'During the bar rush period, the implications of this willingness to pay attention went beyond the mere desire to hear a joke and demonstrated that the audience's interest in the performer was greater than if she or he would listen only to spontaneous humour' (Walle, 1976, p. 211).

The most personal or intimate humorous form observed in the diner was the riddle: that is, a humorous puzzle which could be completed only by means of an active contribution from the recipient. Thus riddles were widely used during the bar rush to establish and sustain direct personal interaction between persons participating in the sexual marketplace. In telling and responding to humorous riddles, actors were able to create and take up opportunities for closer interaction than were furnished by the other humorous forms.

Walle's general argument, then, is that people interested in developing sexual contacts during the bar rush made use of these variations in humorous content and interactional form. By moving from neutral towards more intimate humorous topics, and by adopting humorous forms that required greater social interaction, participants were able to progress to the level of social intimacy required to perform effectively within the sexual marketplace. Walle is proposing, not only that topics and humorous forms entail or imply different levels of intimacy, but also that participants are aware of these implications and employ them for their own purposes. Thus his central argument is that the humorous mode provides a means of exchanging coded messages about sexual availability, and a graded series of transitional devices that are used to enable people to move quickly towards intimacy with considerably less personal risk.

> By attempting to engage the potential companion in certain types of humorous performances, the actor could gain information regarding the possibility of a pick-up without ever mentioning his desires or intentions . . . Humour was used in this manner when the raconteur sensed there was a risk in the pick-up attempt and he or she desired to mask his or her intentions until further information was available . . . any rejection by the audience could be interpreted in general terms which would not smack overtly of sexual rejection. (Walle, 1976, pp. 212–13)

Even when sexual humour and humorous sexual riddles were employed, the raconteur was still not seen to be speaking seriously; and encouragement or disapproval could be elicited from within the relative safety of the humorous mode. For example, if a waitress believed that a customer was using sexual humour in preparation for an unwelcome serious proposal, she could pretend to be 'too busy to listen' or to have 'heard that one before'. In this way, recipients could prevent raconteurs from establishing a relationship at the level of social intimacy implied by that kind of humour; and they could signal to the raconteurs that they should return to a less personal level of discourse. Alternatively, if a recipient wished to encourage a more intimate relationship, he or she could actively display amusement. Typically, such a display would be quickly followed by sexual negotiations in the serious mode, and humour would be abandoned after playing its part in enabling participants to achieve their objectives in the real everyday world. Much information was exchanged and much subtle interaction performed behind the veil of humour. The allusive language and interpretative duality of humour were employed to assess others' suitability as sexual partners and to ensure that open, explicit, serious confrontation and disagreement, rejection and humiliation, were kept to a minimum. For, in one sense, all that had happened when a humorous ploy was unsuccessful was that a speaker had failed to tell a joke. Thus, although participants could themselves furnish serious interpretations of such humorous failures, under normal circumstances any negative implications of a serious kind could be left implicit.

Walle's account of humour in the sexual marketplace confirms, and takes much further, Emerson's preliminary analysis of humour as a serious interactional resource. But, like all analyses of the serious import of humour, it inevitably makes claims that are particularly difficult to substantiate. For instance, when Walle observes a waitress responding to a customer's dirty joke by threatening to call the manager or by exclaiming, 'Oh, my virgin ears!', he may take this as confirmation of his analysis. This, he may assert, is an illustration of a waitress refusing to respond favourably to intimate humour in order to prevent the raconteur from following up with serious sexual proposals. But we may wonder whether the waitress might simply dislike this kind of humour. Furthermore, after such a clear rejection, the raconteur is unlikely to admit to having any serious sexual intent. Could it not be that raconteurs and recipients are merely telling jokes and reacting to them in a perfectly genuine and straightforward manner? Why should we accept Walle's relatively complex analysis in preference to this ordinary, common-sense account? Walle's answer, which I find persuasive, is that we should accept his model, partly because humour so frequently led to explicit sexual negotiation, but also because his analysis explains a whole series of contradictory events which constantly occurred during the bar rush.

In the first place, he suggests, humour cannot be interpreted as being produced for its own sake during the bar rush, owing to the distinct shift in humorous personnel which occurred at this time. Certain skilled and normally active raconteurs regularly ceased to operate during this period, whilst various 'unskilled raconteurs utilized humor during the bar rush in order to size up potential sexual partners, even though they were highly inept as performers of folklore' (1976, p. 213). Walle's analysis makes sense of this switch away from skilled towards unskilled raconteurs, because it regards the interactional implications of humour as being more important than the quality of performance during the bar rush. Skilled raconteurs who were uninterested in sexual negotiation would withdraw from the humorous mode, while less skilled raconteurs would be forced to take it up in the course of their sexual explorations.

Secondly, there were certain features of waitresses' behaviour which are difficult to explain in terms of their direct response to humour. For instance, the same waitress would often respond to similar humorous performances in mutually exclusive ways. She might claim to be 'too busy' to listen to one customer's joke, but yet be able at the same time to listen to jokes from, and to participate in riddles with, another customer. Similarly, a waitress might express indignation about the topic of a joke – for example, if it were racial or political – and then proceed to tell the same joke herself after the original raconteur had gone. It appears from these observations that waitresses were responding primarily to the tellers of jokes, and what those jokes might imply interactionally, rather than to the humour as such.

Waitresses' responses to sexual humour were particularly revealing, because sexual humour was so often the preliminary to a pick-up attempt. Walle notes that all the waitresses in the diner enjoyed sexual humour and often used it among themselves or with customers, yet, on occasion, these same waitresses would claim to be shocked and embarrassed by customers' sexual humour. These variations in waitresses' reactions, he suggests, only make sense if we view them as part of the serious sexual negotiations within which so much humour during the bar rush was embedded. The apparent contradictions in participants' use of, and responses to, sexual and other humour can best be explained by reference to the implications inherent in the performance of specific types of humour during the bar rush. During this period humour was not an end in itself but was employed by participants as a useful resource in the context of changing interpersonal relations. This can be seen quite clearly when one views the fluctuations in humorous discourse in relation to the overall sequence of social relationships within the diner.

The importance of the bar rush context is best dramatized by comparing humor performed during this period with the humor performed during a different time period in the diner. After 2.00 a.m. all the waitresses on duty had just arrived at work and would not be free until 7.30 a.m. or 8.00 a.m. the next morning. The waitresses and customers were no longer considered as immediate sexual objects, for the context of the situation ruled out such considerations. The diner ceased to be a sexual marketplace and became merely the only public place available. For this reason, most of the ambiguities and tensions that existed during the bar rush were eliminated and humor functioned as an end in itself: a series of entertaining folklore performances. The raconteurs tended to be the most skilled performers, not the seekers of information. Since the sexual motivation for a performance was ruled out by the situation, humor was used as a means of 'killing time' not 'making time'. But around 6.30 a.m. men began to drift into the diner from afterhours bars or their all night jobs and again a whole shift of waitresses would soon be off duty. Humor again ceased to function merely as an end in itself. (Walle, 1976, p. 214)

Jokes, teases and serious outcomes

In the last two chapters we have looked in considerable detail at the use of humour in informal settings, and we have seen that both standardized and situational humour can be employed to accomplish serious outcomes. We saw in chapter 4 that standardized jokes, although signalled as belonging to a distinct discursive mode, can be topically linked to the surrounding discourse and are often collectively accomplished and intricately related to the ongoing, serious interaction. In the latter part of this chapter, we have returned to participants' use of standardized jokes and we have seen that they can be employed to achieve more intimate social interaction. Standardized jokes can be a critical resource enabling people to overcome some of the difficulties involved in moving from formal to more personal relationships. Because of its allusiveness, its interpretative duality and its apparent denial of serious intent, the humorous mode can be used artfully by participants to convey messages which can subsequently be denied or developed further, depending on recipients' responses. The humorous mode, in its standardized as well as its spontaneous forms, can operate as a protective device for participants in their pursuit of serious ends.

The appropriate response to a standardized joke is some overt expression of amusement. When such jokes are used for serious purposes, therefore, participants can indicate the extent of their willingness to cooperate in serious matters by finding the joke amusing or not. In a setting where one kind of serious negotiation is particularly prominent, as in the all-night diner, recipients' responses to jokes can be given a very specific interactional significance. As we have seen, in the case of the diner this significance was primarily sexual, at least during the bar rush. Given that so much humour deals with sexual topics (Winick, 1963), it was relatively easy for participants there to focus their humorous remarks on topics that were closely related to their serious concerns. Thus standardized jokes were a particularly convenient transitional device in the context of the sexual marketplace.

But standardized jokes are not always readily available or appropriate. This was the case for the hospital patients studied by Emerson. Formal jokes could not easily be used to lead into discussion of certain topics of major interest to patients, because such topics were prohibited and these prohibitions were widely upheld by staff. Moreover, patients' concerns were often highly personal: for example, the competence of their doctors, the indignity of their medical treatment and the likelihood of their own death. There was no repertoire of jokes available to patients that could be used to breach this interpretative barrier and to allow them to move naturally into helpful personal interchange with staff about these topics. In such circumstances, only by means of spontaneous humour linked directly to the ongoing discourse could patients give vent to certain urgent, but forbidden, queries and observations. As we saw above, they did succeed in employing humour in a relatively basic fashion. The humorous mode was used to enable patients occasionally to allude to 'the unmentionable' without serious impropriety, and to generate reassuring comment from staff which would not otherwise have been offered.

Standardized jokes can sometimes be 'taken seriously'; for instance, the waitresses at Walle's diner sometimes objected seriously to the content of their customers' jokes. But such jokes are so profusely signalled as belonging to the humorous mode that serious responses are probably quite infrequent and may well occur only under rather exceptional circumstances. In contrast, situational humour is very often received in a serious manner and is regularly treated as conveying a serious message. Although it may be tempting on occasion simply to accept without query speakers' signals, and sometimes their explicit assertions, of humorous intent, we must not forget that other participants often respond to humorously signalled remarks with utter seriousness. This, as we saw above, is especially true in the case of teases. Teases follow from and lead to serious discourse. As far as recipients are concerned, most teases are interactionally equivalent to a serious critical comment. On the other hand, they offer a major advantage to the teaser and place certain restrictions on the recipient's response. For teasers, as for people raising awkward topics and for those in pursuit of intimacy, the humorous mode can provide a protective shield against some of the dangers lurking in the realm of serious discourse.

In the last two chapters I have concentrated on serious uses of humour in informal interaction. This does not mean, of course, that all interpersonal humour has some underlying serious intent or that humour among friends, colleagues and acquaintances is never enjoyed for its own sake. In the previous chapter, we saw that humour can be offered and received purely as an agreeable diversion and as a source of that special form of enjoyment which finds expression in collective laughter. After paying so much attention to the serious side of humour, it seems appropriate to enjoy a brief diversion together and to turn our attention now to laughter. Let us devote the next chapter to considering how far laughter can be regarded as a social phenomenon.

6

Laughter as Social Action

I have to begin this chapter with an admission: namely, that very little research on laughter has been carried out by sociologists. Furthermore, there appear to be good reasons why this is so. For, at first sight, laughter seems neither to require, nor to be open to, sociological investigation. Laughter, as we all 'know', is essentially a physiological/psychological process which occurs when people are amused. The *sources* of amusement are certainly, as we have seen, social in character. They arise out of people's organized use of cultural material in the course of interaction. But laughter itself is usually taken to be no more than a physical by-product of participants' social experiences. The possibility that laughter enters into social interaction in a methodical manner or that participants systematically employ laughter as an interactional device is seldom considered.

The widespread adoption of this view of laughter has meant that psychologists, rather than sociologists, have born the brunt of research into laughter. I will devote much of this chapter, therefore, to an examination of two psychological theories of laughter. I will draw attention to various limitations, as well as some advantages, of such theories, and I will try to show that certain aspects of laughter can only adequately be approached from a more sociologically informed perspective. The latter part of the chapter will review the rather small body of research on social aspects of laughter that has been carried out by social psychologists and conversation analysts.

Laughter as a physical reflex

It seems appropriate to begin with Koestler's account of the mechanism of laughter. For Koestler seeks to provide an analysis of laughter which is consistent with the idea that humour depends on the bisociation of interpretative frameworks. Given that the concept of 'bisociation' has been built into my own exposition in previous chapters, Koestler's attempt to link laughter to bisociation is to be welcomed. However, I will argue that Koestler's explanation of laughter is seriously defective and that it draws attention away from certain aspects of laughter which are essential to its understanding.

Koestler begins with the unqualified claim that laughter is a reflex action; that is, it is an involuntary, automatic response to external stimuli of an amusing kind (1964, p. 28). His basic idea is that when something amusing happens out there in the world it triggers a very special kind of physical response within us over which we have very little control. To use Goffman's phrase – when we are amused, laughter seems to come 'flooding out' (1961, p. 55). Koestler recognizes that responses to humour do vary considerably, from an almost imperceptible smile, through innumerable shades of amplitude, to a loud guffaw. But these variations he regards as merely differences of degree. The human reaction to humour, he maintains, is essentially uniform; it varies only in intensity in accordance with the extent to which the stimulus is found to be amusing. Thus human beings' response to humour closely 'resembles the action of a mechanical slot-machine' (1964, p. 29). Whenever humour is experienced, laughter is emitted. Consequently, laughter can be used to identify the occurrence of humour in the same way that 'the tell-tale clicking of the Geiger counter' can be used to indicate 'the presence of radioactivity' (1964, p. 31). Operating within this stimulus/response view of humour, Koestler takes his task to be that of explaining why and how the stimulus of humour produces such a peculiar response. What is it about the comic, he asks, which gives rise to the distinctive physical contortions of laughter?

Before attempting to answer this question, Koestler briefly mentions certain apparently minor qualifications with regard to his basic assumption concerning the reflex, uniform character of laughter. He notes, in the first place, that 'civilized laughter is rarely quite spontaneous' (1964, p. 30), and he goes on, without clarifying what he means by 'civilized laughter', to state that amusement can be 'feigned or suppressed' and generally controlled and 'interfered with' to a greater or lesser extent (1964, p. 30). In addition, he acknowledges that laughter can be used to convey rather different moods and that it is possible, therefore, to distinguish between 'gay laughter, melancholy smile and lascivious grin' (1964, p. 30). Finally, he admits that 'contrived laughter and smiling can be used as a conventional signal-language to convey pleasure or embarrassment, friendliness or derision' (1964, p. 30).

These comments by Koestler himself could be taken to suggest that his basic assumptions about laughter, assumptions typical of stimulus/response analyses in general, are markedly inappropriate or are relevant to only one type of laughter. For example, his acceptance that laughter and smiling can vary from being gay, to melancholy, to lascivious, seems to imply that laughter/smiling is not after all a unitary phenomenon varying only in intensity. Koestler seems to believe that laughter can vary in kind. Secondly, the fact that laughter can be a response to embarrassment or a signal of derision seems to undermine his claim that there is a simple, direct correspondence between laughter and amusement. As others have shown, and as Koestler himself appears to accept at this point in his argument, laughter can occur without humour and humour without laughter (Chapman, 1983). Thus laughter is no 'Geiger counter of the comic' (Douglas, 1968; Morreall, 1983), and any general explanation of laughter would have to deal with its non-humorous forms.

A third, and fundamental, implication of Koestler's qualifying remarks is that, to some unknown degree, laughter is not a reflex action. For Koestler accepts that, at least in 'civilized' contexts, laughter can be controlled. As we can see from his references to laughter being 'contrived' and 'interfered with', he treats such controlled laughter as an unnatural departure from the normal, reflex pattern. But neither Koestler nor more recent researchers can offer us a way of distinguishing spontaneous from contrived laughter.

> Whatever the physiological causes of laughter, it is at times an involuntary reflex action and at times occurs intentionally . . . Yet no criteria have been established for distinguishing between spontaneously occurring natural laughter and laughter that is deliberate, artificial, and acquired as part of the socialization process. (Apte, 1985, pp. 240–1)

If this is so, we have no reliable way of judging whether spontaneous, reflex laughter occurs very frequently or whether it is an occasional, rather unusual event. If it is the latter, then any stimulus/response theory such as Koestler's, even if it were correct, would give a radically incomplete account of the production of laughter.

Finally, in noting that laughter is employed as part of a 'conventional signal-language', Koestler seems briefly to recognize that laughter is generated in the course of social interaction and that it can be used by participants to communicate about and to construct the meaning of such interaction. If one were to explore this aspect of laughter, one would be led to investigate how laughter varies with the social process under way and how it is fitted systematically into the ongoing interaction. But Koestler decides to ignore such analytical possibilities and curtly dismisses from consideration all his own reservations: 'We are concerned, however, only with spontaneous laughter as a specific response to the comic; regarding which we can conclude with Dr Johnson that "men have been wise in very different modes; but they have always laughed in the same way"' (1964, p.

30). Thus Koestler, having drawn attention to certain variable facets of laughter which are inconsistent with his own basic assumptions about its simple, reflex character, chooses to disregard the implications of his own argument. It is not that he has *shown* that participants' ability to control their laughter, to produce different kinds of laughter, to laugh in non-humorous situations, to vary their laughter in accordance with the changing social context, and so on, are analytically trivial phenomena. His procedure is rather to insist on treating the basically reflex character of laughter as self-evident and to refuse to bother seriously with any arguments or observations which do not fit the simple slot-machine model.

Koestler's definition of laughter as a reflex action generates what he calls 'the paradox of laughter'. This paradox or, more correctly, this puzzle is given several different formulations. One version is that, unlike all other reflexes, the 'laughter reflex' serves no apparent biological purpose (1964, p. 31). Laughter seems to contribute in no discernible way to the survival of the human species. But, argues Koestler, if laughter is a true reflex it must make some useful contribution. For if it did not, it would not have been retained by the evolving human organism. Accordingly, a critical goal for any theory of laughter, in Koestler's view, must be to explain how the automatic reaction of the human body to comic situations contributes to its effective functioning and, thereby, to the biological efficiency of the species.

A second formulation of the 'paradox' focuses on the stimulus that produces laughter. Other reflex reactions are physiological responses to very specific changes in the physical environment. For example, a sharp light shone into the eye makes the pupil contract automatically. This contraction occurs because, in the simplest possible terms, the pupil is made up of light-sensitive material. In such cases, stimulus and response appear to operate at approximately the same physical level. But in the case of humour, the stimulus is a complex cultural product which requires complicated mental processing, yet which gives rise to marked reactions in the muscles of the face and violent disruption of the breathing apparatus: 'Humour is the only domain of creative activity where a stimulus on a high level of complexity produces a massive and sharply defined response on the level of physiological reflexes' (Koestler, 1964, p. 31). Koestler is not deterred by this puzzle, nor is he led to reconsider his initial assumption that laughter operates much like other reflexes. Rather, he takes as his central task to explain how the complex stimulus of humour is directly responsible for the unusual physiological processes of laughter.

Koestler establishes a theoretical connection between humour and the physical process of laughter by asserting that all humour contains an element of aggression or fear. This claim has by no means been confined to

Koestler (for useful reviews, see Paulos, 1980; Morreall, 1983). But Koestler develops it in a particularly interesting way. Humour, he argues, necessarily evokes 'an impulse, however faint, of aggression or apprehension. It may be manifested in the guise of malice, derision, the veiled cruelty of condescension, or merely as an absence of sympathy with the victim of the joke' (1964, p. 53). The recipient cannot avoid responding emotionally and physiologically to the 'self- assertive' implications of the humour: 'Emotions of the self- asserting type involve a wide range of bodily changes, such as increased secretion of the adrenal glands, increase of blood sugar, acceleration of the heart, speedier clotting of the blood, altered breathing . . . muscle tension and tremor' (Koestler, 1964, pp. 57–8).

These bodily reactions are primitive and involuntary and derive from mankind's earliest experiences in a hostile world, where they were essential for survival. As a response to humour, however, they are grossly inappropriate. For not only is the aggression and threat contained in humorous discourse merely symbolic; but as the humour unfolds the apparent targets for participants' aggression or self-defence are suddenly and unexpectedly removed as a result of the bisociative structure of humorous discourse: 'The sudden bisociation of a mental event with two habitually incompatible matrices results in an abrupt transfer of the train of thought from one associative context to another. The emotional charge which the narrative carried cannot be so transferred owing to its greater inertia and persistence; discarded by reason, the tension finds its outlet in laughter' (Koestler, 1964, p. 60).

The central argument, then, is that the aggressive element essential to humour generates within those involved a build-up of nervous and physical energy which is suddenly made inappropriate by the unexpected change of interpretative framework required by humour, and which then bursts forth along the line of least resistance – that is, in energetic release of breath and of muscle tension. It is an elegant argument and it undoubtedly provides an answer to Koestler's 'paradox of laughter'. If he is right, it appears that, although laughter has no direct biological purpose, it does have the physiological function of giving relief from the bodily tension sometimes created by man's advanced symbolic capacities. In addition, Koestler combines the idea that humour is aggressive with that of bisociation to provide a plausible explanation of how complex cultural products can elicit a primitive, reflex response. To his credit, Koestler furnishes one of the very few general analyses of humour which include a systematic account of why humorous discourse provokes such a peculiar bodily reaction. Unfortunately, the defects of his theory more than outweigh these advantages.

The first problem with Koestler's scheme follows from his proposal that discourse or action 'will produce a comic effect only if an aggressive-defensive tendency, however sublimated, is present in it' (1964, p. 55). This claim is convincing only if we can show that all instances of humour are recognizably aggressive-apprehensive. There are doubtless many cases where this is a 'reasonable' description. For example, Suls's joke could be said to express aggression against Irishmen (p. 35), and Sacks's joke (pp. 9–10) might be described as expressing aggression against mothers. Similarly, some informal humour, such as Peter's remarks at the dinner party addressed to Deborah and David (p. 69), could be said to express underlying aggression. The most convincing example of all is the laughter of the men in the helicopter over Vietnam, which seemed to be closely associated with release of tension after a fearful experience (p. 53). However, there are many other humorous passages above which do not appear in any way related to aggression or apprehension: for instance, the playful exchange between Boo and Mike (pp. 47–8), the elephant in the fridge joke (p. 85) and the swimming trunks joke (p. 17). It is very difficult to interpret this latter joke as a vehicle for aggression, for example, unless one is willing to believe that every teller of the joke must have had fears about, or aggressive inclinations towards, fish and/or elephants. If we dismiss this possibility, as I think we must, we can defend Koestler's theory only by insisting, as does Koestler himself at one point, that we always laugh at someone else's expense (1964, p. 55). Thus, in the case of the swimming trunks joke, and indeed any other standardized joke, we could be regarded as laughing, not at the humour of its content, but at the recipient's failure to foresee the joke's unexpected outcome. In this sense, even innocent jokes would be told at the recipient's expense.

It is possible, then, to retain the notion that humour is inherently self-assertive, even though its content sometimes seems innocuous, by maintaining that the interactive form of humour is aggressive by its very nature. If this were so, however, we would expect recipients to respond to humour, not with laughter (*displaced* aggression), but with some kind of aggressive retaliation or symbolic retreat. For it would seem that recipients will have been subject in the course of humour to an aggressive act. I suggest that we can account for their reacting with laughter rather than with counter-aggression only if we credit them with the ability to perceive that they are not dealing with *real* aggression. An important defect in theories of humorous aggression, like that of Koestler, is that they pay no attention to the obvious difference between serious and humorous or playful aggression. Participants, on the other hand, evidently do make such a distinction; for they react to them quite differently.

If these observations are accurate, two important consequences follow. The first is that, if recipients are able to register and decode the various signals establishing the operation of the humorous mode, they are not merely responding to humour in an automatic fashion at the reflex, physiological level. Secondly, if recipients can distinguish between humorous and serious intent, we would not expect them to respond to humour with the physiological build-up appropriate to a situation of real physical threat. Consequently, it seems to follow that, where humorous intent is signalled and understood, there is unlikely to be the overwhelming need for the release of tension that is assumed in Koestler's account of the cause of laughter. We can accept that certain *kinds* of laughter do seem to fit Koestler's analysis: for instance, where participants react to unsignalled 'natural humour', as in the helicopter over Vietnam. However, the closer we approach to normal humorous interchange, with its subtle use of meaningful symbols and of signals of intent, the less appropriate does Koestler's reliance on primitive response mechanisms become. Of course, Koestler may well have had such subtleties in mind when he referred in passing to the awkward complications of 'civilized' discourse. But, I suggest, it seems more likely that it is the reflex laughter of the men in battle which is exceptional and that 'civilized', negotiated, orderly humorous discourse is closer to the ordinary state of affairs.

Koestler's use of the word 'civilized' in this context is in one respect rather misleading. For it seems to imply that the ability to regulate laughter and to use it in an organized way as a means of communication are relatively recent human accomplishments. Koestler seems to equate these capacities with the emergence of advanced societies and the creation of a false and contrived culture which tends to conceal man's natural urges beneath a thin veneer of apparent social order. However, this view that controlled, meaningful laughter is a by-product of 'civilized' life has come to appear rather unconvincing in the light of conclusions about parallel behaviour among apes.

> It appears, then, that in the evolutionary process leading from nonprimate mammals to primates, and finally to *Homo sapiens*, the meaning of the teeth-baring display broadened. While it was originally a part of the mainly defensive or protective behaviour mechanism, it became a signal of submission and nonhostility. In some species, the nonhostility signal probably became predominant, so that finally a signal indicating friendliness could evolve. Among primates, the bared-teeth display overlapped with the lip-smacking display, while human smiling appears to have resulted from the combination of both, very nearly replacing the latter. (Apte, 1985, p. 245)

The relationship between primate behaviour and that of humans is bound to remain uncertain. Nevertheless, it now seems clear that, in primate society, actions very similar to laughing and smiling are actively employed as signals of friendliness by participants. As Bateson (1955) and Fry (1963) noted in the course of their earlier studies of 'the play frame', primates are also able to use such signals to indicate that their actions are not what they might appear to be. In particular, facial grimaces are employed as a signal of mock-aggression. It is clear that apes, as well as humans, can distinguish playful hostility from the real thing and can respond appropriately. Thus, even in primate society, actions closely akin to smiling and laughter are part of a conventional sign language that is used to regulate interaction and to play with the distinction between reality and unreality. It seems probable, therefore, that Koestler was mistaken in dismissing these symbolic and interactional aspects of laughter as peculiar to 'civilized' societies and, therefore, as of no more than peripheral interest.

Koestler's analysis of laughter does have some merits. It recognizes the bisociative character of humorous discourse. It suggests a possible link between the semantic structure of humour and the physiology of laughter. It accounts for laughter's lack of biological function. And the basic notion of the build-up and release of tension does seem to apply to certain kinds of laughter. But as a general theory of laughter it is unsatisfactory. Firstly, it ignores the fact that laughter occurs regularly in certain kinds of non-humorous and non-aggressive situations. Secondly, the content of much humour seems quite unrelated to aggression/apprehension. Thirdly, it is difficult to maintain that humorous interaction itself is necessarily aggressive, because it is normally signalled and accepted as being different from genuine aggression. Fourthly, to a considerable extent laughter appears not to be a crude reflex reaction, but a regulated and orderly part of the process of communication and social interaction. Furthermore, it is unlikely that this is a recent or marginal aspect of the production of laughter.

Fifthly, Koestler's argument that 'men have always laughed in the same way' transforms humour itself from a complex and variable cultural process to a simple, utterly primitive phenomenon common to all men. For according to Koestler, when we react to humour, we are not appreciating the subtleties of language or of social action; we are merely giving vent to an accumulation of redundant energy which we have been fooled into producing. I suggest that Koestler has not succeeded in reconciling a high-level cultural stimulus with the production of a reflex response. Rather, he has reduced humour to the level of that supposedly primitive response by eliminating the diversity and complexity of humour from theoretical consideration. Such a slot-machine view of the production of laughter cannot cope even with the actions characteristic of apes.

Finally, there is the fact that Koestler never once offers observational data on laughter. His whole argument is a priori and it takes for granted that we all know exactly what laughter is like, precisely when it occurs, and so on. When Koestler reaffirms Dr Johnson's claim that 'men have always laughed in the same way', he seems to be implying that laughter conforms to one basic pattern. Yet he does not even try to describe what that pattern might be, nor to check whether it occurs in practice. John Morreall (1983) has tried to infer what the pattern would be if laughter was produced, as Koestler and others suggest, through the sudden release of tension. For such theorists, Morreall writes, laughing is analogous to the opening of a safety valve in a steam pipe.

> Just as the opening of the valve releases excess steam pressure built up within the pipe, laughter is supposed to release excess nervous energy built up within the laugher's nervous system. But if this is the case, then we should expect the greatest amount of nervous energy to be released at the very beginning of the overflow, when the excess is at its peak. As the release continues, the amount of energy released, and so the intensity of the laughter, should gradually diminish; just as the steam from a safety valve is at its greatest pressure at the moment the valve is opened, but after that initial outburst gradually diminishes. Now sometimes laughter is like this – there is a powerful outburst that trails off to mild chuckling and then no laughter at all. But often laughter starts out very weak and increases in strength; or there is an initial outburst followed by a period of no laughter, and then more laughter. (1983, pp. 26–7)

Morreall does not provide detailed documentation of these possible patterns of 'laughter emission'. He offers us no more than common-sense reflection on 'what we all know' about laughter. But even with this minimal recourse to empirical evidence, he improves on the efforts of Koestler and the great majority of writers on this topic. In his brief remarks about the variety of humorous patterns, Morreall implies that perhaps laughter is no more uniform than humour. He enables us to imagine that there may be as many kinds of laughter and patterns of laughter-production as there are types of humorous interaction. His remarks also imply that laughter might be carefully observed, its variations and complexities documented and explored, and an analysis developed which was linked to systematic evidence about its production. In the next section, therefore, we will examine Morreall's own theory of laughter.

Laughter and the pleasure shift

Morreall claims to offer a completely general explanation of laughter. His analysis is remarkably simple but quite powerful. It is also a distinct improvement, in several respects, on that of Koestler. Nevertheless Morreall, like Koestler, fails to recognize the limitations of his basic model of laughter-production; and he fails, therefore, to move beyond a narrowly psychological approach to laughter.

Morreall's theory of laughter is built around three basic propositions. The first is that laughter is always associated with some change in the psychological state of the individual concerned. The second is that laughter occurs when this change in state is too sudden for the person to be able to adjust smoothly. Thirdly, the psychological shift leading to laughter must be pleasant. These statements, Morreall proposes, convey the essential characteristics of laughter. Laughter is the physical activity that is caused by, and which gives expression to, the feelings produced by a sudden psychological shift in a pleasurable direction (1983, p. 39).

This theory is an improvement on prior attempts to explain laughter, claims Morreall, in two important respects. In the first place, it applies to all laughter and not just to that associated with humour. Thus it can account, not only for the response to an amusing story, but for laughter produced by tickling, by embarrassment, by running into an old friend in the street, and even that caused by hysteria. Secondly, previous theories of humorous laughter have focused on one kind of humorous situation and have insisted that all humorous laughter is of this type. For instance, Koestler and others have maintained that all humorous laughter involves a release of aggressive tension. Morreall is willing to accept that *some* humorous laughter may arise in this way, but he contends that in many other amusing situations aggression and pent-up emotion are completely lacking. Thus it cannot be the sudden release of tension as such which causes laughter. Rather, he argues, laughter is due to the sudden and pleasurable change of state which accompanies the release of tension, but which can also be created in many other ways. Morreall maintains that his alternative hypothesis includes within its scope all the accurate observations about laughter made by previous analysts, without making the mistake of overgeneralizing on the basis of one limited type of laughter. He claims to have reformulated their findings at a level which is genuinely applicable to all cases of laughter.

Morreall succeeds in making his theory so wide-ranging, despite its basic simplicity, by identifying four analytically distinct aspects of individuals' psychological states: namely, the sensory, the affective, the perceptual and the cognitive. Laughter is so varied, he suggests, because it can be caused by sudden changes of state occurring in each of these psychological dimensions and in every possible combination. For example, the laughter which is emitted by very young babies when they are tickled is said to be produced by sudden, yet pleasant, changes in purely sensory stimulation. In the case of older children and adults, tickling becomes more complex psychologically, but it still operates mainly at the sensory level.

> Older children and adults, of course, can also be tickled; and though more is involved here because a child or adult perceives the tickler, and can often thereby anticipate or even stop the touches, here, too, successful tickling is based on a shift in sensory stimulation. The most important thing in tickling children and adults is that the touch be unexpected in some way – either in its commencement, duration, location, direction, or amount of pressure. For if we can fully anticipate the touch, we can prepare ourselves for it and so eliminate its suddenness, its power to shock us; and in that case there will not be a psychological shift, but an expected bit of stimulation. (Morreall, 1983, p. 40)

In the case of adults, behaviour is always much more complex than in young children and will always involve some combination of sensory input, emotion and cognition. The general applicability of Morreall's theory, however, is assured because it includes any and every conceivable psychological state. The only requirement for laughter to occur is that there must be some sudden and pleasant psychological alteration.

> In the situation where I run into an old friend on the street, for instance, I may be experiencing no emotion before I see him. But then as I recognize his face and rush to meet him, I feel a boost of excitement; my step quickens and even my heartbeat is speeded up. The shift from feeling no emotions to feeling very strong emotions here will be pleasant, and my hearty laughter will be the expression of my pleasure. In much the same way I might laugh on finding out that I have won a lottery, especially if this discovery is accidental and so sudden. Even the shift from a neutral emotional state to simply *thinking* about something that arouses positive emotions can be enough to trigger laughter, as when we laugh in anticipating some enjoyable activity or in recalling some particularly fond memory. (Morreall, 1983, p. 46)

In this passage, Morreall is discussing non-humorous laughter. In relation to humorous laughter, the main advantage of his perspective is that its basic psychological mechanism is so general that it can be said to appear in an indefinite variety of humorous forms. Consequently, not only does the theory cover non-humorous laughter, but it allows for wide diversity within the humorous realm. The psychological shift responsible for laughter may, in some cases, be mainly emotional; and it may sometimes involve aggression/apprehension. But there are many other kinds of emotion and, in principle, every one can give rise to the sudden pleasurable change required for laughter to occur. Morreall emphasizes, in addition, that we should not place undue importance on the emotional shift present in some cases of humour.

> For our enjoyment of an emotional shift is neither necessary nor sufficient for humor, whereas our enjoyment of a conceptual shift is both necessary and sufficient for humor. Though a release of hostile, sexual, or other feelings may be involved in some cases of humor, the essence of humor lies in the enjoyment of incongruity. (1983, p. 47)

One obvious limitation of Morreall's theory, compared to that of Koestler, is that Morreall provides no account of the physical mechanism of laughter. He makes no attempt to explain why sudden, pleasant changes of psychological state should generate the peculiar convulsive movements of laughter. Whereas Koestler sought to devise a theory which brought together the cultural, psychological and physiological levels within one coherent scheme, Morreall concentrates more narrowly on the psychological processes of laughter. In compensation for this exclusively psychological focus, he offers us a theory which should apply equally well to all forms of laughter, yet which avoids oversimplification. Morreall's analysis of the psychology of laughter and humour accepts the complexity and diversity of these phenomena, and recognizes that humorous interplay can be 'pure' and playful as well as emotionally charged. It also gives an account of the psychological process of laughter which could be taken to parallel what we know about the semantic structure of humorous discourse. In other words, we could reformulate Morreall's hypothesis as a proposal that laughter will occur when the discourse fosters a psychological state which is then unexpectedly, but pleasantly, disrupted by the evolution of that same discourse.

Unfortunately, there is a major weakness in Morrreall's theory. This weakness becomes evident when we ask what is meant by the phrase 'pleasantly disrupted'. As we have noted in previous chapters, not all disruptions or incongruities are found to be funny. Morreall is inclined to take for granted that if incongruity or a change of psychological state gives rise to laughter, the experience must have been pleasant. Consequently, his claim that only pleasurable changes of state lead to laughter is somewhat empty. For he offers no independent evidence that an increase in pleasure is involved in such cases. In most of his examples, the likely occurrence of laughter is itself taken as sufficient indication that the experience was pleasant. As a result, the analysis comes close to a tautology.

The wider significance of this aspect of Morreall's analysis will become clearer if we reconsider his example of non-humorous laughter occasioned by meeting an old friend in the street. The emotions depicted in Morreall's description of this meeting are explicitly described as 'pleasant', and the 'hearty laughter' is said to be 'the expression of this pleasure' (see p. 103). I can equally well, however, imagine a quite different psychological state leading to laughter in a similar situation. For instance, I may be very far from pleased at meeting that old fool again, and my heart may sink, but I greet him nonetheless with hearty laughter out of recognition of past ties of friendship. Would this example of a negative change of psychological state producing laughter count as a refutation of Morreall's theory? It appears that it would not. This instance would not be taken to contradict his analysis because, although the change in psychological state did not involve an increase in pleasure, the ensuing laughter would be deemed not to have been natural laughter but merely 'forced laughter' or 'feigned laughter'. As Morreall makes clear, he regards laughter which is not a natural expression of pleasure as a distortion of the primary psychological process. Any situation where people seem to laugh without an increase in pleasure is treated as irrelevant to his basic hypothesis.

> Our formula that laughter is an expression of pleasure at a psychological shift, then, can be seen to cover even the problem cases on our list. Because laughing is not only a natural expression of pleasure, but is also under our voluntary control, and even under the control of unconscious coping mechanisms, it can occur in the absence of pleasure. I can force a laugh to please my boss or to make myself feel less tense. But such cases, as we saw, are parasitic on laughter as the natural expression of pleasure, for they all work by using laughter to feign pleasure, or by breaking into the causal loop between pleasure and laughter to induce pleasure by performing laughter. Because laughter is partially voluntary, too, it can not only be forced when the person is not amused, but can also be suppressed when he is amused . . . There is no one-to-one correspondence, in short, between instances of amusement and instances of laughter. Nonetheless, our formula that laughter is the natural expression of amusement provides the key to understanding all cases of laughter. (Morreall, 1983, pp. 58–9)

In this passage, Morreall's argument closely resembles that of Koestler. For Morreall, like Koestler, insists on regarding the involuntary emission of laughter in response to a pleasant stimulus as the key to understanding all cases of laughter. He does accept that laughter can occur in the absence of such a stimulus and that laughter can be actively employed in the course of social interaction. But this does not lead him either to revise his theoretical hypothesis that 'laughter results from a pleasant psychological shift' (1983, p. 39) or to qualify his claim to be offering a comprehensive theory of laughter. Rather, again like Koestler, he responds by dismissing those kinds of laughter which do not fit his theory as unnatural and parasitic on the so-called natural process.

The central defect of Morreall's analysis, in my view, is that despite its genuine attempt to allow for the diversity of humour and laughter, the theory is confined within a restricted conception of isolated organisms responding automatically to the pleasure derived from external stimuli: 'Laughter, as we have set out to account for it, is a human behavior that is a reaction of the person to his perceptions of the world around him – a motor response, to put it crudely, to sensory input' (1983, p. 57). As we have seen, this simplistic view requires Morreall to disregard a potentially enormous range of situations where laughter seems to be to some degree under participants' control. It also leads him to treat human actors as essentially passive recipients of external stimuli that are intrinsically either pleasure-giving or not. Where he suspects that people are not simply responding to whatever inputs their environment provides, but are acting upon that environment and thereby creating its meaning, he dismisses their actions as feigned, forced, and as being not a source of true laughter. I suggest, in contrast, and in line with the discussion in previous chapters, that participants are continually engaged in giving meaning to the world around them and in making it laughable or not. For example, it seems to me unlikely that the psychological change brought about by hearing, say, the swimming trunks joke, is in itself laughter-inducing. As we will see in the next section, humorous discourse is not inherently laughable. Laughter occurs in a social environment in which participants act to make things humorous. The swimming trunks joke (and much other humour) will give rise to laughter, as we saw in the two previous chapters, only in so far as it has been actively signalled as humour and in so far as participants collaborate to make it laughable. Thus laughter is not merely a motor response by isolated individual organisms to some laughable input. It is necessarily part of an active social process and can be understood only in relation to that process.

Morreall's underlying stimulus-response model leads him, then, to underestimate the extent to which people actively work together to construct the humour and laughability of their 'sensory inputs'. It is also probably responsible in part for his failure to develop his own observations on the possible 'shaping' of laughter in the course of interaction. As we saw in the previous section, Morreall correctly draws attention to other analysts' inability to account for the varying patterns of laughter on different occasions and in different circumstances. This could have led to careful observation of how laughter is actually produced; for instance, one might have predicted that so-called 'forced' laughter was recognizably different in shape from laughter which was a 'natural expression of pleasure'. Rather disappointingly, Morreall does not develop his ideas in this empirical direction. The reason for this, perhaps, is that his basic model implies that contrived laughter is relatively unimportant and that variations in the production of natural laughter must correspond, by definition, to fluctuations in participants' experiences of pleasure. Given these assumptions, empirical research into laughter is quite redundant. As with Koestler, the answers are assumed to be known in advance.

This discussion of Koestler's and Morreall's theories makes it clear that, although laughter may sometimes be a reflex response to changes originating in the external environment, this is not the only, nor even the primary, mechanism of laughter-production. It appears that, even in primate groups, laughter and smiling are actively used as resources in the course of social interaction. We might expect that, in human societies, such controlled and socially accomplished production of laughter would be widespread, if not paramount. In previous chapters we have observed in passing, when we have examined transcriptions of natural interaction, how laughter and smiling are built into social life by participants in an intricate manner and are exchanged as part of a collaborative process. Yet Koestler and Morreall dismiss all such laughter as a marginal phenomenon. In their view, it is obvious that such laughter is no more than a theoretically irrelevant deviation from the 'natural', and 'normal', situation in which a human organism responds automatically to the appropriate external stimulus. But this assumption about what kind of laughter is 'normal' is not based on observation of real, laughing human beings. Neither Koestler nor Morreall takes the trouble to provide empirical support for their assertions about the nature of 'normal' or 'natural' laughter. When, however, we do try to base our explanations of laughter on what can be observed in experimental and natural settings, we are forced to abandon these preconceptions and to accept that laughter is overwhelmingly a product of social processes and can be understood only in relation to such processes. Laughter undoubtedly has, by definition, an important psychological/physiological dimension which requires analysis at that level. But this does not mean that laughter can only be analysed by means of a slot-machine model of human action (Zijderveld, 1983). Laughter is almost always socially mediated. It almost always occurs in a social context and varies, sometimes dramatically and sometimes subtly, in accordance with the interpersonal dynamics of that context. Let us examine some studies of the social production of laughter in which these claims are substantiated and illustrated in detail.

Laughter and the social context

It has long been clear that laughter occurs overwhelmingly in social situations (Chapman, 1983). One obvious reason why this should be so for humorous laughter is that humorous discourse necessarily requires a teller and at least one recipient (Fine, 1983). Standardized jokes, for example, involve concerted action by a participant who already knows and can deliver the comic resolution of the joke, and by one for whom the comic outcome is unexpected, amusing and, therefore, laughable. Moreover, even isolated laughter is likely to be a by-product of the laugher's social experiences, or to arise out of some indirect social relationship.

> For most of us laughter bubbles to the fore only rarely when there is no one else around. These are occasions when we relive amusing accidents or when in day-dreams we conjure up thoughts of others. Sometimes an author can levitate us so that we lose ourselves in the story and imagine ourselves as first- hand witnesses to funny events. When we laugh it is as though we were actually present. Therein lies an explanation as to why laughter, an essentially social response, can find expression when we are on our own: we may be alone physically, but we are not alone psychologically. (Chapman, 1983, p. 148)

Laughter, then, is social in the sense that it normally arises out of real or imagined dialogue between people. There are, however, other more specific connections between laughter and the social setting. Some of these have been revealed in a series of detailed studies carried out since the early 1970s by Chapman and his colleagues (for reviews of this work see Chapman, 1976; 1983). For example, Chapman found that children's humorous laughter is dramatically increased simply by the presence of a companion. When children were presented with humorous material, they laughed and smiled far more in the presence of another child than when they were alone. This was so, even when the companion neither laughed nor smiled and even though there was no observable interaction between the children (Chapman, 1976). In the case of adults, the results were slightly more complex. For it was found that adults' laughter was significantly affected by the companion's behaviour. Subjects who were paired with a partner who was completely unresponsive produced very little reaction to the humorous material. Subjects on their own tended to laugh rather more. But subjects with a responsive companion laughed much more frequently and more enthusiastically than either of the other two categories (Osborne and Chapman, 1977).

It appears from this study of adults that laughter and smiling operate as cues which encourage laughter and smiling on the part of others. It is tempting to infer that participants' laughter and the frequent exchange of humorous cues in the 'high response' situation must have made these subjects' experiences more amusing. But Osborne and Chapman report: 'An analysis of the subjective ratings solicited at the end of the sessions showed no significant differences between the three groups in terms of the perceived funniness of the tape-recordings' (1977, p. 43). Of course, it may be that experimental subjects who laughed relatively little were responding retrospectively to the 'demand characteristics' of the experiment and exaggerating their feelings of amusement. But we cannot know whether or not this was the case. We can only conclude that there is no direct evidence that participants' *amusement* was significantly affected in this study by variations in social context. The extent to which participants laughed and smiled, however, was very considerably altered by the presence of other laughing persons. It seems that, even in situations like this where social interaction is minimal and where humour is not jointly accomplished, participants' laughter can be highly responsive to changes in others' behaviour.

Most of Chapman's studies of laughter have dealt with children, and we cannot be certain that his findings apply equally to adults. But it appears that children's laughter and smiling vary systematically in accordance with a range of interactional and interpersonal factors: for instance, how much a companion laughs, how much the partner looks at the subject, how close they sit together, whether the subject and companions are friends, whether there are several companions and, if so, how much they look at one another, and so on (Chapman, 1983). The general conclusions arising from these studies are that the level of social 'intimacy' among participants is a crucial factor influencing the production of humorous laughter and that the more 'shared' is the situation, the more children laugh (Chapman, 1976). 'Intimacy' and 'sharing' are measured in this research by means of behavioural indicators such as eye contact and physical proximity.

These studies are an advance on the views considered earlier in this chapter in so far as they provide careful empirical documentation for their claims. They certainly furnish ample confirmation of the need to study the production of laughter as a social process. Yet the design of these studies tends to reproduce one of the basic mistakes of writers such as Koestler and Morreall. For Chapman's experimental subjects are always passive recipients, rather than active initiators, of humour. Laughter is persistently treated in these studies as if it can occur only as a behavioural response to external stimuli. The design of the experiments is such that humorous material is always presented to the subjects by the experimenters, and the frequency and duration of their laughter is then measured under controlled conditions. Consequently, we can learn nothing from such studies about participants' active use of laughter and humour in the course of ordinary interaction. Whereas Koestler and Morreall argue theoretically for the irrelevance of laughter which is not an involuntary reaction to humorous stimuli, Chapman and other social psychologists (Chapman, 1983, p. 137) tend to exclude actors' controlled use of laughter from consideration by adopting a particular experimental design.

In addition, although aggregate measurements of the number of laughs or the duration of laughter can be informative, they will never reveal the social 'shaping' of laughter. The work of Chapman and his colleagues clearly confirms that people laugh in response to others' laughter. But aggregate measurements cannot show how the social exchange of laughter works in detail in varying circumstances, nor how laughter may be used in different ways to contribute in a meaningful fashion to the interaction of which it forms a part. If laughter *is* more than a mere reflex response to environmental cues, if it *does* contribute systematically to the sign language of the humorous mode and is employed in subtle ways to communicate about the meaning of the ongoing interaction, techniques must be found to investigate the fine detail of laughter in natural settings. We must find a research perspective which not only allows for the possibility that social actors methodically employ laughter as an interactional resource, but also treats such laughter as a topic for careful investigation. In the pursuit of such a perspective, we will now examine several studies of laughter carried out by conversation analysts.

Making laughter flood out

We have seen that Koestler and Morreall treat occasions where laughter 'floods out' as paradigm cases. Such situations are thought to provide the key to an understanding of laughter. Similarly, Chapman is reassured about the relevance of his data to natural settings by the fact that 'explosive laughter' was very common during his experimental sessions (1976). It should be noted, however, that there are other human reactions which often appear to burst forth spontaneously: for example, clapping and applause. Laughter is by no means as distinctive in this respect as Koestler and others have assumed. Furthermore, clapping and applause have been shown to be collectively managed and to be produced in a socially organized manner (Atkinson, 1984; Grady and Potter, 1985; Heritage and Greatbatch, 1986). Let us turn, therefore, to a paper by Gail Jefferson (1985) in which the 'flooding out' of laughter is viewed as, in some circumstances, a controlled interactional device.

Jefferson starts with the observation that neither participants nor analysts normally describe laughter in the same detail as other aspects of conversation. For example, a participant can normally convey what happened on a specific occasion in summary terms ('He insulted me') or by repeating a version of what was said ('He said, "You clumsy idiot"'). But in the case of laughter, the summary description has to suffice ('He laughed' or 'He laughed heartily'). We do not say, 'He went "*ahh* ha ha *heh* heh heh".' Laughter is very seldom, if ever, reproduced in this kind of detail by participants.

A similar approach to laughter has been adopted by the great majority of analysts. If we look back at transcriptions of informal conversation in previous chapters, we find that the occurrence of laughter is normally indicated by insertion of the word 'laughter' (see pp. 62 and 75). But no attempt is made to reproduce precise details of the sounds of laughter or of its relation to the surrounding discourse. Jefferson acknowledges that this procedure is perfectly adequate for many analytical purposes. However, she suggests that it may obscure interesting features of interaction which can be revealed by means of a more detailed transcription. Her advanced method of transcription is not always easy to read. I will employ it below only for the most critical passages. Jefferson uses a row of 'h's preceded by a dot, ·hhh, to indicate an inbreath. An 'h' in parenthesis, (h), indicates a particle of within-speech laughter.

To illustrate her claim about the analytical value of detailed transcription, Jefferson compares one of her own early transcriptions with a later transcription of the same passage.

First transcription

Ken: And he came home and decided he was gonna play with his orchids from then on in.

Roger: With his *what*?

Louise: heh heh heh heh

Ken: With his orchids. ⌈He has an orchid –

Roger: ⌊Oh heh hehheh

Louise: *(through bubbling laughter)* Playing with his organ yeah I thought the same thing!

Ken: No he's got a great big ⌈glass house

Roger: ⌊I can see him playing with his organ hehh hhh

(1985, p. 28)

In the later transcription of the middle section, the utterance by Louise which had been initially described as being spoken 'through bubbling laughter' is depicted as follows:

Later transcription

Ken: Ee⌈z got an *orch*⌈id

Roger: ⌊Oh: ⌊hehh⌈h a h ·he: h ·*h*eh

Louise: ⌊*h*eh huh ·*hh* PLAYN(h)W(h)IZ

       O(h)R'N ya:h *I* thought the same.

The earlier transcription conveys a clear impression of laughter bursting forth against the speaker's will. Jefferson provides several examples of similar passages, and she illustrates how participants, as well as analysts, can interpret such laughter as an uncontrollable response to the humour of the discourse. For example, in a mildly dirty joke involving a punch line about a 'dick being transplanted', the female teller laughs so much in delivering the punch line that recipients have difficulty hearing what is being said. One of the participants appears to employ a 'reflex' theory of laughter to explain what is causing the problem when she says: 'It's difficult when she gets to the punch line, she can't help laugh.'

Jefferson suggests, however, that this kind of interpretation of Louise's remark in the passage above becomes rather less convincing when we look carefully at the later transcription. For, whereas the first version implied that laughter was uncontrolled and persisted throughout the utterance, we can now see that the laughter is restricted to one part of the utterance and that the remainder is completely free of laughter. At this point in her exposition, Jefferson begins to consider whether the laughter is perhaps not flooding out, but has been deliberately inserted; for it is rather odd that the laughter which seems so difficult to control in 'PLAYN(h)W(h)IZ O(h)R'N' should cease so suddenly and be followed immediately by speech without the least trace of humorous upheaval. Furthermore, given that laughter *can* be inserted and controlled for its interactional effect, it is possible that the impression of laughter exploding out of the speaker's control may itself be intentionally conveyed by actors in certain circumstances.

Jefferson finds support for this interpretation in the way that Louise and other speakers place their laughter. She points out that Louise's laughter in this uttereance begins and ends in exact conjunction with the potentially improper phrase 'playing with his organ'; and she cites other instances where the laughter coincides with what she calls the 'tender' component of the utterance. She gives as another example: 'they'd say catch a n(hh)i(hh)gg(h)er by the toe. ·hh if he hollers let im go.' On numerous occasions, it appears, speakers are able to talk without laughter and with considerable clarity before or after some obscene or otherwise difficult phrase; yet when delivering that phrase they seem to lose control and their speech becomes briefly suffused with apparently uncontainable laughter. In Jefferson's view, the precise placing of the laughter makes it difficult to accept that this seeming loss of control over the impulse to laugh is not itself under the speaker's control.

If participants do sometimes place 'outbursts' of laughter to accompany awkward speech, this is presumably because such placement has interactional consequences. Jefferson's proposal is that the insertion of laughter distorts and hides what is being said. Moreover, the impression that this laughter is out of control makes it 'evident' to other participants that the speaker can do nothing about her inability to speak clearly: 'the presence of laughter can account for the presence of the distortion, not, for example, as a matter of the speaker's reluctance to say the words he is saying and thus in fact not-quite-saying . . . but as a constituent feature of flooding out; of uncontainable laughter invading and incidentally distorting the speech' (Jefferson, 1985, p. 31). Thus tender words, such as 'dick', 'organ' and 'nigger', can be communicated, yet not quite 'said', without the speaker being culpable for her failure to deliver the words clearly. In addition, her 'involuntary reaction' shows that she is not the sort of person who would *choose* to engage in dirty talk. As we saw above, speakers are somehow able, by the nature of their laughter, to make it clear that they 'can't help laugh'. When they are 'flooded by laughter', they can claim the right not to speak properly and not to be held fully responsible for any indelicacy of conduct.

Laughter can be used, as in Louise's remark, to add another level to the allusiveness which is characteristic of humorous discourse. Thus the written phrase 'playing with his organ' does no more than allude indirectly to a possible sexual referent. When it is uttered by Louise as something like 'PLAYN(h)W(h)IZ *O*(h)R'N' it is even further removed from open, explicit discourse. Interactionally, the insertion of laughter focuses attention on the locus of the humour (Nash, 1985) whilst placing the responsibility for extracting its improper meaning even more firmly with the recipient. As so often, the humorous mode is being employed to enable speakers to say and do things without appearing to do so. The careful placing of laughter, revealed by Jefferson's method of transcription, shows that laughter can be used, not merely to signal that the humorous mode is in operation, but also to promote the allusiveness of humorous discourse and to engage in impropriety apparently against one's will.

Jefferson's study of participants' controlled use of 'flooding out' is, of course, no more than a first step towards a sociological analysis of laughter. It seems likely, however, that the 'supposed spontaneity' of laughter may be put to work in many other subtle ways. Schenkein has shown, for example, that brief fragments of laughter can be inserted successfully into conversation in a meaningful way at points where the person responsible would normally be open to the charge of having improperly interrupted the discourse. In Schenkein's words: 'One possible accomplishment of the use of *heheh* then is that a speaker may be immune to some charge of interrupting the ongoing sequencing, of usurping a slot properly available to someone else, while nevertheless accomplishing rather intricate pieces of interactional work' (1972, p. 367). One reason for this immunity may well be that laughter, unlike other conversational inputs, is taken to be, or can be presented as, being beyond one's control. Thus, in the same way that speakers can always deny the serious import of their humorously signalled remarks by claiming that they were 'only joking', laughers can always deny responsibility for their laughter on the grounds that it was a natural, uncontrollable response to the humour of the situation. One general lesson to be learned, therefore, from studies such as those of Jefferson and Schenkein is that we must be careful not to assume too readily that laughter which seems spontaneous really is so; for participants themselves may be artfully engaged in sustaining and making use of this assumption for their own ends.

Inviting laughter and declining to laugh

Neither Koestler nor Morreall offers precise predictions about the location of laughter within social interaction. One might infer from their theories, however, that 'normal', unregulated laughter would be produced mainly by recipients of the humorous stimulus rather than those who deliver the humour. Tellers of standardized jokes, for instance, would already know the punch line and would not, therefore, experience either a sudden displacement of aggression or an unexpected psychological shift when telling the joke. Consequently, the theoretically predicted pattern for standardized jokes would be along these lines:

First speaker: Humorous remark.
Second speaker: Immediate laughter.

In fact, this pattern occurs very seldom in natural conversation, even in the simplest situation where there are only two participants. Furthermore, the recipient's immediate production of laughter, when it occurs, does not necessarily imply that the laughter in such cases is an unregulated, reflex response. For it is clear that participants are expected to laugh after a humorous utterance and that they are aware of this expectation. The two following passages from another study by Jefferson illustrate this nicely.

Example 1

Roger: Well it struck *me* funny
                              (1.0 second pause)
Al: HA, HA HA HA
Ken: hh
Roger: Thankyou.

Example 2

Bill: That wz a jo:ke people
                              (short pause)
Bill: That wz
Ellen: Yeh

(short pause)
Bill: That-En yer spoze tuh smi:le.

(1979, p. 93)

As Fine puts it, 'humor typically requires an immediate audience response' (1984, p. 85), conventionally in the form of laughter or what Fry calls the 'terminal smile' (1963, p. 145). However, actors' production of laughter is no more *determined* by this convention than it is by an involuntary psychological/physiological mechanism. Rather, close observation of natural conversation shows that participants often use laughter itself to invite or solicit laughter from others, and that such invitations can be declined. An important characteristic of participants' 'invitations to laugh' is that they normally remain implicit. Explicit reminders, like the two quotations immediately above, about the obligation to laugh occur very seldom. This is because, by its very nature, laughter must seem to be spontaneous. Recipients are required to laugh; yet they must laugh only if they are genuinely amused. Thus attempts to solicit laughter are overwhelmingly indirect. Nevertheless, in inviting laughter and in declining to laugh, participants continually attend to and make use of other parties' knowledge of the conventional response to humour and to signals of humorous intent.

One regular way in which speakers indicate the need for another party to respond with laughter is to insert within-speech laughter into their own utterance. Jefferson (1979) examines a number of passages in which the use of within-speech laughter elicits laughter from a second party in the middle of talk which has been serious until that point. This is one of her examples:

B: Dju watch by any chance Miss International Showcase las' night?
E: N:no I didn' I waz reading my–
B: You missed a really great
  pro(H)
E: O(hh)h i(h)t wa(hh)s?
  ehh heh heh heh!

(Jefferson, 1979, p. 83)

In this extract, the discourse seems to have been entirely serious until B begins to laugh whilst uttering the word 'program'. Furthermore, the statement 'You missed a really great program' does not appear to accomplish the kind of semantic reversal required by humour. In other words, nothing indicative of humour has occurred during the first three utterances, apart from B's brief interjection of within-speech laughter. Nevertheless, this alone seems to be sufficient to provoke a marked display of amusement on the part of the recipient. It is clear that B's use of within-speech laughter at this stage is not itself a response to humour, but a controlled signal of humorous intent. It is a preparation for humour yet to come. It seems unlikely that E is greatly amused by this signal. However, he immediately signals his own willingness to be amused in due course by emitting laughter of his own. In this way participants use laughter, *in advance of any humorous semantic exchange*, to enter the humorous mode together. In this and other similar cases, laughter is employed in a methodical and collaborative manner to guide interaction in a humorous direction. Both B and E make use of the expectation that recipients of humour will respond with laughter to accomplish their joint entry into the humorous mode.

Conversational replies and laughing responses are normally linked closely to the prior speaker's turn. The second speaker's utterance typically either follows the preceding turn immediately or, as in the last example, overlaps and partially disrupts that turn. Thus when a recipient fails to laugh where a first speaker thinks that laughter is appropriate, first speaker will quickly become aware of the problem (Schenkein, 1972) and will be able to take remedial action. In such circumstances, first speaker's 'humorous' remark is often followed by a pause and then by an 'invitation' to laugh, after which recipient responds in the proper manner. Here is one illustrative example:

> Dan: I thought that wz pretty outta sight didju
>   hear me say'r you a junkie
>   *(0.5 second pause)*
> Dan: hheh heh
> Dolly: hh*heh*-heh-heh.

> (Jefferson, 1979, p. 80)

In this typical extract, the first speaker pauses at the end of a verbal utterance, presumably expecting the appropriate response from his partner. When it becomes clear that this response is not forthcoming, first speaker indicates that laughter is required by laughing himself, thereby drawing attention to the humorous character of his remark and to the convention that humorous remarks should be acknowledged as such by means of laughter. Only at this point, when there can no longer be any doubt that the first speaker has entered the humorous mode and that laughter is conventionally required, does the recipient begin to laugh. In this case, as in similar cases examined by Jefferson, it is clear that neither party is simply laughing in response to humour. Rather, speakers are using laughter to signal the occurrence of humour, to solicit laughter from a partner, to acknowledge a partner's humorous intent, to conform to a conventional pattern of conduct, and generally to manage the ongoing sequence of interaction.

Invitations to laugh, whether by means of within-speech or post-utterance laughter, are not, of course, always accepted. For various reasons, recipients can decline to laugh. Even here, however, both speakers attend indirectly to the obligation to laugh with which recipients have chosen not to comply. The basic pattern in such circumstances, documented by Jefferson (1979), is that first speaker begins to try to elicit laughter from recipient by laughing himself, but is quickly interrupted by second speaker with an emphatically serious pursuit of topics available from first speaker's prior remarks. Given the expectation that humour should receive immediate ratification by recipients' laughter, they cannot simply decline to laugh. As Schenkein (1972) has demonstrated, the withholding of laughter when it is appropriate and expected is likely to be taken as a 'put down', as an expression of ridicule, or as offensive in one way or another. On some occasions, it may be that recipients withhold their laughter in order to cause offence. But if such a negative outcome is to be avoided, recipients of humorous invitations who decline to laugh must act quickly to establish some acceptable, non-humorous alternative. In Jefferson's words: 'In order to terminate the relevance of laughter, recipient must actively decline to laugh. One technique for declining a postcompletion invitation to laugh is the placement of speech, by recipient, just after onset of speaker's laughter, that speech providing serious pursuit of topic as a counter to the pursuit of laughter' (1979, p. 93).

We have seen, in this section, that laughter often occurs before humorous discourse rather than in response to it. Laughter often seems to be used by those initiating humour to signal their humorous intent and to discover whether or not their partners are willing to enter the humorous mode. Even when laughter occurs after a 'humorous' utterance, it is frequently begun by the teller and seems to be used by him to invite laughter from the recipient and to confirm thereby the amusing nature of his preceding remark. In these circumstances, recipient's laughter appears to be, not an involuntary emission, but a voluntary sign of acquiescence. In the course of such negotiations, both teller and recipient use laughter to establish and display the meaning of their interaction. In so doing, they attend to the expectation that humour should be immediately ratified by recipient's laughter (or smiles). But this expectation is in no way binding on recipients. For they may choose to withhold laughter in order to cause offence, or they may decline to laugh in a more active, yet less offensive, manner by quickly exploiting any serious topics contained in their partner's prior discourse.

Controlled spontaneity

As this chapter has progressed, it has become increasingly clear that the production of laughter needs to be seen in relation to its social context. It is undeniable that laughter involves certain fairly distinctive physiological, and presumably psychological, changes in the individuals concerned; and it is possible that these changes sometimes occur as a result of involuntary responses to external stimuli. Even in these cases, however, the nature and extent of the laughter are significantly affected by variations in the social situation. Furthermore, when we carefully examine the details of laughter in the course of ordinary conversation, it is clear that explosive, uncontrolled laughter occurs much less frequently than other forms of laughter, which are fitted in a systematic and intricate fashion into the surrounding interaction. If we are to understand the full range of human laughter we must accept that most laughter is, to a considerable extent, part of the sign language of the humorous mode.

Sociological analysis will never be able to explain the physical contortions of laughter or to convey what happens psychologically when we feel amused. What it may be able to do, however, is to show how laughter is used to help construct the boundary between humorous and serious discourse, and to establish the meaning of participants' conduct in relation to that boundary. Until recently, as I said earlier, very little sociological research on laughter has been completed. But the few studies by conversation analysts have already begun to reveal how participants may regulate the production of laughter and yet artfully contrive to convey the impression that it is an involuntary, uncontrollable reaction. Indeed, although there are strong conventions involved in the production and exchange of laughter, it must always *appear to be* natural and spontaneous (Schenkein, 1972). Participants within the humorous mode are required not to seem to be controlling their own, or other people's, responses to humour. Humour is deemed to be successful only if it evokes what is taken to be a genuine, spontaneous reaction.

The 'primitive' physical contortions of laughter are usually regarded as the clearest indication that a recipient's response is natural and uncontrived. It is in this sense that, in Morreall's words, the natural expression of amusement provides the key to understanding laughter (1983, p. 59). But most empirical researchers as well as most theorists of laughter have taken this appearance of spontaneity at face value. They have assumed that 'real' laughter does flood out in response to humour and, as a result, they have never looked closely at laughter's details. Consequently, they have failed to observe the constant interactional work that lies behind the surface impression that laughter is 'normally' uncontrolled. What seems to be spontaneous is often, on closer inspection, solicited, signalled in advance and produced on cue. Even 'explosive' laughter may be furnished in preparation for humour yet to come, or may be devised to cope with other subtleties of social interaction. It is, perhaps, another paradox of the humorous realm that its inhabitants must appear to laugh spontaneously, whilst exercising a very strict control.

7

The Social Significance of
Sexual Jokes

Sexual matters and the relationship between men and women are perennial topics within the humorous mode. Any representative collection of standardized jokes from our own culture will include a substantial number of 'dirty stories', and all professional comedians, whether male or female, regularly use material of this kind. Some forms of humorous discourse deal with little else. For example, I have in front of me a collection of 'saucy postcards' which is peopled almost entirely by women in a state of undress, women with protuberant busts, honeymoon couples, men lowering their trousers, and so on (*Bamforth's Saucy Postcard Annual*, 1977). I also have a tape-recording of a typical performance by a male stand-up comedian at a pub in Northern England, lasting one and a half hours, in the course of which there is continual obscenity and a wide range of suggestive humour. Similarly Winick (1963) reports, in his content analysis of orally transmitted humour in New York, that 17 per cent of the jokes identified in his study were concerned with sexual matters and that this percentage was significantly greater than that of any other category. It appears, then, that one of the features that distinguishes humour from ordinary, serious discourse is its marked concern with sexual relationships and its frequently obscene treatment of sexual topics.

How can we account for the prominence of sexual themes and obscenity within the world of humour? One clue is provided by the work of Emerson (1973) and Walle (1976) discussed in chapter 5. For their studies suggest that humour is often employed to deal with topics, such as sexuality, which are important, but which are also difficult to handle openly within the serious mode. Difficulties of this kind with the topic of sexuality, it is clear, are not confined to our own society.

> We must bear in mind that Trobriand manners do not ban sex as a subject for conversation, save in the presence of certain tabooed relatives, and Trobriand morals do not condemn extramarital intercourse, except in the form of adultery and incest. The attraction

of the subject and its piquancy is not due, therefore, to the feeling that it is socially and artificially forbidden. And yet there is no doubt that the natives regard bawdiness as 'improper'; that there is a certain strain about it, barriers to be broken and a shyness to be overcome and a corresponding enjoyment of getting rid of the strain, breaking the barriers and overcoming the shyness . . . Sex, like excretory functions and nudity, is not felt or regarded as 'natural', but rather as naturally to be avoided in public and open conversation, and always to be concealed from others in behaviour. (Malinowski, 1929, p. 335)

Like the Trobrianders, we tend to cover sexually relevant parts of our body and to avoid explicit mention, in polite conversation, of sexual anatomy or the intimacies of sexual conduct; and it is precisely these hidden aspects of sexuality that reappear regularly in the discourse of the 'dirty joke'. The use of the terms 'dirty' or 'obscene' in this context reflects the fact that there is a range of topics and words which should not normally be used. Their very existence, however, implies that such topics are sometimes addressed and that such words are sometimes uttered. But they are accompanied by severe restrictions within the serious mode. Their much more frequent appearance within the domain of humour suggests that the sexual themes and obscene words which are unacceptable or restricted in proper, serious conversation are more legitimate and more freely available for use when signalled as humorous (Wilson, 1979). As we noted above, speakers are not taken to be entirely responsible for the content of their humorous remarks. Consequently, by adopting the humorous mode, they can communicate about forbidden aspects of sexuality whilst ostensibly being concerned only to provide amusement.

Of course, entry into the humorous mode does not completely remove the restrictions on sexual converse that apply in the serious realm. For example, dirty jokes are most likely to be told in single-sex groupings and among persons who are on a relaxed and intimate footing (Middleton and Moland, 1959). Nevertheless, within those settings where sexual humour is deemed to be appropriate, participants who address sexual topics or who employ obscene words in the course of humour can be taken to imply, and can always insist, that their discourse should not be taken seriously and that they have not transgressed the rules of proper discourse. Thus it seems likely that the strict limitations on sexual talk in the serious mode, combined with the importance of sexuality in our lives, are in some measure responsible for the prominence of sexual discourse within the domain of humour.

Dirty jokes and the transmission of sexual information

If this line of argument is broadly correct, it implies that sexual humour sometimes, perhaps frequently, operates as a means of communication about sexual topics. It implies, for example, that dirty jokes and other sexual jokes circulate, not simply as sources of amusement, but as carriers of sexual information, attitudes and emotions which have restricted passage within the serious mode. Furthermore, it seems likely that the sexual content deemed to be significant and informative by one social grouping may be of little interest to other groupings where participants' sexual experience is quite different. Consider the following joke:

'The deaf pharmacist'

Teller: There was this woman and she went into a shop and she said, 'Have you got any Tampax?' And the man said, 'Paaardon?' She said, 'Have you got any *Tam*pax?' And he said, um, 'Pardon?' And she goes, 'Have you got any *Tam*pax?' He said, 'Sorry, can you speak a bit louder, I can't hear you.' She said, 'Have you got any *bloody Tam*pax?' And he goes, 'Sorry, we don't sell second hands.'

Recipients: Ha ha ha ha

(Told by a twelve-year-old girl, 1985)

This joke was told by a young girl on the threshold of sexual maturity. Its content is highly relevant to her location in the cycle of sexual conduct. In its focus on tampons and their usage, it resembles numerous other jokes which were circulating freely among her group of friends. The example given above is the simplest and most basic of these jokes. Although the information about tampons contained in any one joke is limited and incomplete, as a set of related jokes they offer these young women a range of information about the control of menstruation. But the material that I have does not demonstrate unequivocally that these particular jokes convey helpful information on this topic to their young recipients. (For further anecdotal evidence see Wilson, 1979, pp. 188–9.) One possible reason for this is that they were recorded in a way which minimized the social interplay which normally occurs during a joke's telling. In addition, those involved were already very familiar with these tampon jokes. In order to glimpse the kind of interaction and information-exchange that sexual jokes can engender on a first hearing, let us look again at Madeleine's joke (told by a slightly older adolescent girl to two of her friends).

(1) A: Have you heard the one with the woman at the doctor's?

(2) B: Might have. I dunno till you tell us.

(3) C: Go on tell us anyway, it don't matter if we've heard it.

(4) A: Right, At the doctor's

(5) C: Don't tell me, there was this woman

(6) A: Oh shut up.

(7) C: All right, all right.

(8) A: At the doctor's this woman with a

(9)   baby was shown into the surgery for a check-up.

(10)   Doctor asks, 'Is he breast-fed or bottle-fed?'

(11)   'Breast-fed,' she says.

(12)   'Right,' he says, 'Strip to your waist.' When she'd

(13)   took her clothes off, he started to touch

(14)   her boobs

(15) B: (*giggles*)

      C: (*giggles*)

(16) A: Then he started to suck 'em.

(17)   'No wonder this baby's ill. You've got no

(18)   milk.' 'I'm not surprised,' she says, 'It's me sister's

(19)   baby.' 'Oh dear you shouldn't have come then.'

(20)   'I didn't till you sucked the second one' hahaha.

(21) B: Eh?

(22) A: She didn't come until he sucked the second boob.

(23) B: Oh hhe hahah

(24) C: heheyheheh

(Told by an adolescent girl, 1985)

One particularly interesting feature of Madeleine's joke is that it has two punch lines, one of which is ignored by both teller and recipients. The first punch line occurs in line 18. At this point the joke could have terminated, for line 18 suddenly transforms the meaning of what has gone before by revealing that the doctor has been examining the breasts of 'the wrong woman'. But the teller does not pause here and the recipients make no response. These three young women take no notice of the sub-joke about mistaken identity. For the teller, the point of the joke is to do with the sexual significance of the female breast. It is conveyed in lines 19 and 20 with the revelation that the woman had not only been sexually aroused by the doctor's sucking her breasts, but had 'come', that is, had reached a sexual climax. For the recipients, however, although they display an interest in the joke's central theme at line 15, when they giggle at the reference to the doctor's touching the woman's 'boobs', the meaning contained in the main punch line does not seem to be immediately evident. C fails to respond at all at line 21 and B seems to indicate that the point of the joke has escaped her. The teller then clarifies by extracting what had been implicit in the direct speech of the last two lines of the joke and by summarizing succinctly what had happened sexually to the woman in the joke. Once this has been done, the sequence concludes with both recipients registering that they have now understood.

This transcription clearly suggests that the telling of this joke on this occasion did involve the transmission of sexual information. In this respect it is typical of much of the material in my possession documenting the passage of such jokes among adolescent females. As in Madeleine's joke, recipients regularly reveal a pronounced concern with the sexual dimensions of the humour – for example, by responding audibly to words describing sexual parts. In addition, they sometimes fail to understand the punch line or some other part of the joke, which is then explained to them by fellow participants. During the telling of a joke, such explanations are undertaken in order to enable recipients to see the point of the joke: that is, to decipher the sexual meaning implicit in the punch line. But, clearly, any such explanatory gloss provided by other participants can also help recipients who are ignorant or doubtful about aspects of the sexual conduct depicted in a joke to understand that conduct more fully. For example, it seems that the recipients of Madeleine's joke were able to learn from that joke's telling that it is possible for women to achieve sexual climax when a man sucks their breasts.

Because the language of humour is allusive and the conventional response to humour so diffuse, we cannot know for certain what conclusions were drawn by the two young women on hearing Madeleine's joke. But it is precisely the allusiveness of humour which makes it such a suitable vehicle for the transmission of sexual information. For instance, in responding to sexual jokes, recipients can receive information without having to admit sexual ignorance. When the meaning of a joke is explained, it is not usually assumed that the recipient lacks the basic sexual knowledge to understand the joke, but rather that she has simply failed to solve the specific interpretative puzzle contained in the joke in question. Thus when recipients fail to see the point of a joke, they will typically be given an explanatory gloss in which the sexual knowledge on which the joke depends is made more accessible – although it is seldom made fully explicit – without either party engaging in open discussion of sexual topics.

The content of sexual jokes and the interactive work accomplished by participants as they are told make possible a transfer of sexual information in such a way that neither tellers nor recipients need acknowledge, or even recognize, that this sexual transmission is taking place. However, a major disadvantage of this method of communication is that it is left to recipients to disentangle fact from fantasy. As we have seen, this is far from easy within the humorous mode. Thus Madeleine's joke alone will not reveal to the naive hearer whether sexual climax by oral stimulation of the breast actually occurs in the real world or whether it is a typical humorous misrepresentation. Moreover, no single joke will deal comprehensively with a young woman's doubts and uncertainties about menstruation or the sexual activities of adults. Her knowledge of these topics has to be gradually built up, revised and extended as she hears new jokes from her friends, as she tries to understand the sexual innuendoes that they contain and to solve the sexual puzzles that they pose, and as she compares the pictures of sexuality presented within the domain of humour with those available from various kinds of serious discourse. It seems likely that the active interpretation required in response to sexual humour forces and assists adolescents to become skilled in the interpretative subtleties of sexual discourse, and helps them to acquire that understanding of sexuality which they require as they approach adulthood, but which is not available within the restrictions of serious discourse. If this line of argument is correct, it provides an explanation, and perhaps some justification, for the particular enthusiasm shown among adolescents for sexual humour and dirty jokes.

The sexual nucleus and its semantic packaging

So far in this chapter, I have concentrated on the transmission of sexual humour among young women. I have done this in order to help to correct a mistaken view that is widespread among men and also in the secondary literature on humour: namely, that women very seldom tell jokes and that they have a less developed sense of humour than men (Kramarae, 1981). I have tried to illustrate in the previous section that sexual jokes particularly relevant to their concerns as females do regularly circulate among young women and that, within single-sex groupings, young women can act as competent raconteurs. The impression that women are not active producers of humour and that they contribute insignificantly to its dissemination is almost certainly due to the fact that women tend to contribute noticeably less to humorous discourse in the presence of men (Coser, 1960; Middleton and Moland, 1959).

There are several interrelated reasons why women are less humorously active than men in sexually mixed groups. Firstly, there is the fact that men tend to control interaction in such situations and to regulate the production of discourse in general, including humour. Secondly, it seems likely that women's view of the social world is systematically different from that of men, and that they are amused to some extent by different things (Kramarae, 1980). As a result, it may be that women refrain from

distinctively female humour into social situations dominated
ilst often finding typically male humour to be unsuited to their
arae, 1981). Thirdly, in relation to sexual humour, it is clear
gative consequences of overstepping the boundary between
polite conversation and 'dirty talk' are more serious for women than for
men. In our culture, men tend to assume that women 'do not talk like
that'. Consequently, women will be careful to avoid dispelling that
illusion, and will normally refrain from telling sexual jokes in mixed
company.

It may also be that sexual jokes are likely to be seen as invitations to, or
explorations of the possibility of, more intimate sexual relationships
(Legman, 1968, p. 218; Walle, 1976); and that women, on the whole,
avoid becoming involved in discourse which may be seen as implying that
they are taking the sexual initiative or that they are receptive to men's
sexual overtures (see chapter 5). A further possibility is that women's
signals of humorous intent are more often ignored than those of men and
that their potentially humorous contributions receive less social recognition in mixed groups. Finally, it may well be that much of the humour
produced by men gives expression to men's sexual domination of women
and that women are, on the whole, less willing to participate actively in a
discourse which often involves, for them, a form of extreme self-
denigration.

In the next chapter, I will focus on the relationship between sexual
humour and the domination of women by men. For the moment,
however, I wish to explore the implications of the claim made above that
male humour and female humour differ in certain significant ways. If this
is so, it could be taken to imply that the sexual humour that circulates
among adolescent males operates differently from that which passes
among adolescent females, and perhaps, that the conclusions reached in
the last section do not apply to young men. Unfortunately, to my
knowledge, there have been no extended studies of adolescent humour in
natural settings and no careful comparisons of the jokes told by young men
and young women. My discussion of these issues, therefore, must be
regarded as tentative. Nevertheless, my own observations combined with
the fragments of data and analysis to be found in the published literature
lead me to conclude that, although there are important differences
between the sexual humour circulating among young women and that
which circulates among young men, in both cases sexual jokes act as
vehicles for sexual information which is not easily available within the
serious mode.

We can begin to explore the operation of dirty jokes among adolescent
males by returning to Sacks's joke discussed in the first chapter. This joke
was said by its seventeen-year-old male teller to have been passed to him

by his twelve-year-old sister. When we examine the collective reaction to this joke, we find that the young men spend twenty conversational turns debating, not only what the joke meant, but also whether the younger sister could possibly have understood its sexual meaning. The nature of their response strongly suggests that they are extremely interested in what the joke reveals about sexual conduct. It also suggests that the idea of oral sex is fairly new to them, that they are uncertain about their knowledge on this topic, and that they are surprised by the younger sister's apparent ability to extract the joke's hidden sexual message. For instance, at one point Ken, the teller, says: 'For twelve years old tellin me – *I* didn't even know.' To which Roger replies: 'How do you know she's just not repeating what she heard and doesn't know what it means.'

In this exchange, both speakers seem to assume that twelve- year-old girls would not normally know about oral sex. For Ken, this assumption seems to be linked to his own relatively recent acquisition of this kind of sexual knowledge. His reasoning seems to be: How can this young female know about oral sex, when I have only just heard about it? Roger's contribution is to suggest that the young girl may simply not have understood what she was saying. This neatly, but implausibly, reconciles her telling the joke with his assumption that she cannot yet have attained his own level of sexual sophistication. After this exchange, Al and Roger proceed to make fun of Ken by implying that his younger sister seems to be more sexually knowledgeable than him and by challenging him to provide an explanation of the joke's meaning. Although Ken becomes increasingly disturbed by the allegations of sexual ignorance and by the suggestion that he does not understand the joke, he is unwilling or unable to say in a straightforward manner what the joke is about. It appears that, although the young men are intrigued by the topic of oral sex and, perhaps, eager to explore it further, they are unable to discuss it openly in the serious mode. As a result, the sequence comes to an end with the unanswered chant of 'Explain . . . explain . . . explain . . .'

It seems clear to me that the young men involved in Sacks's joke, like the young women participating in Madeleine's, focus collectively upon and pay special attention to the sexual information implicit in their sexual humour. Yet Sacks reaches a rather different conclusion in his examination of the joke presented in chapter 1. It is necessary, therefore, to consider Sacks's account of what dirty jokes communicate to their hearers.

Sacks argues that dirty jokes are 'rational institutions' designed to package and transmit information efficiently. He insists, however, that it would be wrong to infer:

> that the information in a dirty joke is its obscene information. That would be irrational, since their obscene character serves as a

restriction on their passage. A vehicle which, by virtue of its obscenity, has a restriction on its passage, would be rationally exploited if it were used to pass information other than that which restricts that passage. Thus, if there are any sorts of information which it's relevant to pass, which it's also relevant to pass restrictedly, then such things could be put into dirty jokes, where the obscenity serves as a 'cover' for other information. (1978, p. 262)

In other words, the dirtiness of Sacks's own joke and of dirty jokes generally is taken to be a device for regulating the passage of other, 'non-sexual' information contained in the joke.

In view of this argument, it may seem surprising to find that Sacks does accept that the young men in his transcript interpret the joke 'by reference to its oral sex' (1978, pp. 268–9). But in so doing, he argues, they are *mis*understanding a joke which was not designed for circulation among males. The younger sister and her friends, Sacks proposes, would have understood the joke differently, and indeed properly. For they would have been much more aware of the non-sexual information specially relevant to twelve-year-old females that is contained in the joke, and they would have responded to this information rather than to the joke's superficial, sexual meaning.

This part of Sacks's technical considerations of a dirty joke seems to me unconvincing and seriously defective. In the first place, although Sacks claims that dirty jokes generally are vehicles for the restricted transmission of non-sexual information, the one example for which he provides documentation appears to be a counter-instance. For on Sacks's own admission, in the transcript under discussion, both recipients and teller focus on the topic of oral sex. Secondly, although Sacks maintains that twelve-year-old girls would see the joke in a different way, this is no more than supposition. Sacks offers no evidence to support this assertion. Moreover, we have examined data above which show that girls of this age are quite capable of displaying an active interest in the sexual meaning of dirty jokes. Thirdly, Sacks dismisses the boys 'sexual interpretation of the joke as a misunderstanding (1978, p. 263). This seems to imply, not only that there is only one correct understanding of a dirty joke, but also that the analyst can claim the right to define the procedures by which such jokes should be interpreted by participants. This latter implication seems to me to go beyond the proper scope of sociological analysis. In my view, if participants choose to understand a dirty joke in sexual terms, this must be accepted by the analyst as a proper and legitimate reading.

The major argument offered by Sacks to support his claim that the boys have misunderstood the joke is that quoted above in which he asserts that dirty jokes must be 'rational institutions'. But why must we accept that dirty jokes have to be 'rational' according to Sacks's conception of rationality? Sacks insists that dirty jokes will be rational only if their obscenity is used to regulate the transmission of information which is not obscene. But would it not be equally plausible to argue that dirty jokes would be even more rational (that is, efficient and economical) if their obscene components both restricted their passage *and* contained the relevant information? Sacks's view of dirty jokes as semantic packages in which the obscene content regulates the transmission of non-sexual information seems to imply a rather high level of inefficiency (or irrationality). For there can be no guarantee that the boundary restricting the movement of obscene discourse will coincide with that required by the non-sexual information contained in the wide variety of dirty jokes. However, these a priori arguments about the rationality of dirty jokes are, in my view, largely irrelevant. I am persuaded by the details of Sacks's transcript and by empirical material of my own, such as Madeleine's joke, that young people of both sexes regularly attend to, and learn from, the *sexual* content of dirty jokes.

As we have seen, an important part of Sack's analysis is that the obscenity of dirty jokes restricts their circulation in such a way that their non-sexual information remains with the social grouping for whose members it is significant. In the case of his specific joke, he maintains that it is designed for circulation among twelve-year-old girls and that the critical information which is transmitted by the joke concerns the way in which parents, and particularly mothers, employ rules unpredictably to regulate their daughters' conduct. But, once again, the joke under examination appears to contradict Sacks's claim. For the obscenity of Sacks's joke does not prevent that joke from being passed outside the social network of twelve-year-old girls. Sacks insists that the boys do not understand or like the joke, and that once it has got into their hands it is going nowhere (1978, pp. 263, 269). He provides no evidence, however, to show that the joke's circulation stops here. Furthermore, the transmission of the joke from younger sister to older brother was not prevented by the joke's obscenity; and the brother found it sufficiently interesting to retell it within his own age and sex grouping. All the evidence we have seems to suggest, therefore, contrary to Sacks's analysis, that the joke's obscene content does not stop it from circulating. Clearly Sacks is right to insist that there are limitations on the movement of dirty jokes. In particular, as I suggested above, they tend to be told within single-sex groups. However, this is by no means always the case and, despite restrictions on their telling, dirty jokes are not rigidly confined by their obscene content within specific social groupings (Middleton and Moland, 1959; Winick, 1963).

When the boys respond to Sacks's joke, they pay no attention to the way in which the third daughter turns the tables on the mother and uses one of the mother's own rules in an unexpected way to undermine her authority. In Sacks's view, however, this component contains the covert message of the joke which the boys fail to grasp: namely, that all mothers apply rules selectively in order to control their children. Sacks may well be right to identify this as an important part of the humorous package which has presumably been circulating among the younger sister's friends. But his argument goes much further. For his general account of dirty jokes as 'rational institutions' implies that this information about mothers' use of rules is transmitted in joke form because it cannot be passed around openly and because its circulation must be carefully controlled. However, not only have we seen that the joke's obscenity does not prevent its transmission, but in addition it is difficult to accept that twelve-year-old girls are unable to complain openly among themselves, and indeed to their brothers, about their mothers' use or misuse of rules. Thus Sacks's suggestion that twelve-year- old girls' critical appraisal of maternal authority has to travel under cover of a dirty joke seems unconvincing.

Finally, it is worth noting that, toward the end of his analysis, Sacks appears to revise his initial argument and to propose that it is not the sexual content alone, but both sexual and non-sexual components, which govern the circulation of a dirty joke: 'obscenity can provide an initial restriction [on a joke's transmission], but it is other aspects of it which discriminate among that initially located population and find a still narrower population, among which the joke circulates' (1978, p. 268). In relation to his specific joke, Sacks argues that what the seventeen-year-old boys do not like about this joke is not its sexual content, but the way in which the joke about oral sex is packaged. In particular, the joke deals exclusively with the relationships between women; and the men feature in the joke as no more than sexual ciphers. This latter observation is clearly correct. Sacks's joke is a sexual joke virtually without men. It seems likely, therefore, that this formulation of the joke has been produced by females and, as Sacks suggests, may well circulate effectively among females.

We have no further detailed evidence about the circulation of Sacks's joke. I can, however, provide an alternative version published quite recently in a wide-ranging collection of jokes (Knott, 1985).

Sacks's joke: alternative version

These three men went for a drive in the country and their car broke down, so they went to the nearest farmhouse to ask for shelter for the night. 'Sure, lads,' said the farmer, 'you can spend the night here, but you've each got to sleep with one of my daughters, because they don't get much company out here'. The men all agreed, and during the night the farmer got up to make sure they were going through with their part of the deal.

The next morning the men went on their way and the farmer called his daughters together.

'Linda, why were you laughing last night?'

'Because it tickled, Daddy'.

'Susie, why were you crying?'

'Because it hurt, Daddy'.

'Lizzie, why was your room silent?'

'Because you always told me not to talk with my mouth full'.

(Knott, 1985, p. 63)

It seems that the core of Sacks's joke is still on the move some twenty years after the telling recorded by him. In the light of Sacks's analysis and the discussion above, it is interesting to note how the joke about oral sex has remained constant, whilst the packaging has changed. In this alternative version, intended for widespread public distribution, men have come to occupy a much more prominent role. For instance, the male ciphers of the 'original' version have become more clearly defined and operate as the dominant figures during the first part of the joke. In addition, the mother has been replaced by a father. A more subtle change is that, although the father's authority is challenged in the punch line as was the mother's in the previous formulation, the father is depicted in the alternative version as exercising firm control over his daughters' sexual activities. The alternative version still contains the same implicit information about oral sex. But in the process of wider transmission, the packaging appropriate for young women has been replaced with a more male-centred representation of sexuality and of sexual relationships.

This suggests that the sexual component of a dirty joke constitutes a relatively stable nucleus which embodies and is capable of furnishing sexual information. Indeed, as Sacks himself demonstrates, the humorous structure of such a joke is created out of a precise arrangement and sequencing of sexually relevant scripts which leaves little room for alteration. Some of the non-sexual packaging, however, can sometimes be changed without destroying that structure and, as Sacks finally acknowledged, this non-sexual content may be critical for the circulation of the central, sexual component. It seems likely that the female focus of the 'original' version of Sacks's joke was particularly suitable for circulation among young women, and that the non-sexual packaging has been refashioned in accordance with the assumptions and requirements of a wider audience as the joke has come to circulate more widely. Thus non-sexual content is probably highly relevant to the dissemination of specific versions of a dirty joke. But in cases where this element can be revised, it is unlikely to restrict the social transmission of the sexual nucleus of the joke to any great degree.

Let me bring this chapter to a close by offering a few conclusions. In the first place, it appears that jokes especially relevant to the sexual concerns of specific age and sex groupings circulate among young women and young men. For example, menstrual jokes of various kinds are popular among girls approaching puberty, but very seldom appear in published collections of humour or among the jokes told by adolescent boys. Although they have not been examined here, it seems likely that jokes about prostitution, masturbation and the size of male genitals are particularly common among young men (for examples, see Legman, 1968; Raskin, 1985a). Not only do dirty jokes deal with sexual topics of special interest to the members of the groups within which they circulate, but they also provide information or clues about sexual topics such as oral sex, adultery and homosexuality, which are difficult to broach within ordinary, serious conversation, whilst helping participants to develop interpretative skills related to sexual conduct. Although men and boys often assume that females are lacking in humour, and are especially surprised to find women, particularly young women, participating in obscene humour, women of all ages make active use of the humorous mode. However, females' humour does tend to differ to some extent from that of males in its sexual focus and in the representation of social relationships it conveys.

As dirty jokes pass from one group to another and across sexual lines, their semantic packaging tends to change. This humorous repackaging will reflect, in particular, certain differences between men and women with regard to sexuality. Women's humorous culture, however, appears to be much less visible than that of men. For example, such an authority on sexual humour as Gershon Legman can write as follows:

> One fact strikingly evident in any collection of modern sexual folklore, whether jokes, limericks, ballads, printed 'novelties', or whatnot, is that this material has all been created by men, and that there is no place in it for women except as the butt. It is not just that so preponderant an amount of the material is grossly anti-woman in tendency and intent, but also that the situations presented almost completely lack any protagonist position in which a woman can identify herself – *as a woman* – with any human gratification or pride. (1968, p. 217)

Legman is wrong, I suggest, if he is claiming that women do not create humour (see Johnson, 1973). Nevertheless, he is undoubtedly correct in maintaining that the great bulk of sexual humour that is publicly available – in published collections, for example – seems to have been produced by men and to reflect a distinctly male view of sexuality. Some of the reasons for this are fairly obvious. Humour in television and publishing is largely produced and controlled by men. For example, until very recently, female comics were entirely absent from our TV screens. The main audience for humour, sexual or otherwise, is taken to be male ('Women have little sense of humour'); and male topics and the male perspective on sexual humour have become widely established, thereby furnishing the interpretative framework within which such humour is generated and distributed. However, Legman goes further than this. He asserts that the sexual humour which is culturally dominant in our society is not only male-centred, but also 'grossly anti-woman in tendency and intent'. In the next chapter I will examine how far this is true of adult sexual humour.

8

Sexual Humour and Gender Relationships

Adolescent sexual humour is likely to be rather different from that of adults. Adult humour will be less involved in the passage of basic sexual information because, on the whole, adults will have experienced a wider range of sexual activities and will have acquired a more adequate stock of sexual knowledge than adolescents. However, the sexual humour circulating among adults will still employ, give expression to and transmit the underlying sexual assumptions of those concerned. For we know from the preceding discussion that standardized sexual humour is embedded in semantic packages which are created out of the sexual and social conceptions of those among whom it passes. Thus Legman's (1968) wide-ranging and detailed examination of the dirty jokes produced by men, from which I quoted at the end of the previous chapter, may not only reveal the major features of male sexual humour, but also provide insight into the basic assumptions about the relations between men and women that enter into men's serious sexual discourse. Legman's study of male sexual humour is too extensive to be discussed here in full, so I will concentrate on just a few of his more important conclusions regarding the structure and content of dirty jokes.

The basic principles of men's sexual humour

One of Legman's main observations is that, within the discourse of the dirty joke, men approach women with the sole aim of achieving sexual congress. The men appearing in dirty jokes are overwhelmingly represented as being interested in women solely as a source of sexual pleasure. Legman refers to this semantic principle, in terms of which dirty jokes are constructed and understood, as the principle of 'the primacy of coitus' (1968, p. 236). A second principle identified by Legman is that of 'the general availability of women'. According to this principle, all women are available as partners for any man, even when they pretend not to be (1968, pp. 221, 236). Legman provides copious documentation of the use of these two principles in men's humour. They are combined with great economy in the following joke:

Verbal rape: 1

Salesman: Listen, I'm only in town for a couple of hours, and I can't kid around. Do you screw or don't you?

Girl: (*shyly*) Well, I don't usually, but you talked me into it.

(Legman, 1968, p. 222)

The tone of this joke is captured perfectly by Legman's phrase 'verbal rape'. The joke seems to be a great favourite among men. The version reproduced by Legman was heard in New York in 1939. The basic joke, however, has continued to circulate since at least that date, and it reappears in several published collections. Here is a transcript of a comedian's presentation recorded in Yorkshire in 1985:

Verbal rape: 2

Chubby Brown: I go into this club the other night, a fucking *great* club, honest. I get fixed up with this tart. And I walked across dead casual, you know what I mean. I said, 'Hiiii, do you *fuck?*'

Chorus of male voices from the audience: *Haha*haha hurr*aah*, ha ha (*5 seconds*)

Chubby Brown: She said, 'I suppose I'll *have* to, you smooth-talking bastard.'

Audience: Ha haha ha (*4 seconds*)

Legman's two principles are clearly illustrated in both versions of the verbal rape joke. The man is depicted in both as choosing, on this occasion, not to engage in small talk about non-sexual matters, and as revealing without prevarication or pretence his exclusively sexual interest in the woman (in any woman). In the fantasy world of humour, the man has been able to step outside the restrictions of normal interaction between men and women and to express in the most direct fashion what he really wants from women – namely, sexual gratification. As we can see from the live recording of version 2, many men in the audience respond enthusiastically to the first half of the joke in which this symbolic transformation is accomplished. They appear to find this move from the normal script of sexual restriction to that of uninhibited sexual discourse to be highly amusing, even deserving of applause. Similarly, the largely male audience actively expresses its collective enjoyment of the joke's punch line in which the woman, in accordance with Legman's second principle, reveals that her normal resistance to men's advances is a sham and that she also is really interested only in sexual pleasure.

A third, related principle evident in men's dirty jokes is that women can be represented adequately by reference to the sexual, domestic and other services which they provide for men. In the world of the dirty joke, women often become no more than objects designed to cater for the needs of men. This is made particularly clear in jokes which provide humorous definitions of womanhood or of specific female roles. Although Legman provides numerous examples of jokes in which this principle operates (see 1968, p. 239), he does not give it a name. We may call it the principle of 'woman as object'. The following example is taken from Legman:

WIFE: a gadget you screw on the bed to get the housework done.

(1968, p. 239)

It is clear that the 'you' in this joke is male. For only husbands can 'screw their wives on the bed'. This is a joke for men alone. It provides a definition of a basic female role that is intended to be passed from one man to another. Not only are women defined as objects designed to serve men's interests, but they are also excluded from active participation in the act of humorous definition.

This instance seems to date from the 1940s and Legman traces its origins back to 1919. Let me bring us up to date by providing another definitional joke which was circulating in written form in 1985 among working men in Yorkshire.

'The perfect woman'

What's the definition of a perfect woman?
A She's three feet tall, has a round hole for a mouth and her head is flat, so you can put a pint glass on it.
B The sports model has pull-back ears and her teeth fold in.
C The economy model fucks all evening and at midnight turns into a roast beef sandwich and a six-pack.

This joke was contained in a list of jokes entitled 'Jokes Guaranteed to Offend Anyone'. There is no doubt that many people will find this joke offensive, as I do. One reason why this, and many other, dirty jokes are experienced as offensive is that they convey ideas and sentiments that are normally regarded as unacceptable, as outside the bounds of proper discourse – which is what we mean by calling such jokes 'dirty'. We may feel that this joke, like the previous one, is particularly unpleasant in the way that it seeks to amuse by removing all trace of humanity from womankind. However, although we, the analyst and his readers, may be offended by its humour, *participants'* characterization of the joke as 'guaranteed to offend anyone' cannot be taken literally. For, although some of them may have thought it distasteful, it has nevertheless been read and passed on so that it could eventually arrive on my desk. Moreover, Legman's researches show that jokes of this kind have been widely available in North America, and presumably in Britain, since the early years of this century. It seems clear that the principle of 'woman as object', like those of 'the primacy of coitus' and 'the availability of women', is an enduring part of men's humorous culture within our society.

The final principle that I will extract from Legman's analysis can be called the principle of 'the subordination of women's discourse'. As Legman makes clear, one pervasive formula for the construction of a dirty joke is to make the female character utter some remark which can then be reinterpreted in sexual terms, to the woman's presumed discomfiture, by a man. For example:

Manicurist: Shall I skin back the cuticle for you, sir?
Customer:　No, just kiss me, honey, and it'll take care of itself.

(Legman, 1968, p. 227)

Legman comments that the punch line in this kind of joke 'is supposed to floor and destroy the person spoken to. This point has been made before, but must not be lost sight of. The old standbys in the punning proposition field do not give this weapon to the woman. Sometimes she hardly speaks at all' (1968, pp. 225–6). In men's dirty jokes, it is not only women's bodies and services that are at men's disposal, but also women's language. Women's words, through which women's versions of the relationship between men and women might be expressed, very seldom triumph in the dirty joke. They are persistently subject to what Legman calls a 'purposeful perversion' which transforms their meaning and replaces it with that preferred by men. Thus dirty jokes depict the relationship between men and women in terms of a radical form of sexual, social and linguistic domination of women by men. The very words used to refer to women endorse and exemplify this domination. For instance, in male jokes, women are persistently referred to in terms which express men's superiority and contempt, such as 'tart', 'babe' and, most frequently, 'girl'. The domain of humour is a world where the male voice constantly triumphs over that of the female and where women are made to exist and act only as appendages to men's most basic sexual inclinations.

Così fan tutte

This account of the main characteristics of the representation of sexuality
and sexual relationships in male humour is accurate, in my judgement, not
only for the material supplied by Legman, but also for the great majority
of instances of dirty jokes available in published collections as well as those
which have come into my hands informally. Let us accept, then, that
much of this humour is accurately described by the four principles of 'the
primacy of coitus', 'the availability of women', 'woman as object' and 'the
subordination of women's discourse'. What are we to conclude from this
finding? In previous chapters, two basic points have been made that may
have some bearing upon our conclusions. On the one hand, it has been
stressed that humorous discourse is significantly different from serious
discourse and that it is a mistake to try to understand humour in the same
way that one understands serious discourse. This line of argument might
seem to imply that men's dirty jokes should be regarded as mere fun and
that their content is largely determined by the requirements of the
humorous realm. On the other hand, however, I have also argued that the
separation of humour from serious discourse is often put to serious use. I
have maintained that one of the paradoxes of humour is that its removal
from the serious domain actually makes it useful for certain serious
purposes. This line of argument would seem to imply that men's dirty
jokes may play an important role in their serious discourse and, perhaps,
that they can be understood only in relation to that discourse. Let us
consider these two possibilities in turn.

The first possibility is that the four semantic principles identified above
are unavoidable if participants are to succeed in constructing dirty jokes.
The principle of the primacy of coitus comes closest to meeting this
requirement. For if we are to generate *sexual* humour, we must employ
active agents in our humorous discourse whose motivation is unequivocally sexual. Furthermore, as we saw in chapter 1, standardized jokes have
to depict actions in a highly simplified manner, with all interpretative
irrelevances removed. Thus one might reasonably argue that the
prevalence of the primacy of coitus in much of men's humour implies
nothing about men's serious perspective on the relationship between men
and women. For a crude representation of men's sexual motivation is
required by the very form of the dirty joke.

This seems to be a powerful argument. If we reduce it to its simplest
formulation, it becomes self-evident: namely, that sexual humour has to
focus on sexuality. There is, however, the issue of *whose* sexuality is taken
to be primary. In most dirty jokes, the humour centres unambiguously
around the sexuality of the male. Men are taken to be the active agents of

sexuality and women the largely passive recipients. Even in Sacks's joke, for example, where women are more prominent than usual, they are nevertheless depicted as responding to the sexual actions of their men. Yet there seems to be no good reason why men's sexuality *has* to be primary in the dirty joke. The principle of availability, in fact, seems to imply that women have powerful sexual drives and this idea could be used, if men were not otherwise inclined, to construct a larger proportion of jokes in which the sexual initiative was taken by women.

Although the three remaining principles, concerning the sexual availability of women, the depiction of women as objects and the subordination of women's language, also operate to support the asymmetrical assumption of men's sexual dominance, it seems quite clear that alternative principles could be, and occasionally are, employed. For example, in a few jokes, the woman's voice wins out over the man's. In such jokes, women's discourse is dominant without, presumably, any great sacrifice of humorous effect (see, for example, Legman, 1968, p. 223). It appears, therefore, that the subordination of women's discourse is not essential to sexual humour and cannot be explained as being required by the form of the dirty joke. Similarly, there is no compelling reason why women, but not men, should be regularly portrayed as objects. For instance, it seems to me that my own reformulations below of the definitional joke quoted on p. 136 are just as effective as that furnished by Legman, even though they represent men as objects and express (my version of) possible female perspectives on sexuality:

HUSBAND: a gadget you screw on the bed to obtain a fur coat/to feed the kids/to stop getting hit/to protect your friends.

However, although the principle of 'men as objects' can be used to construct sexual humour, I know of no previous instances where it has actually been employed.

Finally, we must consider 'the availability of women'. In order to do so, let me turn to genuine female humour. The sequence of cartoons below is taken from Christine Roche's *I'm Not a Feminist but* . . . (1985). I have provided the caption. This cartoon clearly addresses and makes use of the principle of the availability of women, as well as that of the primacy of sexual interest on the part of men. To that extent, it resembles male humour. However, my interpretation of this joke is that it challenges men's assumption that women are available and reveals, humorously of course, men's hypocritical denial, when thwarted, of sexual intent. Whereas the principle of availability is typically used in men's jokes to create situations in which women are shown to be interested in virtually any man solely for sexual purposes, no matter what they may say – in Roche's joke the humorous effect is achieved by first implying this

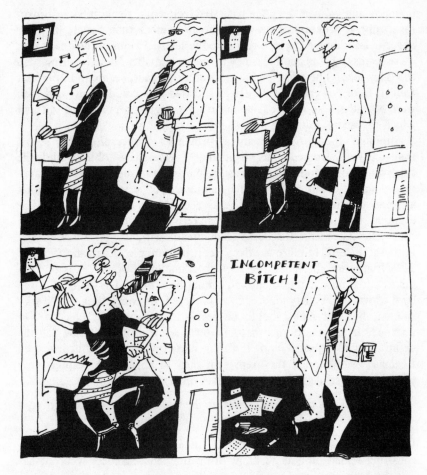

'The unavailability of women'

assumption and then switching from the man's to the woman's perspective in order to show that, for her, the principle does not operate at all. In this cartoon, 'the availability of women' has become subordinate to a contrary principle, 'the unavailability of women'. In Roche's humorous creation, the interaction culminates in the assertion of this latter principle and in the man's discomfiture. Once again, therefore, it is evident that neither the semantic principles customarily used by men to construct their sexual humour nor the male-centred application of those principles are required by the form of the dirty joke, as such, but by the peculiar tradition of sexual humour that has grown up as part of male discourse.

If the generative principles identified above are not essential to sexual humour, if they are not required to create the dirty joke, it seems reasonable to suggest that their origin lies outside the realm of humour. In other words, we are led to conclude that the content of men's humour derives from their serious discourse and from their serious relationships with women. If this is so, we must ask: What do men's jokes tell us about these relationships? The answer, I think, is that men treat these relationships as fundamentally asymmetrical. My conclusion is that men, in constructing their sexual humour, take over from the serious realm the assumption that women are subordinate to men, that women exist for men, and that this is the natural relationship between men and women which women, on the whole, recognize and accept. The parallel between what I have shown to be the case for men's sexual humour and masculine discourse in general is supported by much recent research.

> The imperious 'he' is rooted in Western discourse to such an extent that even when an attempt is consciously made to avoid its use, we either have to invent a new language, or have to deconstruct our present usage. Language, written or spoken, is saturated with 'masculinity'. Not only do men make history, but they write and speak that history. It is only recently that feminist writers have begun to reclaim and reconstruct women's past. (Brittan and Maynard, 1984, p. 195)

Elsewhere, Brittan and Maynard emphasize the theme of domination of women by men which is built into our ordinary language, as it is into so much of our humour.

> Male control of language . . . conveys implicit sexist messages to the girls [in schools] concerning their lack of importance and status in comparison to their male peers. However, it is not simply sexism which is being transmitted here, nor just the benign signalling of the existence of two complementary gender roles. Rather, girls are learning that the relations between the sexes are power relations where men are dominant and in control, while women are subordinated and inferior. (1984, p. 165)

The discussion so far brings to our notice an aspect of our own culture the significance of which is in danger of being overlooked, perhaps because it is so utterly taken for granted: namely, that in the domain of humour man's control over and sexual domination of women is exceptionally stark and unrestricted. As I noted in chapter 3, the scripts for specific terms can be radically different in the humorous mode compared with the realm of serious discourse. We saw, for example, how the meaning of the term 'bishop' is altered within humorous discourse for comic effect. In the case of terms denoting femininity, too, we note a change. But the difference between the two modes appears to involve not a radical reversal of the basic female script, but rather a humorous exaggeration of, and simplification of, elements that are already pronounced within serious discourse. In other words, in the world of humour the script for 'woman' differs from that operative in serious discourse in being even more narrowly confined to a few basic semantic elements – in particular, to those of female subordination to, and sexual use by, the male.

If this is so, it appears that, to some extent, Sacks was right to draw our attention to the 'non-sexual' message contained in the dirty joke. In the case of adult sexual humour, where the transmission of basic sexual information is relatively unimportant, the humorous mode seems to be used to give comparatively unrestrained voice to an exploitative conception of the relationship between men and women which cannot normally be expressed so forcefully within serious discourse.

The basic message of the dirty joke is 'non-sexual' in the sense that its implications extend well beyond the realm of sexual reproduction and related topics. However, we must be careful not to try to separate too strictly the 'sexual' from the 'non-sexual' here. For men's domination of women can never be entirely divorced from the ways in which women's bodies are used by men, nor from the ways in which this use is given meaning through men's, and women's, use of language. The use of, and attitudes towards, a human being's body by other persons can involve a fundamental form of domination. It is this kind of domination which is most clearly evident in the discourse of humour where, of course, it is not to be taken seriously. It is another paradox of humour that men's most basic, serious assumptions regarding women and sexuality are probably most clearly visible, if we care to look closely enough, in the world of humour.

If this discussion is broadly correct, we can understand more fully women's reluctance and/or inability to participate as prominently as men in the sphere of humour. For it seems that such participation will normally require women to collaborate in a discourse which employs extremely derogatory assumptions about the characteristics of females. This discourse will require them to accept, albeit for humorous purposes, that *così fan tutte*, or in plain English – 'women are like that.' We can reasonably infer, therefore, that women will often find men's humour to be alien (Kramarae, 1981). But we have not, so far, seen how humour is actually used by men and women in the course of interaction. In order to complete our examination of the nature of sexual humour we must now attempt to do this by adopting a more ethnographic approach and by turning to observational studies of the use of situational humour in specific social settings. In the next section, I will examine one such study in detail.

The cocktail waitress

The most detailed study available of the humorous interplay between men and women in a particular locale is contained in *The Cocktail Waitress* (1975) by James Spradley and Brenda Mann. This study provides careful observation of the relationships between bartenders, waitresses and their clientele in an American drinking establishment called Brady's Bar during the 1970s. Although there are few other comparable studies (see, however, Coser, 1960; Sykes, 1966; Leonard, 1980), there is no reason to think that Brady's Bar is in any relevant way unique. I will assume, therefore, that Spradley and Mann's conclusions apply in many similar locations in our society and, probably, in a wide variety of situations where men and women come into close contact. I will concentrate on what the analysts tell us about the joking relationship between bartenders and waitresses.

Spradley and Mann observed that the serious interaction between waitresses and bartenders in Brady's Bar was frequently, although irregularly, punctuated by humorous exchanges. They mention no instances where formal jokes were employed in the course of such exchanges, so their analysis appears to deal exclusively with what was termed earlier situational or spontaneous humour (see chapter 4). Although the humour was spontaneous in the sense that it was constructed out of the ongoing discourse and did not make use of pre-arranged humorous anecdotes, Spradley and Mann stress that it had several ritual aspects. Firstly, it was limited to specific categories: in particular, those of 'bartender' (male) and 'waitress' (female). Similarly, it was deemed to be appropriate only in certain specific settings. For example, it could take place at the bar when clients were present, but not in private in the kitchen. Thirdly, the form and content of the humour were rigidly restricted to the exchange of ridicule, sexual insults and lewd words. Spradley and Mann argue, following Radcliffe-Brown's (1940) analysis of ritual joking in preliterate societies, that this joking relationship has grown out of structurally created conflict between bartenders and waitresses in the bar, and that the exchange of humour serves, in part, to alleviate this conflict (1975, pp. 88–9, 97, 100).

The first step taken by Spradley and Mann in their attempt to explain the joking relationship in Brady's Bar is to identify certain problems faced by waitresses as a result of their position in the social structure of the bar. These problems arise, they argue, because waitresses have to deal with two conflicting pressures. On the one hand, they are required to cooperate with the bartenders, as a result of which they develop close personal ties with them, sometimes culminating in sexual liaison. On the other hand, the waitresses' low status in the bar means that they are subordinate to the bartenders and that all their actions in the bar must be designed to meet the bartenders' needs. These socially generated but opposing patterns of conduct are difficult to reconcile. Fortunately, however, Spradley and Mann propose, humour is available to make their difficulties less oppressive.

> This structural conflict creates powerful but often ambivalent feelings in the girls. They all recognize the ambivalent nature of this relationship and would as quickly defend the bartenders as criticize them. When they talked together about their work, the most frequent discussions centered on this relationship and its significance to them personally. As we listened to these descriptions and observed the social encounters that took place, it became clear that the conflict was mediated, in part, by the joking aspect of this complex relationship. (1975, p. 89)

Spradley and Mann argue that humour helps to resolve waitresses' problems by furnishing a safety valve for the release of their frustrations. At the same time, however, although humour is of assistance to the waitresses, it also helps to sustain an authority structure in which the bartenders can continue to exercise control over their female subordinates. Humour, they conclude:

> serves to resolve the deep structural conflict in the social structure of the bar. Anger and frustration are dissipated and feelings of inequality felt by the waitresses are deflected away from the relationship. It creates a buffer between the waitress and bartender in potential conflict situations and provides a means for handling inadequate role performances that occur in full public view.
>
> But the joking relationship also maintains the status inequality of female waitresses and reinforces masculine values. By providing a kind of 'safety valve' for the frustrations created for women in this small society, joking behavior ensures that the role of female waitresses remains unchanged. (1975, p. 100)

Spradley and Mann's study is particularly valuable because it is based on careful observation of the use made by men and women of humour in the course of direct interaction. The detail of their observational work enables us to examine their data for ourselves and to draw our own conclusions. Mine do not not coincide entirely with theirs, and I will develop a somewhat different interpretation of their material.

The analysts focus in their study on what humour does for the waitresses. They decide, as we have seen, that humour operates as a safety valve which allows the waitresses to find relief from their frustrations. But consider whether this conclusion is consistent with their own reconstruction of a typical conversation among the women working in Brady's Bar concerning a bartender's humorous insults.

'Rob made some reference about my chest'.
'Same here. But I don't know what we can do to get him back'.
'Maybe we could all get together and try grabbing him'.
'That's silly. We aren't strong enough and they would just make a joke out of it'.
'We could all ignore him, but that wouldn't work because he would just pick at us until we responded. If we ignore him, we're admitting defeat'.
'There's no way we can get them back. We can't get on their level. The only way to get them back is to get on their level and you can't do that. You can't counter with some remark about the size of his penis or something without making yourself look really cheap'. (Spradley and Mann, 1975, p. 97)

Spradley and Mann comment immediately after presenting this passage, that 'although the joking helps to alleviate some of the conflicts between bartenders and waitresses, it is an asymmetrical relationship, one that continues to express the accepted cultural definitions of sexual identity in the bar' (1975, p. 97). To describe the relationship between waitresses and bartenders as asymmetrical seems entirely appropriate. In this respect, informal humour in the bar resembles the discourse of the dirty joke. But I find it difficult to see how the conversation above shows that joking, at least the joking performed by the *men*, helps to alleviate the waitresses' problems. It seems, rather, that the bartenders' humour creates yet another, somewhat intractable, difficulty arising out of the men's social and linguistic dominance. From the women's point of view, the humour of their male partners is an additional and particularly offensive consequence of their own structural subordination to the bartenders. If the passage above is typical, as Spradley and Mann claim, men's humour does not serve as a welcome release for the women, but as an added unpleasantness which is especially troublesome because it takes place within the humorous mode.

One way in which we might try to retain the authors' analysis, with only minor revisions, would be to propose that it is not the *bartenders'* humour which helps the waitresses, but their own humour. Unfortunately, we are not provided with any estimates of the frequency with which men and women initiated humour in the bar, nor of the frequency with which the humorously insulting exchanges ended to the advantage of either party. Nevertheless, we can try to compensate for this lack of information by examining the sixteen examples of humorous interchange actually provided by the analysts in their chapter on joking relationships. When I did this, I found that twelve of the sixteen exchanges were started by men and that thirteen ended with the men as victor. In contrast, four were begun by women, in only three of which did the female emerge as dominant. It seems, therefore, that joking in Brady's Bar is overwhelmingly initiated by men and that it is mainly the men who benefit from it. If humour was primarily a mechanism enabling women to cope with their subordination and their ambivalent relationship with the bartenders, we would surely expect that women would play a much more active role in the production of humour and that joking exchanges would work in a way which enabled women to emerge, at least in play, as the dominant partners. But, if the observational material presented by Spradley and Mann is at all representative, the exact opposite seems to happen. Far from being a safety valve for women's frustrations, humour is used mainly by men in such a way that it further reinforces their control over the women with whom they are in direct contact.

We can understand how this happens, if we look in greater detail at one kind of situation in which humour is especially likely to occur. Spradley and Mann note that jokes very frequently arise out of the mistakes made by members of the bar staff. In such circumstances, they report, employees use humour to hide their error by humorously insulting the colleague who drew attention to it, or by jokingly attributing the error to that person or to some other member of the staff. In the two instances described by the analysts, the mistake is made by a bartender in his dealings with a waitress. On each occasion the bartender adopts the humorous mode as soon as the error is made evident by the waitress and, playfully of course, makes the waitress appear to be at fault. In one case, for example, in which the bartender has given the wrong change to the waitress, the sequence ends with the bartender admonishing the waitress with the words, 'Okay, chesty. Next time, get the amount right so I don't have to go to all this trouble.' In reply, the waitress helplessly sticks out her tongue, picks up the money which is now the correct amount, and retreats to her tables in defeat.

Given that bartenders are required constantly to respond to the orders placed by the waitresses, they will inevitably make mistakes which will be drawn to their attention by their female partners. (For a general discussion of such problems in restaurants, see Whyte, 1973.) We may speculate that, when these mistakes occur, the bartender's authority is momentarily in jeopardy.It is clearly difficult for him to re-establish that authority immediately within the mode of serious discourse. For within that mode, his only suitable response is to admit his own incompetence and the passing superiority of the waitress. Within the fantasy world of humour, however, where reality and illusion are interchangeable, that mistake can be made to disappear by a mere change in the bartender's tone of voice; or if a fault is acknowledged, it can easily be attributed to the other member of staff involved in the incident – namely, the waitress. Because the bartender is 'only joking', it is, as we know, difficult for the waitress effectively to challenge his reallocation of blame. For any serious reply can be taken to be an inappropriate response to the bartender's humorous remark. Yet if the waitress also enters the domain of humour, she thereby accepts the unreality of the bartender's error. Thus his rapid switch from the serious to the humorous mode has a serious outcome for both parties. For the waitress, the result of the joking exchange is that the bartender's very incompetence has become an occasion for a further display of her subordination, whilst for the bartender, it has made possible a reassertion of his control over the female staff in a situation where that control was under threat.

Spradley and Mann's study leads me to the conclusion that the humour in Brady's Bar is produced or initiated primarily by the men, and that it is used by them to sustain their domination of the women. For the men, humour is a valuable interactional resource. In contrast, for the women, it is a source of continual frustration and one of the means by which their subordination is maintained. Spradley and Mann are probably correct in claiming that the sexually toned insults which occur persistently in Brady's Bar are used to deal with problems created by the regular patterns of interaction between waitresses and bartenders. I suggest, however, that they provide a solution, not to the difficulties of women, but to those experienced by men in maintaining their formal authority. As the analysts show with great clarity, the joking relationship between these men and women is fundamentally asymmetrical (Spradley and Mann, 1975, p. 97). They show, for example, that whereas women are not allowed to take offence at men's humorous or ribald remarks, men can and do object when a 'girl' 'goes too far'. 'Even when joking, girls must maintain a subordinate position, careful that their ritual insults do not denigrate a male bartender' (1975, p. 93). Similarly, the humorous language used by the women must be much more restrained than that employed by men. 'The waitresses must be careful not to say things that would appear course or crude. The males have much more latitude in what they do and say' (1975, p. 97; see also Sykes, 1966).

This asymmetry is also evident in the way that the customary repertoire of humorous terms focuses on the sexual attributes of women rather than those of men, particularly on the female breast. As Spradley and Mann report, 'public joking behavior in Brady's contains only vague and metaphorical comments about genitalia and almost never includes references to males in this regard' (1975, p. 96). One final aspect of this pervasive asymmetry within the discourse of the humorous mode is that humorous talk regularly 'involves calling attention to the waitress as sexual object' (1975, p. 98). This even extends to the analogues and metaphors used by men to make fun of the women's bodies. For instance, in the two following fragments from bartenders' jocular repartee, waitresses are insulted by being likened to inanimate objects:

1 'It'd look better if you had some tits! Who wants to pull down a zipper just to see two fried eggs thrown against a wall?' (1975, p. 97)
2 'Who wants two ball bearings on a steel board, anyway?' (1975, p. 98)

The parallel with the discourse of the formal joke is obvious.

The asymmetrical joking relationship of Brady's Bar closely resembles the interpretative asymmetry noted above which is characteristic of male humour in our culture. Spradley and Mann comment that the humour of Brady's Bar reflects masculine values as defined by that culture (1975, p. 98). Yet they also try to argue that this male-centred humour largely benefits the female participants. I suggest, in contrast, that the joking relationship found in Brady's Bar, and presumably in many other places, is best seen as part of a wider pattern of male domination and female subordination that is widespread in society at large. I am quite sure, for example, that if Brady's Bar had employed a team of waiters instead of waitresses, the humorous asymmetry would have been much less pronounced and the language of sexual denigration would have been entirely absent. In other words, the insulting and lewd language used by the bartenders is not addressed to the waitresses simply as subordinate members of the bar staff, but as women, who are taken to be inferior by the bartenders in a much more comprehensive and basic manner. This, I think, is well illustrated by an exchange which occurred on one occasion when a waitress exceeded her authority and advised the bartender not to serve a customer who had been drinking heavily:

Bartender: What would you know? You're just a female and anything you say is nothing more than idle chatter.
Waitress: Okay, then. I won't tell you how handsome, charming, and intelligent you are.
Bartender: Don't be redundant. I already know.
                                          (Spradley and Mann, 1975, p. 95)

It is clear that interactional problems do arise in the bar as a result of the structure of the relationships between waitresses and bartenders. But the solution which has evolved in response to these problems cannot be separated from the relationships between men and women in the bar, nor from the relationships between men and women in the wider society. It is no accident that the position of formal authority in the bar, that of the bartender, is occupied exclusively by men, whilst the subordinate position is reserved for women. Thus the problems experienced by the bartenders in maintaining their control undoubtedly arise in part from the fact that their subordinates are women. It is not surprising, therefore, that their repertoire of humorous discourse is heavily sexual in content and extremely derogatory in tone. This is so because it is a discourse designed to assert and reassert the subordination of women.

If I am right in taking the asymmetrical, humorous interplay in Brady's Bar as arising out of participants' interaction as men and women, and not just as waitresses and bartenders, we can reasonably infer that the pattern observed there will occur widely throughout society; although clearly, the use of sexual humour will vary to some degree from one social grouping to another, from one person to another, and from one occasion to another. Thus this appraisal of Spradley and Mann's study provides strong support for the conclusions derived in previous sections from the examination of dirty jokes. Like the humour of the dirty joke, men's informal humour constantly denigrates women's bodies and stresses their inferiority as social beings. It seems likely that much of the humour which has become partially fossilized in the standardized dirty joke has its origin in the widespread asymmetry of direct interaction between men and women, as illustrated in the humorous interplay in Brady's Bar.

Humour and the critique of gender relationships

In the preceding chapter, I suggested that women's humour tends to differ from that of men. This is likely to be true, however, only to a limited extent. For women operate as cultural producers within the context of a dominant discourse and a pattern of social relationships which are premised on a male view of the world. Consequently, although the humour used by and circulated among women will tend to have certain distinctive features, it will also resemble men's humour in many ways and will draw upon similar interpretative resources. For instance, we saw in Madeleine's joke (p. 123) that the critical component of the humour was the handling, by a man, of a woman's breasts and that the young women found this amusing. Similarly the joke that I have called 'Sacks's joke', but which originated, as far as we are concerned, from an unknown twelve-year-old girl, depicts women as passive recipients of male sexuality: 'It *ti*ckled,' said the first daughter, 'It *hu*rts,' said the second. According to one commentator, it can be read as a joke 'in which women are presented as objects of pleasure whose capacity to satisfy male desire is enhanced by their incapacity to distinguish between a dinner table [where the mother's rule about not speaking with one's mouth full would have been appropriate] and a bed' (Thompson, 1984, p. 117). Our attention is drawn by this reading of the joke to the fact that, although Sacks's version comes from a young girl and although women predominate in the joke's text, it still depends on a male- centred conception of sexuality and on the notion of female stupidity which features widely in men's jokes about women.

Because women's humour is created within a society where men's discourse and men's humour are dominant, the growing involvement of women in the production of mass humour will not, in itself, bring about a change in humorous style. For instance, Joan Rivers is a very popular TV comedienne in Britain and the USA, but her humour is firmly within the male-centred tradition, relying heavily on insulting sexual innuendo. This is clearly illustrated by her comic book (1985), the guiding theme of which is implied in the book's prefatory quotation: 'You show me a woman with a naturally beautiful body, and I'll show you a tramp!'

The clearest sign of a changing approach to humour, and particularly to humour dealing with the relationships between women and men, is to be found in humour which has been influenced by the women's movement. It would be misleading to suggest that those involved in the women's movement have emphasized the need for analysis or corrective action in relation to humour. They have concentrated, probably correctly, on serious analysis and serious areas of conduct. However, the discussion above indicates that it would be a tactical error on their part to ignore humour entirely. For, as we have seen, the male-centred view of sexuality and of women is formulated and transmitted in a most potent form within humorous discourse. Humour can allow the most unadulterated expression of sexist views because, when we speak humorously, we are not fully responsible for what we say. From the outside, from within the realm of serious discourse, the messages of humour are extremely difficult to oppose successfully. Yet the messages conveyed by humour may have very serious consequences. It seems, therefore, that the development of an 'alternative humour' is an important task to be faced by the women's movement.

Some female humorists have recognized the cultural importance of humour and, informed by ideas drawn from the women's movement, have sought to address and make fun of the basic assumptions of men's views of women, which are linked to the basic assumptions of men's sexual humour. In a previous section (p. 140), we saw Christine Roche's cartoon sequence in which the principle of the sexual availability of women was shown to be ludicrous. This chapter ends with another of her cartoons, in which Roche beautifully displays the infantile character of the male-centred conception of women which, with minor variations, is shared by many men as well as boys. In the cartoons that I have chosen, Roche is still

operating partly within the dominant tradition of male humour. However, her humour does not endorse the assumptions of that humorous discourse, but seeks to challenge them by giving expression to the potentially different perspective of women. As I argued above, there is nothing inevitable about the sexual humour of our culture. Quite different assumptions can be used to create humorous incongruity on this topic. Roche's work is a sign that a movement may already be under way towards the creation of new principles for producing humour about sexuality and about the relations between women and men.

9

Humour and Social Structure

We have just looked at the way in which certain aspects of sexual humour are linked in our society to the structured relationships between women and men. One broad conclusion of that chapter was that much sexual humour arises directly out of the social structure of gender relationships and that, on the whole, sexual humour works to reproduce this structure. I now intend to explore the connection between humour and social structure in more general terms. I will attempt to provide an analysis which can be used to elucidate the structural sources and consequences of humour in a wide range of social settings.

Jokes in the social structure

The most relevant and useful discussion in the existing literature with which to begin this chapter is that by Mary Douglas (1968; reprinted in Douglas, 1975). Her examination of the link between humour and social structure starts with a review of the writings of Freud (1905) and Bergson (1911) on the underlying structure of 'humorous thought'. She extracts from these authors what she calls a 'formula for identifying jokes'. This formula appears to be another version of the concept of 'bisociation'.

> A joke is a play upon form. It brings into relation disparate elements in such a way that one accepted pattern is challenged by the appearance of another which in some way was hidden in the first . . . any recognisable joke falls into this joke pattern which needs two elements, the juxtaposition of a control against that which is controlled, this juxtaposition being such that the latter triumphs. (Douglas, 1975, p. 96)

This formulation captures the interpretative duality of humour on which I have placed great emphasis. It stresses that humour is produced, not merely by the incongruous combination of opposing patterns, but also by the revelation of an alternative, hidden meaning.

Douglas's analytical task is to demonstrate how humour, thus defined, is linked to social structure. She establishes this link by proposing, in the first place, that actors' perception and understanding in general are determined by the range of conceptual possibilities furnished by the social structure in which they act. Thus their ability to recognize and appreciate the interpretative oppositions and ambiguities required in the realm of humour is also structurally constrained. It follows, she argues, that a joke will be seen and allowed only 'when it offers a symbolic pattern of a social pattern occurring at the same time' (1975, p. 98). In Douglas's view, 'humorous' discourse cannot even be recognized as such, let alone found to be amusing, unless it expresses the social situation in which it occurs. Accordingly:

> The one social condition necessary for a joke to be enjoyed is that the social group in which it is received should develop the formal characteristics of a 'told' joke: that is, a dominant pattern of relations is challenged by another. If there is no joke in the social structure, no other joking can appear . . . I would go a step further and even suggest that the experience of a joke form in the social structure calls imperatively for an explicit joke to express it. (1975, pp. 98, 100)

The central idea, then, is that there is a direct correspondence between humour and social structure. Joking takes place because the organized patterns of social life themselves involve contradictions, oppositions and incongruities which find expression through the medium of humorous discourse. One might have expected, at this point in the analysis, that Douglas would have argued that joking, in giving symbolic expression to structural 'strains' and 'tensions', helps to lessen these strains and thereby to maintain the established structure of social relationships. There is, indeed, a well developed tradition of anthropological interpretation, stemming from the work of A.R. Radcliffe-Brown (1940; reprinted 1952), in which institutionalized joking is regarded as a device for resolving structural tensions in a manner that enables participants to engage in collaborative activities which are critical for the existing structure. Douglas, however, adopts a completely opposite position. She stresses that humorous utterances necessarily involve a confrontation with the dominant social pattern. Joking, she suggests, is an activity that is generated by the social structure, but which challenges and disrupts that structure by giving voice to its inconsistencies and irrationalities. In order to emphasize this aspect of humour, she compares jokes with standard rites. Rites express and impose order and harmony. They create a sense of unity. They assert hierarchy and convey the necessity of the established social patterns. In contrast, she maintains, humour disorganizes. It destroys hierarchy and order. Joking does not affirm dominant values, but denigrates and devalues them. In the course of humorous discourse, the accepted patterns of social life are shown to have no necessity. 'Essentially a joke is an anti-rite' (1975, p. 102).

Let me illustrate how Douglas's analysis can give insight into specific social situations by briefly reconsidering the humorous interplay between waitresses and bartenders in Brady's Bar that was described in chapter 8. If Douglas is right in stressing that joking will occur only when there is a joke in the social structure, it should be possible to identify a joke in the social structure of Brady's Bar; that is, we should find that in the bar the dominant pattern of social relationships is challenged by an alternative pattern which is 'hidden in the first'. It seems to me that this is a reasonable way of describing what was, in fact, observed. For we saw that the joking among waitresses and bartenders was centrally concerned with the latter's attempts to maintain their position of formal authority in a situation where this was threatened by a degree of interactional subordination to the waitresses. Speaking figuratively, we can say that the social structure of Brady's Bar had played a joke on the bartenders; that is, it had vested in them authority over the activities of the other staff within the bar, but it had then placed them at the beck and call of their subordinates. We might even say that the social structure at large had played a joke on the bartenders. For it had given them the dominant status of men and had then forced them to behave like women; that is, it had required them constantly to cater for the needs of others, including waitresses as well as clients. The bartenders, it seems, responded to this joke in the social structure, of which they were the victims, by adopting the humorous mode of discourse themselves and by using it to reaffirm the domination that was 'properly' theirs.

If we accept that it is possible to identify a joke in the social structure of Brady's Bar and that much of the humour that took place there grew out of this structural joke, it follows that Douglas's analysis applies, at least in part, to this specific social setting. It may be, therefore, that it applies much more widely and may provide a useful framework for understanding the relationship between humour and social structure in general. Douglas's argument appears to suggest that the relationship between humour and social structure is fairly straightforward and that, in order to understand any particular instance of humorous interchange, we need do little more than locate the structural joke from which it arises and to which it corresponds. However, before we can reach this optimistic conclusion, we must examine several analytical difficulties that Douglas leaves unresolved.

In the first place, although Douglas suggests that the presence of a joke form in the social structure 'calls imperatively' for explicit humour to express it, she makes no attempt to describe the mechanism whereby this call is put into effect. Her phrasing seems to indicate that she expects explicit joking to be a direct 'expression of' structural incongruity; and, indeed, there are situations where this seems to be the case. In some preliterate societies, institutionalized joking relationships exist which appear to take the form of playful displays of the interpretative ambiguities inherent in a tribe's complex kinship relationships and kinship terminology. Among the Gogo of Tanzania, for example, joking between male cross-cousins involves the reciprocal use of overlapping and potentially ambiguous kinship categories in a way which enables participants to pretend to be, not cousins, but father and son or nephew and mother's brother (Rigby, 1968). This, and similar examples (see Sharman, 1969), can reasonably be described as straightforward 'expressions' of jokes that are partially hidden in the social structure. (For a review of research on 'joking relationships', see Apte, 1985.) But Douglas gives no clue as to why such structural ambiguities are used as the basis for explicit humour, nor whether all such potential jokes are put into practice. Furthermore, it is clear from Brady's Bar that, in certain circumstances, a joke in the social structure may not be given voice at all, but may itself be confronted and suppressed as the more powerful participants respond within the humorous mode to its structural implications.

The evidence from Brady's Bar forces us to reconsider Douglas's claim that joking necessarily disrupts the dominant pattern and threatens hierarchy and order. It is true that what I have called 'the joke in the social structure of Brady's Bar' – namely, the control exerted by the waitresses over the bartenders' activities – challenges and threatens to disrupt the dominant structure. However, the pattern of joking initiated and sustained by the bartenders does the exact opposite. The bartenders' actual humour counters the joke in the social structure and works to reinstate the formal pattern of authority which had been put in jeopardy by the 'hidden pattern' implicit in the structured relationships taking place in the bar. If the processes operative in Brady's Bar are typical in this respect, it would follow, contrary to Douglas's proposal, that humorous discourse tends to support and maintain the dominant structure rather than to subvert it.

Douglas's analysis is presented as a completely general account of the relationship between humour and social structure. It must, therefore, encompass groups as different as the Gogo and the denizens of Brady's Bar. In both these settings, and in many others, there does appear to be a connection between the occurrence of humour and the existence of the kind of structural ambiguity or incongruity that Douglas calls a joke in the social structure. In addition, within groups like the Gogo, certain joking relationships do seem to involve fairly direct expressions of ambiguities in the kinship structure. Even here, however, participants' actual humour does not appear to challenge that structure or to reveal its arbitrary character. Gogo cross- cousins only *pretend* to be father and son within the protected confines of the humorous mode. Their humour does confront the dominant structure with its ambiguities. But it does this only in play. The structural challenge thus expressed is no more than a mock challenge. It has no serious consequences. In this respect, institutionalized joking among the Gogo differs significantly from that occurring in Brady's Bar. For in the latter case, humorous interchange does seem to have a serious consequence: namely, that of supporting the formal pattern of authority within the bar.

We need no further examples to conclude that Douglas has oversimplified the relationship between humour and social structure. In order to build upon her analysis, we must recognize, to begin with, that there are different kinds of humour. The playful exchanges of Gogo cross-cousins are markedly different from the insulting sexual banter of Brady's Bar – for participants as well as for analysts. The former is analogous to what I called 'pure humour' in chapter 4: that is, humour which is taken by participants to have no implications beyond the realm of humorous discourse. Joking in Brady's Bar, in contrast, seems to involve 'applied humour', in the sense that it makes a discernible contribution to serious interaction and is seen, at least by some participants on some occasions, as having serious consequences. Pure humour may be generated by the social structure, but it will, by definition, neither disrupt nor support that structure. Applied humour, however, may do either of these things. It may operate to maintain the dominant structure, as in Brady's Bar, or it may in different circumstances have the opposite effect.

We must accept that there are different types of humour, with varying effects on the social structure. But our amendment of Douglas's argument cannot stop here. Given that we, and Douglas, are seeking a universal formulation of the connection between humour and social structure, we must also respond to the fact that we are faced with a potentially enormous variety of different social structures. Clearly, we cannot hope to deal adequately with this structural diversity from the outset. We must be content for the time being with crude approximations. Nevertheless, it seems to me essential to recognize from the start that social structures do vary in significant ways. This means that different types of structure may create different sorts of structural joke, may provide different social contexts in which these jokes have to be handled and may, thereby, generate quite different reactions from participants.

It is clear that we must abandon Douglas's unduly simple idea that jokes in the social structure call imperatively for humour that challenges the structure which gives it birth. I suggest that we replace it with the following more complex and, I think, more realistic proposals: namely, that some, but not necessarily all, humour is directly generated by structural jokes; that humour so generated can be pure as well as applied; that applied humour can, in principle, have positive as well as negative consequences for the structure within which it occurs; and that the relationship between humour and social structure is different in different kinds of social setting. I will assume that these general points have been established in the course of the discussion so far. However, I also wish to make one more proposal: that the structural generation of humour is significantly affected by the degree of formality of the structural context in which it occurs and by the nature of the social hierarchy in which it is located. The two aspects of this claim will be substantiated and developed in the next three sections of this chapter.

Degrees of structural formality

If we are to understand how humour alters in accordance with variations in social structure, we must clarify what is meant by the statement that 'there is a joke in the social structure.' In the previous section, I suggested that it was reasonable to make this claim with respect to Brady's Bar as well as to the kinship structure of Gogo society. But I made no attempt to explain how a structural joke can be recognized. In order to do so, we have to combine what appear to be two rather different concepts. On the one hand, we have a joke, that is, a linguistic formulation displaying the characteristics identified in previous chapters. On the other hand, we have a social structure, that is, a pattern of recurrent meaningful interaction between the occupants of specific social positions. If we are to identify jokes in the social structure, we must be able to reconcile these two notions. We can do this, I suggest, by interpreting the phrase 'pattern of recurrent meaningful interaction' as equivalent to 'pattern of linguistic exchange'. As soon as we accept that both 'social structure' and 'joke' refer to organized patterns of discourse, we have no difficulty in allowing that social structures may reproduce the linguistic form of a joke.

Even if we insist that 'social structure' is something more than the mere exchange of words, it is undeniable that social scientists identify and describe social structures primarily by interpreting what people say, and in some societies write, to each other. (For a more extended discussion, see Gilbert and Mulkay, 1984, chapter 1.) For example, the claim that there is a formal authority structure in Brady's Bar in which bartenders exercise control over waitresses depends on the investigators' having observed that bartenders regularly give orders to waitresses, that waitresses almost never challenge those orders, that waitresses frequently complain to each other about the way in which bartenders treat them as inferiors but seldom complain directly to the bartenders themselves, that bartenders use various phrases which imply waitresses' subordination and express their own position of dominance, and so on. The phrase 'social structure of Brady's Bar' refers to such patterns of regular, organized discourse.

If a social structure is a pattern of organized discourse, it follows that it can be organized in the form of a joke; that is, in Douglas's words, it can be arranged in such a way that one accepted or dominant pattern is challenged by the existence of another pattern which in some way is hidden in the first. In the case of Brady's Bar, the two conflicting patterns occur because the waitresses, although subject in many respects to the bartenders' control and obedient to their orders, are also required to pass on to the bartenders the 'orders' of the most powerful social category in the bar – namely, the customers. (It seems that jokes in the social structure can involve puns.) Because waitresses regularly speak to bartenders as the customers' representatives, and thereby exercise control over bartenders' actions, a secondary pattern of reciprocal discourse exists which implicitly contradicts the dominant pattern and sometimes gives rise, as we have seen, to genuine interactional difficulties (Whyte, 1973). It is the clash between these patterns of discourse that creates the joke in the social structure of Brady's Bar.

If this argument is correct, our analytical task has been simplified to some extent. It seems that, in exploring how variations in social structure give rise to humour, we must focus on the organized patterns of discourse which are characteristic of different social settings, and we must examine how contradictory patterns are generated and handled by participants within these different settings. However, the task may still appear to be dauntingly complex. For discourse varies along so many different dimensions, all of which may have some bearing on the generation of humour. I will try to create order out of this diversity by concentrating on the degree to which discourse is formalized in various social situations.

At one end of the spectrum of formality are ritual ceremonies. We saw earlier that Douglas regarded ritual discourse as being fundamentally different from humour. Unlike humour, ceremonial discourse is internally coherent, uniform and highly predictable. In the extreme case, as in marriage ceremonies in our own society, every word to be uttered is known in advance and, if the exact pattern of formal discourse is not reproduced, what takes place does not count as a proper ceremony (Austin, 1962). In such a setting, as long as participants make no mistakes, humour is impossible. It is excluded by the rigid formality of the discourse.

As we move away from such extremely formal settings, humorous discourse begins to occur. In Nobel ceremonies, for example, although the range of discourse and the basic forms of verbal exchange are pre-established (Mulkay, 1984), there is greater room for discursive variety than in the case of the marriage ceremony. It is this slight reduction in the level of formality that makes humour possible. However, the humour that takes place in Nobel ceremonies is, as we will see in the next section, closely linked to the standard forms of ceremonial discourse by the relative formality of the occasion. In this setting, participants are unable to move away from the central focus of the ceremony. As a result of this restriction on the variability of ceremonial discourse, Nobel humour never challenges or disrupts the dominant pattern of the ceremony. It appears that, in this respect, it is typical of humour in highly formalized social structures. To put this in general terms, the more formalized the structure, the stronger is the connection between humour and the prevailing pattern of discourse. Moreover, in formal settings, where humour is most directly linked to the social structure, it is highly unlikely to be used to express opposition to that structure. In contrast, in situations where the pattern of interaction is less formal and the discourse less structured, the less will participants' humour be generated directly in response to structural contradictions.

Since, in informal settings, the relationship between humour and social structure is relatively weak and indirect, the humour that occurs can range more widely and, frequently, in a highly creative manner. Even in these circumstances, however, when participants' discourse is largely free from direct structural restraint, humour is rather seldom used to undermine the dominant patterns of social life. Although the humour that takes place in unstructured situations does occasionally touch upon issues of structural importance, we will see that the interpretative duality of the humorous mode, together with the separation of such humour from the major social structures, reduce its significance as a source of social disruption or challenge.

Ceremonial humour

There is, in fact, little humour during the annual ceremonies at which Nobel Prizes are awarded. During the period 1978–81, I was able to identify only twelve instances of humorous discourse in the published transcripts – that is, an average of three per ceremony (Mulkay, 1987). One reason for this low level of humorous content is that the ceremonies are by their very nature solemn ritual events devoted to the celebration of mankind's highest and most serious achievements in the realms of science, literature and human welfare. In addition, the ritual interaction is strictly pre-ordained and the discourse of individual participants varies from year to year only in relatively minor respects (Mulkay, 1984). Nevertheless, there are always a few isolated fragments of humour. Let us see how this humour is related to the relatively rigid structure of ceremonial discourse.

Nobel ceremonies are organized around three symbolic acts: that of describing and praising the achievements of each Nobel laureate named in a particular year; that of awarding the prize to each laureate; and that of responding after receipt of the prize. These acts are performed by means of a fairly simple linguistic exchange, of which the basic structure is as follows (Mulkay, 1984). First, various non-laureates speak on behalf of one or more social entities: for example, the Nobel Foundation, an academic discipline, the younger generation, and so on. The speech of these non-laureates is addressed both to the ceremonial audience and to the laureates themselves. It consists overwhelmingly of admiring descriptions of laureates' accomplishments and enthusiastic endorsements of the significance of their contributions to knowledge, to world culture or to peace among nations. After this, the prizes are awarded and the laureates respond to the ritual praise of the non-laureates and to the ultimate compliment of the prize itself. The laureates' responses, like the speech of the non-laureates, are rigidly formalized. Their central features are the scrupulous avoidance of self-praise, the downgrading of their own achievements, the regular use of return compliments addressed to Alfred Nobel or to the Nobel Foundation and, most notably, the reassignment of praise by the laureates to their colleagues and families, and to wider social groupings of which they are members (Mulkay, 1984; 1987).

We do not need to understand why the Nobel ceremonies are organized in this way (see Mulkay, 1984). Our task is to consider whether there is a joke in the structure of Nobel discourse and whether the humour that occurs intermittently during the ceremonies is linked to that joke. It seems to me that the ceremonial discourse gives rise to a very obvious structural joke. For much of what the laureates say, when downgrading their own work and reassigning credit for their achievements, can be taken to contradict the fulsome praise bestowed on them by the non-laureates and, in many cases, to challenge the very idea of granting the prizes to particular individuals (Mulkay, 1985, chapter 8). We can, therefore, formulate the structural 'joke' or interpretative contradiction of Nobel discourse in a rather crude fashion by means of the following imaginary exchange:

Non-laureate: I give you this prize for your marvellous achievement.
Laureate: Thank you very much. I accept the prize and, in so doing, I accept your judgement of my cultural contribution. But actually my achievement is rather insignificant and, anyway, other people did most of the work.

Thus both laureates and non-laureates, in their different ways, endorse the dominant pattern of Nobel discourse and cooperate in bringing about the award and acceptance of the prizes. However, the laureates also challenge the validity of the dominant structure by implying, but never fully revealing, an alternative, hidden pattern.

If this account of the joke in the structure of the Nobel ceremony is correct and if, as I have suggested, the humour in highly formalized settings is closely linked to structural jokes, we should find that Nobel humour focuses on the attribution and denial of merit with respect to the Nobel laureates. As I have shown elsewhere, this is in fact the case (Mulkay, 1987). Let us examine two humorous passages taken from the ceremony held in 1979, one from a laureate and one from a non-laureate, in order to understand in more detail how Nobel humour and the surrounding context of ceremonial discourse are related.

The following quotation is taken from the banquet speech of one of the two recipients of the prize for physiology and medicine. The prizewinners were being honoured for their contributions to the development of computerized tomography, a technique for constructing three-dimensional X-rays.

'The Nobel prescription'

There is an irony in this award, since neither Hounsfield nor I is a physician. In fact it is not much of an exaggeration to say that what Hounsfield and I know about medicine and physiology could be written on a small prescription form!

While there is an irony in the award, there is also hope that even in these days of increasing specialization there is a unity in the human experience, a unity clearly known to Alfred Nobel by the broad spectrum of his awards. I think that he would have been pleased to know that an engineer and a physicist, each in his own way, have contributed just a little to the advancement of medicine. (*Les Prix Nobel*, 1979, p. 41)

For several reasons, I take the first paragraph of this passage to be 'not entirely serious'. In the first place, the speaker mentions the irony of the award, thereby drawing attention to the possibility of attributing more than one meaning to his receipt of the prize for medicine. In addition, he engages in the kind of distortion characteristic of humour. He tells us that what he is about to say 'is not much of an exaggeration'. But this informs us that what is to come is *some* kind of exaggeration and is, therefore, not literally accurate. The 'non-serious intent' of the punch line is further confirmed by what I take to be a playful replacement of the standard humorous phrase 'what he knows about X could be written on a postage stamp' with 'what we know about medicine could be written on a small prescription form'.

These indications that 'the Nobel prescription' is not to be taken entirely seriously are incorporated in a passage that expresses an emphatic self-deprecation. Self-deprecation, as I have stressed, is part of the normal pattern of laureates' discourse; in this respect, the speaker is conforming to the established pattern. However, there is a problem facing any laureate who states openly and without qualification that he has done nothing to deserve the Nobel Prize. This problem must be resolved even when the statement is made in the relatively relaxed atmosphere of the ceremonial banquet. For such an outright denial of merit by a laureate clearly contradicts the laudatory pronouncements made by non-laureates in the course of the prize-giving ceremonies, and is hardly consistent with his acceptance of the prize. For example, if this laureate had said in a straightforward, serious manner that he knew nothing about physiology or medicine and could not properly be given the prize under this heading, his very participation in the ceremony would have been put in question. The challenge to the ritual structure implicit in the pattern of Nobel discourse would have become 'no laughing matter'.

In the quoted passage, however, the laureate succeeds in employing irony and the humorous mode to deny his competence in the area for which the prize is being awarded, without producing these serious consequences. He uses the interpretative duality of humour to assert his incompetence without thereby challenging his right to receive the prize. The award of the prize is said to be 'ironic', but not actually 'wrong'. This passage is typical of laureates' Nobel humour in that humour is used, not to challenge and confront, but to avoid the potential difficulties built into the conflicting patterns of Nobel discourse.

Let us now turn to an example of humour produced by a non-laureate.

'Christopher Columbus'

Scientific research has old traditions. Throughout the ages, man has striven to gain new knowledge, searched for new paths to follow. To many people, Christopher Columbus is an early and worthy exponent of this tradition. When he set off for America, he didn't know where he was going. When he reached that continent, he didn't know where he was. And safely back in Europe again, he didn't know where he had been. And as if this wasn't enough, he did not even travel at his own expense!

This is very often the dilemma in which science finds itself. (*Les Prix Nobel*, 1979, p. 43)

This is the opening of the banquet speech delivered by the representative of the students of Stockholm. The first three sentences seem to be entirely serious, and no explicit indication is furnished at any stage that the passage is not intended to be taken literally. However, the account given of Columbus's explorations seems to me to be recognizably humorous. On a literal reading of this joke, Columbus appears to be subject to strong criticism. The underlying contrast structure of the joke seems to be that between ignorance and knowledge: Columbus was pursuing knowledge, but ended up in a state of ignorance. In the introduction to the joke, he is depicted as representing the tradition of scientific research, and in the following paragraph his dilemma is said to be the dilemma of science itself. Thus on a literal reading, it appears that the student representative, in remarks addressed directly to the laureates, is proposing a general criticism of science or is at least drawing attention to certain limitations of the enterprise of scientific research. Needless to say, criticism of science or of the laureates is not typical of student representatives' discourse at the Nobel ceremonies. The normal pattern is that, along with all the other non-laureates, they pay profound homage to the laureates' achievements and to the attainments of science. On a literal reading, this passage contravenes normal expectations.

However, if I am right in suggesting that 'Christopher Columbus' is clearly humorous, a literal reading is prohibited. The joke is apparently critical of and disrespectful towards science, but we are instructed by its humorous form not to take these criticisms entirely seriously. I suggest that the joke is a temporary pretence of criticism that is reinterpreted subsequently and used as the basis for a conventional allocation of praise to science and scientists. The speech continues:

> Often, scientific progress has been the result of less specific basic reasearch. At the same time, it is difficult to combine free and independent research with the demands that may be placed upon this activity by providers of research funds . . . The freedom of the scientist is being curtailed in many parts of the world. If Columbus had been fitted out for a voyage to Cyprus by his patroness, probably not even he would have reached North America! . . . In a democratic society, free and independent research will always benefit all mankind. (*Les Prix Nobel*, 1979, p. 43)

In the course of this serious passage, the student representative proceeds to tell her audience how she interprets the Columbus joke. She draws an analogue between Columbus's wanderings and the unpredictable explorations of free and independent basic research. Columbus is depicted as having been successful in discovering America, despite his initial errors, because he was free from direct external control. It follows that science, similarly, should be left free to follow its own objectives, even though outsiders may be unable to understand scientists' conclusions. If scientists are not subject to outside constraint it can be guaranteed that, like Columbus, they will benefit all mankind.

In this passage, then, the apparent criticism of science implicit in the joke is transformed into a glowing compliment. The apparently misguided wanderings of Columbus and of scientific research are now seen to be an essential prerequisite for fundamental advances in understanding and in human welfare. Thus the student representative ensures that the meaning of the Columbus joke does not remain equivocal for long. Like the laureate in 'the Nobel prescription', who immediately transforms his playful self-denial into a serious return compliment to Alfred Nobel, she quickly makes it clear that the joke was only a pretence of criticism. By formulating that criticism as a joke, she avoided any possibility of being seen as seriously infringing the normal patterns of Nobel discourse. Although her apparent criticism of the science laureates was at no stage 'to be taken seriously', her subsequent gloss re-presents the Columbus joke as having been an expression of praise 'all along'. Columbus, and by analogue scientists and the laureates, are shown to be Protean figures of knowledge and beneficence. Through this subsequent interpretative work, the student representative re-establishes her unambiguous conformity to the requirements of Nobel discourse.

At the banquet, the student representative briefly adopts the pattern of alternative discourse that is recurrent within the Nobel ceremony. Allusively, through the figure of Columbus, she represents scientists collectively as confused, ignorant and expensive. In so doing, she makes visible the secondary pattern hidden in the ceremonial social structure. But she is careful to express this potentially dangerous idea in humorous form. Her humour, like all humour at the Nobel ceremonies, necessarily focuses on the attribution of credit for cultural achievements. For this topic is the overriding concern of Nobel discourse, and the speech of all participants is required to deal exclusively with cultural accomplishment and the bestowal of appropriate reward. Because her remarks are humorous, they have to deviate in some way from the standard pattern of Nobel discourse, and they do so, like all Nobel humour, by endorsing the pattern already implicit in much of what laureates themselves say. Within the Nobel ceremony, as within any highly structured situation, humour is inevitably restricted in this way. Within formalized social contexts, any appreciable departure from recurrent forms and their central focus would not be treated as humour, but as a serious misdemeanor or breach of etiquette. Thus in the Nobel setting, neither laureates nor non-laureates can make any significant use of humour which is not linked to the joke in the social structure.

Although humour within the formal context of the Nobel ceremonies is closely linked to the structural joke, and although it relies on the contradictory possibilities implicit in the alternative pattern of discourse, Nobel humour never challenges the dominant pattern. It is always used, as in the two examples given above, in a way which sustains and reinforces that pattern. Thus Nobel humour is not imperatively called forth by structural incongruities that threaten to disrupt the existing structure. The very infrequency of humour, despite the existence of an evident joke in the structure, shows that participants can handle the difficulties of Nobel discourse, when they so wish, without recourse to humour (Mulkay, 1984). We must not reify the social structure and treat 'it' as an agent that calls particular responses into being. Rather, it seems that participants make use of the humorous possibilities of Nobel discourse when it suits their purposes. For example, it is surely no coincidence that Nobel humour is especially likely to occur in the course of speeches at the ceremonial banquet. Participants presumably regard humour to be particularly appropriate at the banquet as a way of lightening the atmosphere and making the occasion more relaxed and enjoyable.

It seems that Nobel humour, despite its infrequency, is an organized and significant social phenomenon. Whether it appears during the more solemn parts of the ceremonial proceedings (Mulkay, 1987) or during the banquet, it is employed, as we have seen, as a protective device which enables speakers to deviate from the normal pattern of discourse without giving offence. Even during the banquet speeches, the humorous mode is employed to perform what is, in that setting, the 'serious' work of creating a little amusement and discursive variety out of the narrowly restricted interpretative resources that are available within a highly formalized social setting.

Hierarchy and humour

In this section we will move away from the extreme formality of ritual occasions, and examine the social sources and social consequences of humour in a setting which, although highly structured, is much less rigidly organized than are the Nobel ceremonies. The discussion will be based on Rose Laub Coser's study of the 'social functions of humor among the staff of a mental hospital' (1960, p. 81) in the USA. This study took place about ten years before Douglas's paper was published. Consequently, Coser makes no reference to Douglas's concept of a 'joke in the social structure'. Nevertheless, Coser's view of the social production of humour is very similar to that of Douglas; that is, they both argue that humour is generated by ambiguities in the social structure. However, Coser's conclusion about the social consequences of humour is closer to my own: namely, that in highly structured situations humour works to maintain the existing pattern.

> The meaning of humor, then, is to be detected primarily in the common concerns of the group, and can be understood only by examining its content and themes in the context of the network of role relationships among those who laugh together . . . attention will be given to humor as a means of mutual reassurance in an area of work that seems to be fraught with uncertainties, and to the group support it provides for facing ambiguities in role performance. (Coser, 1960, pp. 82, 83)

Coser does not speculate about the social production of humour in other kinds of social setting, and she does not herself distinguish between groups with different degrees of structural formality. Her concern is rather to provide a detailed empirical study of the place of humour in a series of meetings among a specific group of psychiatric staff. The purpose of these meetings was to allow collective discussion of case material presented by junior staff members. The meetings were, Coser emphasizes, formally structured (1960, p. 82). Nevertheless, it is clear that neither the patterns of interaction, nor the form nor the content of the discourse, were pre-arranged to the same degree as in the Nobel ceremonies. The presentation and discussion of case material relating to individual mental patients were inevitably less predictable than the ceremonial circulation of praise. Thus social interaction during these staff meetings was more flexible, and probably more complex, than that at the Nobel ceremonies. There certainly appears to have been a greater variety of structural ambiguities. As we would expect, therefore, humour was more frequent and more varied than that generated within the more narrowly confined repertoire of Nobel discourse. Coser reports a total of 103 examples of humour that she noted in the course of twenty staff meetings. Although this rate of humorous production is not high, the average of five items per meeting clearly exceeds the three per ceremony observed during the much longer Nobel rituals.

Participants at the staff meetings occupied one of four social categories: namely, senior psychiatric staff, junior psychiatric staff, visiting psychiatrists and auxiliary staff. Coser maintains that the members of each of these categories faced structurally generated difficulties in their dealings with other participants, and that most of their humorous remarks were related to these difficulites. A major problem facing senior staff, for example, can be said to have arisen from their often being obliged to say two contradictory things at once to junior staff. This was necessary because the meetings were intended to help junior staff to learn from their mistakes and to become increasingly competent as psychiatrists yet, at the same time, to provide support so that they could continue to perform demanding tasks in the hospital for which they were not fully qualified.

Since the implementation of these aims fell upon the senior staff, the speech addressed by senior to junior staff at these meetings had to convey reprimand and criticism – so that junior staff might learn – along with support and reassurance, so that they might not become unduly discouraged. Coser does not report on whether it was possible for senior staff to accomplish this subtle task of interpretative reconciliation within the serious mode of discourse. We do not know, in other words, whether this discursive duality could be achieved only by means of humour. She maintains, however, that humour was 'especially suited for this task because it combines criticism with support, rejection with acceptance' (1960, p. 91).

Coser gives several examples of the use of humour by senior staff. In the following instance, a junior psychiatrist has just reported to the meeting that he has adopted the therapeutic technique of accepting a patient's delusion of having killed someone. Upon hearing this, the senior member presiding at the session asks him in a humorous tone: 'When was it that you reassured her that she was a murderess?' (1960, p. 90). This remark is greeted with laughter from the group. But Coser regards it as doing the serious work of drawing the recipient's attention to what the senior speaker regards as a therapeutic error. The comment is taken as conveying to the junior member that delusions of this kind should not be endorsed by the therapist. By adopting the humorous mode, and by eliciting laughter from the group, the speaker is able to display to the assembled participants that the younger psychiatrist's action is incongruous, without engaging in open criticism. Subsequently, the same senior member of staff employs the humorous mode again, in relation to the same case. On this occasion he uses humour in a manner which combines correction with reassurance and with collective amusement at the incongruity of others' actions in similar circumstances: 'Let me mention that there were precedents of your method. There once was a patient who went around barking like a dog [laughter starts here] and the therapist barked back . . . [the rest of the sentence is drowned in laughter]' (Coser, 1960, p. 91). The use of humour to generate group laughter also operates, Coser suggests, to add collective weight to the implied criticism and to make the offending party less likely to ignore the advice being offered by the senior person.

Coser reports that about 40 per cent of the humorous remarks of senior staff are directed at junior staff, and that this humour regularly conveys a critical or corrective message along the lines illustrated above. When humour is used in this fashion at the meetings, it appears to be a means of coping with the implicit joke built into the routine discourse of senior staff in this social context. In other words, much of the humour of senior staff seems to be designed to enable them to point out their juniors' mistakes, whilst simultaneously requiring recipients to respond with laughter rather than with resentment or with self-justification. If Coser is right, humour is used to a considerable extent by senior staff to accomplish correction without confrontation.

Coser's analysis of the humour of visiting psychiatrists and junior staff is similar to that of senior staff's humour. Visiting psychiatrists are usually present at the meetings when they have been unable to deal with the problems of one of their own patients and when the patient has had to be taken into hospital. Thus, when they attend staff meetings, visiting psychiatrists speak as supposedly qualified, competent psychiatrists whose competence is, on this occasion, a matter of possible doubt. Coser shows that much of their humour focuses upon and resolves this discursive uncertainty. It does this, she suggests, by humorously asserting the speaker's professional skill at the expense of patients and of others associated with patients. In other words, visiting psychiatrists' humour treats patients and those related to them as 'scapegoats'. Whatever has gone wrong is, jocularly, attributed to them. In Coser's view, the implicit message of this humour is that the visiting psychiatrists, despite any appearances to the contrary, are not responsible for what has happened. In short, this joke in the structure of discourse, this potential challenge to the established pattern of professional dominance, is persistently resolved in a manner which dissipates that challenge and sustains the visitors' appearance of professional competence at the staff meetings.

The structural joke with which junior staff have to deal at the meetings is perhaps the most blatant. In Coser's words: 'Junior members . . . find themselves in a contradictory status position. In relation to patients they act as practising psychiatrists. Actually, however, they are still in training; in relation to senior members, they are advanced graduate students' (1960, p. 92). Thus at meetings, junior staff have to speak as students about things they have done and said elsewhere when they were acting as 'practising psychiatrists'. It is hardly surprising, therefore, that much of their humour is self-deprecatory, taking the form of joking denials of the legitimacy of their actions and discourse in the hospital wards: 'At the meetings, the junior members must show their seniors that they are good psychiatrists and good students, but these two roles are paradoxical – and the paradox may seek its solution in self-aggressive humor' (1960, p. 93). In making fun of themselves when reporting to their seniors, junior staff represent their professional discourse and actions as something that should not be taken entirely seriously. Thus it seems that the joke in the social structure to which junior members have to respond is normally resolved to their disadvantage in the sense that, at the meetings, their own humour operates to confirm their formal subordination.

In this respect, junior staff's humour converges with that of senior staff. Whereas senior staff are particularly likely to direct their humour at junior staff, the latter are strongly inclined to focus their humour on themselves. Although four out of every ten jokes by senior members deal with the actions of one or more juniors at the meeting, Coser reports that not once in twenty meetings 'was a senior staff member present a target of a junior member's humor' (1960, p. 85). Similarly the ancillary staff, who occupied the lowest formal status at the meetings and all of whom were women, virtually never joked. Their contribution to the operation of the humorous mode was to laugh enthusiastically in support of their seniors' witticisms (1960, p. 85).

In our examination of humour at the Nobel ceremonies, we saw that it was never employed to challenge the dominant social pattern. The same is clearly true of the departmental meetings studied by Coser. Indeed, she stresses that humour is no different from any other interpretative resource in this kind of hierarchically structured setting; that is, it is employed strictly in accordance with participants' location in the formal hierarchy. In so far as these meetings are typical of other hierarchical settings, it appears that humour is overwhelmingly directed down the hierarchy. (For a review of supporting evidence, see Wilson, 1979, chapter 12.) For not only do senior members focus their joking upon juniors, who in contrast tend to make fun of themselves or of outsiders, but senior staff are much more likely than their subordinates to make use of humour. 'Thus it would seem that not only the frequency with which humor occurs, but the direction which it takes, tends to meet the requirements of the authority structure. Humor tends to be directed against those who have no authority over the initiator' (Coser, 1960, p. 85).

In highly formalized ceremonial situations, the formality of the discourse ensures that humour is seldom, if ever, allowed to be disruptive. In somewhat less formal settings, the disruptive potential of humour may appear to be greater. For the interaction characteristic of such settings is more open-ended and involves a more variable pattern of discursive exchange. However, in situations where there is a formal hierarchy and where proceedings are guided by participants occupying positions of authority, it seems likely that humour will be employed routinely to support the authority structure, in a way which maintains the dominant social pattern. Humour will be steered towards what those in control regard as the proper concerns of the group, and will, on the whole, take the form of fairly standardized solutions to the recurrent interpretative problems generated by the structured discourse of the group.

In such hierarchically regulated situations, much of the humour that occurs can be said to be already available in the social structure, in the sense that participants seldom draw upon discourse external to the setting in order to create humorous incongruity. Humour is produced primarily out of ambiguities, contradictions and interpretative difficulties that occur regularly in the particular context. What we may call 'non-structural' humour, that is, humour that is not directly linked to the group's normal discourse, does take place occasionally in such settings, as Coser illustrates (1960, p. 88). But such playful departures from the customary concerns of the group are infrequent, and are available almost exclusively to those in positions of authority (1960, p. 86). In short, their exploitation is subject to control by those participants who are dominant within the serious domain. As Coser concludes: 'humor helps . . . to overcome the contradictions and ambiguities inherent in the complex social structure, and thereby to contribute to its maintenance' (1960, p. 95).

In the light of the discussion so far, we might infer that, in order to find humour which operates to challenge and confront the dominant patterns of social life, we need only turn to situations where social organization is much less formal and where participants are less subject to direct structural constraints. We might expect that, in such relatively unstructured settings, people are not only more humorously playful, but also more humorously critical and disruptive. In practice, it seems, this expectation is only partly fulfilled.

Humour in unstructured situations

In order to compare the social production of humour in ceremonial and hierarchically structured situations with the processes operating in less structured settings, let us return to Tannen's dinner party, with which we are already familiar from the discussion in chapter 4. One very obvious difference is that the rate of humorous production is so much higher at the dinner party. During this meal, the six participants uttered a total of 202 remarks that were taken by Tannen to be humorous or ironic (1984, p. 131). Her figures show that about 7 per cent of the total recorded utterances were recognizably humorous. We cannot conclude, of course, that all informal interaction involves such a high output of humour. A dinner party is likely to be exceptional in this respect. Nevertheless, the contrast with our two previous examples is dramatic. Moreover, it seems clear from Tannen's account that this high level of humorous production was made possible by the relative informality of the occasion. In other words, it was possible because there was no pre-established agenda, no formal pattern of interaction, and no specific, serious objective to be attained. Accordingly, participants were able to enter the humorous mode at will, in pursuit of any potential interpretative reversal that became available.

We have seen earlier in this chapter that the humour occurring in structured contexts tends to be applied: that is, it merges with the dominant patterns of serious discourse and contributes significantly to participants' serious interaction. In informal settings, such as Tannen's dinner party, there tends to be much more pure humour, which seems to be generated for its own sake and makes no direct contribution to serious interactional work. The pursuit of pure humour is more prominent in informal settings because there are few direct structural constraints on participants' discourse.

At the dinner party, the only two identifiable roles in operation seem to have been those of 'host' and 'guest'. The formal requirements of these roles are relatively vague within the social milieu of middle-class American society inhabited by Tannen and her friends. There is, therefore, much more room for individual variation in conduct in such a setting than there is at the Nobel ceremonies or at the hierarchically organized staff meetings. Nevertheless, even an informal dinner party requires a certain minimum of structured interaction and discourse. Here this residual social structure consists mainly of interchange between the host and his or her guests. As we would expect, some of the humour observed by Tannen appears to have grown out of this interchange and, in particular, out of interactional difficulties experienced by the host.

Tannen reports that the host, Steve, persistently adopted the humorous mode when he was speaking as host. For example, sometimes he 'ordered' his guests to do things in a 'clipped, tough guy manner' whilst at other times he assumed a mock Jewish accent and, in an obviously exaggerated fashion, displayed an abject concern to cater for their every need (Tannen, 1984, pp. 132–6). Tannen summarizes his behaviour: 'In addition to affecting exaggerated hosting style, Steve stylizes the bossiness that his host role entails' (1984, p. 133). It seems likely that this use of humour is linked to a basic contradiction in the pattern of discourse required of the host in such a setting. This contradiction resembles that experienced by the senior psychiatrists studied by Coser. For the host must maintain a minimal level of control over the conduct of his guests in accordance with his own conception of how the meal should proceed, whilst appearing not to dominate them but rather to be entirely responsive to *their* wishes. The contradiction facing the host is essentially that between dominance, or what Tannen calls 'bossiness', and subjection.

If we accept that this interactional problem is built into the structure of informal dinner parties, Steve's use of the humorous mode can be seen to provide a reasonably effective solution. For it enables him constantly to influence what his guests say and do during the dinner without seeming, seriously, to be interfering with their inclinations. By acting the role of 'host' in a humorous, and frequently self-mocking, fashion Steve can exercise a degree of control over his guests whilst appearing to be, or at least being able to claim to be, merely playing the fool and doing nothing serious at all. His complaints about the tape recorder and the bottle of salad dressing that were discussed in chapter 4 clearly illustrate this use of humour. On this occasion, at least one of the guests was not convinced by Steve's humorous 'performance' and maintained that Steve was really angry at the guests' refusal to comply with his wishes. Steve's use of the humorous mode, however, enabled him to insist that he was 'just picking up on a fleeting impression he got and exaggerating it for comic effect' (see pp. 69–71). Whatever Steve's motives, it is clear from Tannen's text that his regular use of humour during the dinner party made it possible for him to direct the proceedings more than any other participant, yet to do so in a way which fostered amusement and which was accepted, on the whole, as an expression of good fellowship (Tannen, 1984, pp. 132–6).

It is clear, then, that some of the humour occurring at Tannen's dinner party was structurally generated; that is, it arose out of attempts to deal with contradictions that are implicit in the patterns of discourse required on such occasions. Although the solutions devised by Steve were undoubtedly idiosyncratic in certain respects, they originated in an interpretative difficulty that is structural in the sense that it is present in the basic forms of discourse routinely adopted by participants at informal dinner parties of this kind. However, it is important to note that the great majority of humorous utterances produced during the dinner party appear to have been unrelated to this structural feature or to any formal requirements of the specific situation. The guests, in particular, appear to have been relatively free of formal constraints and of structural contradictions. As a result, because neither the form nor the content of their discourse were prescribed in advance, they were able to create a great deal of diverse humour out of the vagaries of unstructured personal interaction.

This relative lack of formal constraints in unstructured situations means that participants can draw freely upon standardized comic resources. It also means that humour can become more inventive, fantastic, and – as we all know – on some occasions, 'plain silly'. We have already examined 'the Pope's nose', 'smoking after sex', and the spontaneous joke about the absence of misunderstandings, which illustrate how participants at the dinner party were able to engage in various forms of pure humour (see chapter 4). Humour of this kind appears to have no serious interactional consequences nor to grow out of patterns of discourse required by the occasion. To take another example provided by Tannen, at one point in the dinner party David spoke about a fictitious organization that he and his friends had invented, called NORCLOD (Northern California Lovers of the Deaf). This fantasy generated much amusement, and the humorous possibilities initiated by David were taken up and elaborated by other guests, as in the following fragment:

David: u:m . . . and . . . um the way we were gonna have the uh the officers of the organization the higher up you go . . . the more hearing people there would be and then the . . . the . . . the: chairperson of the organization was gonna be a hearing person.
Deborah: That didn't know sign language.
David: That didn't . . . Yeah. That didn't know sign language.
          (*laughter*)

(Tannen, 1984, p. 137)

Most of the humour at the dinner party was of this kind; that is, it was unconnected with any specific patterns of discourse required of participants as host or guest. It makes no sense to treat such humorous make-believe as a response to contradictions in the social structure.

If Tannen's dinner party is representative of other relatively unstructured contexts, we can conclude that the less structured the social situation, the less frequently will humour be generated by jokes in the social structure. Formulated in this way, my conclusion may appear self-evident. For it seems obvious that, where social structure is at a minimum, there will be few or no structural jokes present to set humour in motion. However, this idea that humour varies inversely with the degree of structural formality was not obvious to Douglas, nor to other social analysts of humour. It has, perhaps, only come to appear self-evident as a result of the detailed comparison of specific cases that has been presented in this chapter. Moreover, we have also observed that the level of humorous production may be much higher in unstructured settings. If this is generally the case, and if levels of humorous output are lower in formally structured contexts, it follows that Douglas's concentration on social structure as the source of humour was rather misleading. For it seems likely that much, perhaps most, non-professional humour will be generated in circumstances where structural constraints are weak and indirect. (Professional humour will be considered in the next chapter.)

Douglas maintained that the 'one social condition necessary for a joke to be enjoyed is that the social group in which it is received should develop the formal characteristics of a 'told' joke . . . If there is no joke in the social structure, no other joking can appear' (1975, p. 98). This claim does seem to apply to formally structured groupings. But in those relatively unstructured settings where humour occurs much more frequently and where the humorous mode is much more prominent, structural factors appear to be less relevant. In such settings, humour is not only too frequent, but also too variable, idiosyncratic, wide-ranging, and sometimes too fantastical, to be explained solely by reference to structural contradictions. Thus, it was only when we came to examine the informal setting of Tannen's dinner party that a wide range of humorous forms, varying from standardized jokes to witty remarks and extended humorous fictions, began to appear. Highly structured situations restrict and confine humour, both in scope and quantity. Humour blossoms, it seems, when the course of social interaction is neither prescribed by convention nor regulated from above. I suggest, therefore, that most informal humour has its origin, not in structurally pre-established contradictions, but in creative interpretative work that is possible in situations where participants are relatively free from structural constraint.

Humour and structural critique

One important implication of Douglas's original idea about humour and social structure was that humour would necessarily tend to challenge and disrupt the dominant patterns of social life. We have not found this to be so in the case of humour in structured situations. It seems that when humour is located within a context of formal interaction, participants' inclination and ability to employ it in a disruptive manner is severely limited. We might expect, therefore, that humour produced in unstructured contexts, in the course of unregulated interaction, would tend to be more critical of the dominant patterns of social life. This may well be so under certain circumstances. There can be no doubt, for example, that when presidents run into trouble or when prime ministers become unpopular, there is often a surge of informal humour in which the offending parties are ridiculed mercilessly. But on the whole, I suggest, the humour that is produced in unstructured situations is predominantly mild and playful rather than critical and subversive. Let me substantiate this claim.

There is one particular form of humour that is produced in a situation where the direct impact of social relationships is at an absolute minimum – namely, that of humorous graffiti. Many, perhaps most, graffiti are produced by individuals acting in isolation or, at least, in very small groups. This is obviously so of those found in toilets (Bruner and Kelso, 1980), but is probably also the case with other kinds of graffiti. On this assumption, we can take graffiti to represent a form of humour that occurs in a context where producers, and indeed recipients, are not directly involved in a social structure.

Graffiti are, by their very nature, widely dispersed geographically and, for that reason, rather difficult to collect. On the other hand, they are written down in public or semi-public settings and are potentially available for collection. Fortunately, since 1979 Nigel Rees has amassed and published five collections of graffiti (so far) from around the world, but particularly from English-speaking countries (Rees, 1979, 1980, 1981, 1983, 1986). These volumes contain over six hundred pages of humorous material. I do not intend to offer a detailed analysis of this mass of data, but rather, to make one major point based on a careful examination of these items: namely, that there are remarkably few which seem to express any significant challenge to the dominant forms of social life. The vast majority seem to me to resemble closely the kind of playful creation of incongruity that pervaded Tannen's dinner party. The following examples are, in this respect, typical:

1 Give masochists a fair crack of the whip. (Rees, 1979)
2 Keep incest in the family. (Rees, 1980)
3 To do is to be – Rousseau.
  To be is to do – Sartre.
  Dobedobedo – Sinatra. (Rees, 1979)

These humorous quips differ from ordinary informal humour in being more epigrammatic and self-contained. But they resemble such humour in that they create a playfully humorous reversal of meanings out of commonly available cultural resources. I describe them as 'playful' because, in my view, it requires a wilfully perverse reading of these texts to interpret numbers 1 and 2 as genuinely endorsing masochism and incest respectively, or number 3 as proposing any kind of serious point. It is, in fact, remarkably difficult to discover graffiti in Rees's wide collection that seem to express a powerful rejection of society or of any of its major institutions. The three following examples seem to me to be as socially relevant as one can find:

4 Don't vote. The government will get in. (Rees, 1979)
5 Military intelligence is a contradiction in terms. (Rees, 1979)
6 Keep Britain tidy – kill a tourist. (Rees, 1979)

These items could be taken to convey a more serious message than the previous examples and to contain a more effective challenge to government, the military and tourism. It might well be that number 6 in particular, because it is both clever and unexpected, could briefly shock an unsuspecting tourist or bring a grim smile of satisfaction to the lips of long-suffering natives of one of Britain's cathedral towns. But do such humorous formulations amount to a challenge to or a confrontation with the established patterns of social life? I suggest that they do not, and cannot, for the following reasons.

In the first place, any serious message implicit within a humorous graffito is bound to remain uncertain as a result of the interpretative duality of the humorous mode. Self-contained humorous statements are inherently ambiguous. They play with meanings, and with the boundary between reality and unreality. Isolated fragments of humour, such as graffiti, can be made clearly relevant to structural issues only if they can be placed within a serious social context. But, for the great majority of graffiti, this is made impossible by the very nature of their production – that is, by their removal from any discernible context of social interaction. The separation of humour from any specific social location removes the interpretative context without which humour cannot be given serious meaning and cannot be used to exert an effective challenge to dominant social patterns. Any serious intent or import that may lie behind an ordinary graffito is heavily obscured by the anonymity of the speaker, the fragmentary nature of the discourse and the lack of a context within which to give it meaning. Unless we know who is speaking and why, and unless we can locate an utterance in some wider framework of discourse, the humorous epigram is doomed to remain inert except as a source of fleeting amusement.

It follows from this line of argument that graffiti will acquire serious significance only in so far as they can be linked, despite their anonymity, to specific social categories and to social confrontations that are operative in the realm of serious action. It is for this reason, I suggest, that anti- German graffiti were washed from the walls by the occupying troops after the invasion of Czechoslovakia at the start of the Second World War (Obrdlik, 1942). Similarly, it is for this reason that feminist graffiti have become distinctly more influential in recent years than other items in this genre. Their challenge to the existing structure of social relations has become recognized as such because they have been incorporated into a wider programme of critical discourse and organized action. There is, for example, the by now famous graffito added to an advertisement for a well known make of car:

> 7 If this car was a lady it would get its bottom pinched.
> *If this lady was a car she would run him down!*

It is not that this clever semantic reversal has an obvious and inherent serious message. Viewed as an isolated fragment of discourse, as are most graffiti, it is potentially amusing, but it need not necessarily be taken as a genuine expression of resentment about the relationships between women and men in our society. However, the visual version of this item has been reproduced in large numbers as a postcard and widely distributed by those with feminist commitments. It has also been included in a book entitled *Off the Wall: A Collection of Feminist Graffiti* (Bartlett, 1982). In this latter context we know that this graffito, and the others in the collection, are to be given a feminist, that is, a serious, interpretation as well as a humorous one. No longer are we dealing with an isolated, anonymous, possibly merely playful, comment. We are back in the world of structured social relationships. We are being addressed by a representative of an identifiable social category. The provision of this context has made it clear that these graffiti are being used to display, from a variety of perspectives, one of the most fundamental 'jokes' in the social structure of our society:

> 8 Every mother is a working mother.
> 9 Mummy, mummy, what's an orgasm?
> I dunno, ask your father.
> 10 Behind every great woman there's a man – who tried to stop her.
> 11 When God created man she was only experimenting.
> 12 To be successful at anything a woman has to be twice as good as a man
> . . . luckily this is not difficult. (Bartlett, 1982)

The cumulative impact of this discourse is unequivocal. Its underlying serious message offers a clear challenge to one of the dominant patterns of our social world. However, this challenge has been made effective, not by leaving these unconnected speakers to operate alone beyond the margin of organized social life, but by bringing them together to speak as a collective female voice and by linking that voice's humour to the serious struggle of the women's movement within the established social structure.

One conclusion to emerge from this chapter is that much humour is directly linked to the social structure; but that even more is not. The humour that occurs in formal structures is closely linked to their inherent contradictions. Overwhelmingly, however, this humour is employed in accordance with the requirements of the existing system, and in a way which supports that system. The lack of formal restraint that is characteristic of unstructured situations allows participants to be humorous more frequently and to be more humorously imaginative and fanciful. But this interpretative freedom in informal settings does not enable participants to use their humour to confront and contradict the dominant structure more effectively. For the less structured the social situation in which humour occurs, the more ambiguous does its message become and the more uncertain its interpretation. In completely unstructured situations, the only unambiguous characteristic of humorous discourse is that it is not part of the serious domain. Thus humour can be used effectively to perform serious work only within reasonably well defined social contexts. However, within such contexts, humour normally comes to be used to conserve the dominant pattern of social relationships. Humour *can* be used to challenge the existing pattern, as we saw in the case of the women's movement – but only when it is given meaning in relation to criticism and confrontation that is already under way within the serious realm. It is yet another 'paradox of the humorous mode' that, although semantically humour involves confrontation with and subversion of a dominant pattern, it is used most effectively for serious purposes mainly in structured situations where it works to maintain that pattern.

10

The Mass Production of Humour

In chapter 9, I concentrated on the structural origins and social consequences of humour in situations where producers and recipients are in direct contact. Such situations are critical to an understanding of humour as a social phenomenon. Even in the large, amorphous societies in which we live today, a substantial proportion of humorous discourse is produced in contexts of this kind. However, we cannot ignore the fact that humour, like many other cultural products, is now in considerable measure mass produced and distributed to mass audiences. In other words, a great deal of present-day humour is created by professional humorists who are employed, wholly or in part, by the media of mass communication and whose contact with the consumers of their products is often rather indirect.

The mass production of humour takes a slightly different form from the mass production of consumer goods. In the latter case, each item is more or less interchangeable. Each refrigerator, say, of a given make and model is taken to be the same, for practical purposes, as any other. The professed aim of the manufacturer is to make all his refrigerators work equally well and in an identical fashion. In contrast, each item of mass humour has to be recognizably unique. Today's cartoon must be different from yesterday's; this week's episode of a situation comedy must be distinct from the one televised last week; this year's comic film must not employ the same plot as the one distributed a year ago. In this respect, mass humour resembles humour exchanged in face-to-face situations. However, the producer of mass humour, unlike the informal raconteur, cannot ask each new recipient, 'Have you heard the one about . . .?' He has to assume that his public is relatively constant and that at each performance he must devise something fresh and original.

The 'mass production' of humour, it appears, takes the rather odd form of the regular production of unique cultural items. It might seem, therefore, that 'mass production' is a misleading term, and that 'mass communication' or 'mass distribution' would be more suitable. These phrases are certainly applicable. If we define 'mass communication' as a situation where individual persons, or small groups, pass their cultural products by some indirect means to a much larger audience, it is clear that a great deal of humour in modern societies is part of the world of mass communication (Gruner, 1976). But such terms are not entirely satisfactory. For they fail to capture the fact that, despite the essential requirement of humorous uniqueness, there is a pronounced element of repetition in the production of humour for a mass audience. Although the surface features of each joke, each cartoon, each TV series, are distinctive, the underlying formulae of humorous production change more slowly. Each comedian, cartoonist and sitcom writer develops recipes for generating humour in which repeated use is made of a restricted range of techniques, themes and semantic scripts. In addition, the variation amongst producers of a given kind of product at a particular point in time is quite limited. For instance, although no two television sitcoms will have identical characters or exactly the same story line, they will often be remarkably alike in their basic form and in many aspects of their presentation. In these respects, the mass production of humour closely resembles the mass production of consumer goods (Golding and Murdock, 1977). In both cases, there is organized production for an anonymous aggregate of consumers of a range of products which vary in stylistic detail, but which are strikingly similar in overall conception and design. The mass production of humour in technically advanced societies is too complex a topic to be investigated fully in this book. The discussion which follows, therefore, is intended to be no more than illustrative. I will focus on two contrasting forms of mass produced humour. In chapter 11 I will deal with the political cartoon, as it occurs in newspapers and satirical magazines. In this chapter, I will examine the televised sitcom series. I will explore in particular how far these types of mass humour operate to subvert or to conserve the patterns of serious belief and conduct to be found in the wider society.

Humour as a commodity

Humour and comedy are officially identified in Britain as essential constituents of any 'balanced' television service. In the reports of the various television agencies, however, there is no formal distinction between serious and humorous output. Programmes with a high level of humour are usually treated as part of 'light entertainment', which is assumed to appeal to a large-scale audience whose members need periodic relief from their own serious activities and from the more demanding discourse of serious television programmes (for example, *Independent*

Broadcasting Authority Annual Report, 1983–4, pp. 18–19). As Barry Curtis puts it in his discussion of television comedy: 'Entertainment as a rationale for television implies an alternative to work, education, seriousness' (1982, p. 11). The amount of time assigned to 'light entertainment' varies from one channel to another, but is consistently below 15 per cent of total output in Britain and has remained at much the same level for the last decade or so (see Williams, 1974; *British Broadcasting Corporation Handbook*, 1980). 'Humour programmes' are a sub-section within light entertainment. My own estimate of the proportion of time devoted to such programmes on British television, based on the published details of all television programmes for one week in January 1987, is about 8 per cent.

This figure is, of course, extremely crude and is undoubtedly an underestimate of the total proportion of humour on television. A much more refined measurement is provided in Joanne Cantor's careful and systematic study of the frequencey of humour on American television (Cantor, 1976). She and her colleagues viewed and examined in detail all programmes broadcast during one week by the three commercial network affiliates and the Public Broadcasting Service affiliate station in Madison, Wisconsin. (The study does not state when the observations were made, but the manuscript was accepted for publication in October 1975.) Her aim was to identify every item in every broadcast during that week which seemed to be 'designed to elicit a humorous response in the audience' (1976, p. 502). She found that 81 per cent of the 310 programmes studied contained at least one attempt at humour. In this minimal sense, humour is widespread on television. Even programmes with a markedly serious focus, such as news-information (70 per cent) and drama (80 per cent), were very likely to include at least one brief transition into the humorous mode. Nevertheless, it appears that, if Cantor's findings are generally representative, television discourse is overwhelmingly serious. For her study showed that in only 9 per cent of television time were contributors trying to be funny and that 'more than 90 per cent of programming time was non-humorous' (1976, p. 506). In six out of ten programme categories, the percentage of time devoted to humorous utterances was well below 10 per cent; and only in variety programmes (19 per cent of time), children's programmes (23 per cent) and situation comedies (34 per cent) was a substantial portion of the discourse clearly identifiable by Cantor's coders as being intended as humorous.

Cantor's study suggests that the overall contribution of humour to television output is quite modest. However, like my figure of 8 per cent, her 9 per cent of programme time could also be regarded as an underestimate. For instance, she excludes from the category 'humour' much of the material in sitcoms, despite the fact that these programmes are clearly signalled and framed in their entirety as non-serious. But even if we compensate for this possible underestimate by reallocating *all* the time occupied by sitcoms in Cantor's data to the category 'humour', the total percentage of television time directly involving humour rises no higher than 13 per cent. Broadly speaking, therefore, we can conclude that the amount of television programming devoted to humour is likely to be, roughly, between 9 and 13 per cent; that the balance between humour and serious discourse on British and American television seems to be quite similar; and that, although isolated humorous items do occur across the full range of programme types, television humour tends to be concentrated within specific kinds of 'light entertainment' programme such as variety shows and situation comedies, which are treated officially as providing temporary relief from the rigours of the serious world.

The basic structure of the sitcom

Television humour includes cartoons, the comedy of the variety routine, the repartee of the quiz show, and so on. But these kinds of humour also occur elsewhere. The distinctive contribution made by television to humorous form is the creation of the situation comedy (Lovell, 1986) out of the vaudeville sketch. This evolution took place on American television during the 1950s (Eaton, 1981). In the early days, the basic 'situation' used to generate humorous dialogue was built around the social relationships of domestic life, as in 'The Burns and Allen Show', transmitted by CBS. But since then, although the family and the small work group have continued to be the primary locations, the range of specific settings employed in sitcom has expanded enormously, as producers have striven to meet the demand for humorous uniqueness. For example, sitcoms have been set in such varied, and sometimes unlikely, situations as a military medical team ('MASH'), an American bar ('Cheers'), space travel ('Come Back, Mrs. Noah'), life in prison ('Porridge'), the British 'Home Guard' during the Second World War ('Dad's Army'), and so on.

Although the content of television sitcoms has ranged far and wide, the basic structure has changed very little over the years. One reason for this is that the sitcom is designed for, and restricted by, the commodity production line of television broadcasting. Sitcom can be defined 'as a comic narrative in series format' (Lovell, 1986, p. 152). Television requires humour in the form of series partly because of the bureaucratic character of the process of TV production. Personnel, scripts, physical locations, production teams, all have to be organized in advance in order to produce relatively brief transmissions. There is, as a result, a strong pressure towards limiting the range of variation wherever possible. The repeated use of the same comic figures in the same setting is one effective way of reducing the problems of bureaucratic coordination in such a situation (Alvarado and Buscombe, 1978). In addition, the organizations concerned, whether publicly or commercially financed, are locked into a struggle for the mass audience. In order to capture and retain this audience, it is assumed, television output has to be standardized and reproducible so that recipients know what goods are being offered and can make their programme choices, and their long-term viewing commitments, accordingly.

> The process of scheduling generates a uniformity which also favours the series/serial format. The schedule creates a grid of programme slots, or units of time, classified according to the size and composition of the audience who will be watching at that time. These pre-given slots must be filled with material deemed suitable to that audience and that time of day. (Lovell, 1986, p. 150)

The sitcom, then, is a means of packaging humour which is suited to, and is used by all the major participants in, the battle of the television ratings. A successful sitcom recipe guarantees its originators a large and predictable section of the mass audience for the duration of the series (Eaton, 1981). It is sometimes argued that sitcom is no more than a way of packaging other routine forms of humour; in other words, that sitcoms 'can be reduced to a series of jokes, gags, etc., strung out along a facilitating narrative which is not in itself funny' (Lovell, 1986, p. 153). But this view is, I think, mistaken. In the first place, sitcoms, like standardized jokes, are clearly signalled as comic narratives – often by the nature of the graphics and the introductory music, but also by the regular insertion of tape-recorded laughter (Lovell, 1986, p. 154). The viewers of sitcom are reminded every few seconds by the hilarity of the unseen studio audience that they should be amused by the happenings on their screens. This repeated cueing operates as an instruction to recipients to search for humorous interpretations of the evolving text.

Equally important to the humorous character of the sitcom is the nature of the basic 'situation' out of which all action is generated throughout the series. Some analysts have maintained that the generative situations employed in sitcom are very general, and that they could therefore just as easily be used as the basis for serious narratives. 'The situations of sitcom are usually defined quite broadly, and are rarely in themselves inherently funny. Consider some of the more famous sitcom situations: imprisonment, marriage, family life, shopwork, the Home Guard. All of these might serve just as readily to generate melodrama, adventure, or some other non-comic fictional form' (Lovell, 1986, p. 154).

The problem with this argument is that it remains plausible only as long as we accept the analyst's vague references to 'imprisonment, shopwork and family life' as providing satisfactory definitions of the 'situations' of sitcom. It seems to me, however, that these supposed definitions are irrelevant to the process of textual construction required in the production of specific television programmes. It is quite misleading, I suggest, to propose that the 'situation' which provides the thematic continuity of, say, 'The Burns and Allen Show', is 'marriage' or 'family life' in some generic sense. The events, and the comedy, of this show arise not out of such generalities, but out of the particular forms of contradictory or incongruous discourse which are characteristic of the main figures in the narrative. As Mick Eaton puts it, the heart of 'The Burns and Allen Show' is that 'George is . . . dry, wise-cracking and laconic, and Gracie is the woman with a logic of her own, causing confusion (and comedy) by the misunderstanding generated by the lack of that logic's intersection with the other characters in the drama' (1981, p. 29).

It is, of course, true that the conduct of Gracie and George is linked to stereotypes of women and men, wives and husbands, that are widely available in our culture. To that extent, their comedy is acceptable to its audience as a recognizable version of 'family life'. But the family life of 'The Burns and Allen Show' is organized in a very specific way; and it is this specific structure, involving the conjunction of humorously signalled and contradictory perspectives in relation to a series of shared events, that constitutes the 'situation' out of which humour, rather than melodrama or tragedy, is necessarily generated.

I suggest, then, that the sitcom is a distinct form of visual narrative which is recognizably humorous, not simply because it is signalled as such or because it contains specific humorous exchanges, but because it consists of a series of separate, but related, episodes, each of which is generated out of the same basic 'root joke' (or, occasionally, a small set of interconnected jokes). The phrase 'root joke' is taken from Nash's analysis of extended written texts (1985, p. 68), but it is just as applicable to the linked episodes of a sitcom series. A text can be said to have a root joke when it is organized in a way which continually combines the same two (or more) incompatible discourses within a textual framework that is marked as humorous. It is this kind of combination of specific, contradictory discourses that provides the situation or generative context for every television sitcom. There is, therefore, a close parallel between the root jokes of situation comedy and the structural jokes characteristic of certain social situations. However, any television representation will necessarily involve the exaggeration and simplification essential to humorous discourse. Thus the basic recipe for creating a sitcom is always the same: Take two (a few) stereotyped characters whose views/interests/inclinations are discordant; place them in a context of interaction from which they cannot escape; set in motion a course of events which leads them to formulate interpretations which clash, but without serious consequences; vary the action from one episode to another, but maintain the setting and the underlying patterns of conduct; provide clear and repeated signals of humorous intent; and arrange each episode in the form of a prolonged joke sequence with an 'unexpected' semantic reversal at the end (see British Film Institute, 1982 for supporting evidence).

It follows from the basic structure of the sitcom that the main characters in any series 'are somehow stuck with each other' (Eaton, 1981, p. 37). If any of them were to escape, or even significantly to alter his or her typical discourse, the operation of the root joke would be put in jeopardy. Small changes can and do occur within the social relationships involved in specific sitcoms. For each episode has to contain a series of events in the course of which things happen: and, sometimes, an overall story line can unfold throughout a series. But these developments can never be allowed to disturb the series' basic generative mechanisms. Gracie, for example, can never come to speak and act like George – at least, not for any prolonged period. To create a situation involving two dry, sardonic commentators might be briefly amusing in ˙contrast to the normal dynamics of 'The Burns and Allen Show'. But to maintain such a unified discourse would be to remove the basis for the contradictions and incongruities on which that show depends. Without the opposition between Gracie's enthusiastic 'illogicality' and George's detached 'wit', there would be no confusion and no divergent perspectives on a sequence of events experienced in common. In short, without the two (or more) opposing discourses, the interpretative duality required by humour would be lacking.

The sitcom is a remarkably flexible form, in that it has been possible to apply its basic formula to a wide variety of social locations. Within any particular sitcom series, however, it is a rigid and static textual form. Each series must operate so that 'its basic parameters can be taken up without change, without narrative progress from week to week' (Eaton, 1981, p. 33). Within the constraints of the sitcom, it is never possible to evolve any effective reconciliation of the opposing discourses which it employs. Participants with discrepant views are allowed, indeed they are required, to coexist; but they can neither resolve their differences nor learn to speak with a common voice. In this sense, the very form of the sitcom can be said to be inherently conservative. It is conservative in that it takes over existing social differences, embodies them in specific, unchanging characters, and makes them seem amusing and enjoyable. In 'The Burns and Allen Show', for example, the crazy illogicality of Gracie is closely bound up with her being a woman; it grows out of and is associated with her involvement in female activities. At the same time, George's cool, detached amusement is yet another expression of the masculine assumption that 'women are like that.' Other television sitcoms operate in a similar fashion. Collectively, they display the discrepant discourses of various kinds of supposedly typical social actors. But they do this in a way which exaggerates these differences, prevents any textual resolution and makes them appear to exist in an eternal present (Eaton, 1981, p. 34).

We have seen in chapters 4 and 5 that humour can be used, in the course of certain kinds of informal interaction, as a protective device which makes it easier for participants to address difficult topics and indirectly to correct or condemn others' statements and actions. It may well be that the mass produced humour of television is sometimes used in an analogous fashion to criticize and, implicitly, to challenge established patterns of conduct in the wider society. But our observations so far concerning the humour of the sitcom – that is, the humour of the one distinctive comic form to be employed in television broadcasting – suggest that this is likely to be the exception. For much television humour depends on the constant repetition of the same underlying joke and on the repeated representation of the same unchanging stereotypes. This structural tendency towards social conservation rather than critique may well be strengthened by the reluctance of mass producers, in a competitive situation, to run the risk of alienating their audience by suggesting that its members' perspectives on the world might be in error. If this is so, it seems likely that much television output, and especially its 'light entertainment' will be designed to express and confirm those social presuppositions which are most widespread and most firmly entrenched within the population at large (Golding and Murdock, 1977).

However, it may be that the analysis so far has been simplistic in failing to recognize that several different kinds of narrative structure are employed within the overall sitcom genre; and that different types of sitcom may have different potentials as vehicles for social critique. For example, Lovell (1986) makes a useful distinction between naturalistic (or realistic) and non-naturalistic sitcom narratives. Naturalistic sitcoms are those which 'obey the conventions of social realism' (Lovell, 1986, p. 155; see Cook, 1982, p. 16). They create fictional worlds in such a way that their audience can accept that the events of that world can happen in reality. In naturalistic sitcoms, comedy is portrayed as a natural outcome of typical patterns of conduct in situations which can and do actually occur. At the other end of the spectrum, in non-naturalistic sitcoms, utterly implausible events are allowed to happen and sometimes to dominate the text. For instance, in one episode of 'The Young Ones', Buddy Holly is found alive and hanging from a bedroom ceiling, a genie is inadvertently produced when one of the characters rubs the kettle, and various household utensils in a cupboard under the stairs converse together in mocking parody of a popular television soap opera called 'Upstairs Downstairs'.

The range of comic potential is much greater in non-naturalistic sitcoms, where utterly implausible happenings can be woven around the more realistic interplay of the main characters in the series. But, Lovell argues, the possibility of using the freedom of non-naturalistic representation to mount an effective critique of the wider society is greatly limited by that very departure from the constraints of realism. For the obviously fictional components of non-naturalistic sitcoms encourage the audience to treat the overall product as having little or no relevance to the serious realm. As Lovell says, 'Paradoxically, unless the audience can be brought to see the relevance to politics and social reality of non-realistic forms, they will remain innocuous. And where they succeed in doing this, they will no longer retain the privileges of comic licence' (1986, p. 165).

In contrast, Lovell maintains, more realistic sitcoms, because they are taken to represent the real social world in which the members of the audience live, can have a more critical edge. But they do not necessarily do so. On the one hand, by exposing the inconsistencies and contradictions of the social world to laughter, naturalistic sitcom narrative may enable its audience to see flaws and inadequacies which would not otherwise have been so clearly visible. In this way, television sitcom may have a subverting influence and may provide an impetus towards social change. On the other hand, Lovell suggests, realistic sitcom may strengthen recipients' sense that the existing social order, with all its problems, failures and incongruities, is more or less inevitable. If this is so, even realistic sitcom will be more likely to encourage amused detachment than serious concern (Lovell, 1986, p. 165).

In order to explore which of these rather different outcomes seems the more probable, let us examine a highly popular naturalistic sitcom which has been widely credited with using the resources of comedy to reveal damaging truths about the inefficiency of the state apparatus and about the hypocrisy of political actors in a democracy.

Sitcom politics

'Yes Minister' is a British sitcom which was first shown on BBC television in 1980. In the course of the next few years, twenty-one episodes were transmitted. In 1983, 'Yes Minister' became the first programme ever to win the British Academy award for best comedy series in three consecutive years. The series was eventually discontinued, but only to be reborn without alteration to the basic formula, as 'Yes Prime Minister'. At the time of writing, the latter series is still running and still popular.

'Yes Minister' has clearly been one of the most successful sitcoms ever produced in Britain. Moreover, it may appear to disprove those who have argued that mass popularity can be achieved only by appealing to the lowest common denominator of public taste and by pandering to the prejudices and basic presuppositions of the mass audience (see Golding and Murdock, 1977; Alvarado and Buscombe, 1978; Lovell, 1986). It may also appear to show unambiguously that sitcom can have a critical, and potentially subverting, impact on the area of social life with which it deals. For 'Yes Minister' has received particular acclaim because it is said to combine sophisticated humour with a damaging exposé of some of the fundamental deficiencies of the British political system (Oakley, 1982; Lynn and Jay, 1984). Thus the humorous text of 'Yes Minister' is depicted as conveying serious information of a novel and challenging kind. It is described as 'a satire on the way the country is run', as 'an eye-opener', as providing 'accurate observation of detail and penetrating insight into political and bureaucratic motivations', as 'a great deal nearer the truth than the official myth', and even as, somewhat paradoxically, 'fantastically true to life' (Oakley, 1982, p. 69). In short, this series seems to be a prime example of naturalistic sitcom being used to deliver to the general public a serious critique of existing political practice.

If we were to accept this picture, we would have to conclude that television sitcom can and does contribute to, and perhaps lead to changes in, the socially important domain of political action. But before we jump to such a hasty conclusion, we must look a little more closely at the structure and content of 'Yes Minister'. In addition, as Giles Oakley emphasizes in his examination of this sitcom, if we are to understand its social impact we 'need to see how the series fits into wider patterns of cultural and especially political life' (1982, p. 67), in order to observe how the humour draws upon and is created out of available cultural resources. Only when this has been done with some care can we judge whether 'Yes Minister' is more likely to conserve or to subvert existing social patterns. In the discussion which follows, I will draw heavily on Oakley's (1982) detailed study. Furthermore, I have at my disposal the scripts of the twenty-one episodes of 'Yes Minister' which have been revised and published in the form of a 'political diary' (Lynn and Jay, 1984). This text is particularly helpful because, in transferring 'Yes Minister' from the screen to the printed page, the authors have been led to describe explicitly much that was left implicit in the television presentation or that was conveyed indirectly through the mannerisms, phrasing and deportment of the actors.

The first episode of 'Yes Minister' takes place at a time when a new government has just been elected to office. Jim Hacker, a career politician, is appointed as Minister for Administrative Affairs. Lynn and Jay write:

> Theoretically [this appointment] gave Hacker a roving brief, to investigate and control administrative inefficiency and overspending throughout the system of state administration, wherever it was to be found. Unfortunately the Department of Administrative Affairs was not only created to control the Civil Service [i.e., the body of permanent state administrators], it also had to be staffed by the Civil Service. Readers will therefore be well aware of the inevitable result of Hacker's labours. (1984, p. 9)

The implication is that, as a result of his dependence on the Civil Service, Hacker's labours will have no result at all.

The central relationship in 'Yes Minister', which generates a large proportion of the humour (Klika, 1982), is that between Hacker, the politician and formal head of the ministry, and Sir Humphrey Appleby, his Permanent Secretary and *de facto* controller of the ministry's operations. In Oakley's words: 'The series is in the classic situation comedy mould of two people locked into a perpetually adversarial relationship.' (1982, p. 66). The root joke of the series centres on the fact that Hacker, the politician, is officially the boss and that nobody ever openly challenges his formal authority. However, he is utterly dependent for information and for the implementation of his decisions on precisely those administrators, or civil servants, over whom he is trying to exercise control.

In almost every episode, Hacker is covertly manipulated by his more skilled and more knowledgeable subordinates, and particularly by Sir Humphrey, in such a way that, without understanding how it has happened, he fails to put his intentions into effect or to bring about any change in the existing system. Typically, each episode ends with Sir Humphrey appearing to agree with, and to acknowledge the authority of, his political superior. However, for the audience, whose members are more fully aware than Hacker of the course of events, Sir Humphrey's 'Yes Minister' is subject to a humorous reversal. In other words, the root joke around which the series is built is that 'Yes Minister' really means 'No Minister' (Oakley, 1982, p. 67).

Let me briefly illustrate how the root joke works in practice. In the first episode Hacker takes over his new office at the ministry, where he encounters Sir Humphrey and another civil servant, Bernard Woolley, who is the Minister's personal assistant. The following account is given in Hacker's supposed diary:

> I decided to take charge at once. I sat behind my desk and to my

dismay I found that it had a swivel chair. I don't like swivel chairs. But Bernard immediately assured me that everything in the office can be changed at my command – furniture, decor, paintings, office routine. I am unquestionably the boss. (Lynn and Jay, 1984, p. 15)

In this passage, the politician's wish to take control is clearly depicted. But his apparent success is immediately deconstructed by the less senior of the two civil servants.

Bernard then told me that they have two types of chair in stock, to go with two kinds of Minister – 'One sort folds up instantly and the other sort goes round and round in circles.' (Lynn and Jay, 1984, p. 15)

Hacker is unsure whether this remark is innocent or whether it is intended to make him look silly. This is typical of the politician's failure to understand the discourse of his subordinates – a failure that recurs throughout the whole series. His response is also typical: that is, he attempts to exert his authority. In this case, he does so by bluntly declaring his intention to cut through the red tape of government administration and to streamline the 'creaking old bureaucratic machine'. In the rest of this episode Hacker strives with growing desperation and eventual panic to put this policy of more open and more efficient administration into effect. But he is foiled by Sir Humphrey, whose overriding concern is to maintain the existing pattern of government administration and to prevent any erosion of his own long-established position of practical domination. As events unfold, it becomes clear that Sir Humphrey's ability to win the struggle for control arises in part from Hacker's inexperience and stupidity, in part from his selfishness and hypocrisy, but most of all from the fact that two forms of political discourse are at work and that Sir Humphrey, but not Jim Hacker, is fully conversant with them both.

For example, when Hacker and Sir Humphrey are first introduced, Bernard Woolley reminds them that they met once before when Hacker was a member of the opposition party. Hacker describes the event in his 'diary' as follows:

Sir Humphrey said, 'Yes, we did cross swords when the Minister gave me a grilling over the Estimates in the Public Accounts Committee last year. He asked me all the questions I hoped nobody would ask.' This is splendid. Sir Humphrey clearly admires me. I tried to brush it off. 'Well,' I said, 'Opposition's about asking awkward questions.' 'Yes,' said Sir Humphrey, 'and government is about not answering them.' I was surprised. 'But you answered all my questions, didn't you?' I commented. 'I'm glad you *thought* so,

Minister,' said Sir Humphrey. I didn't quite know what he meant by that. (Lynn and Jay, 1984, p. 14; my italics)

This very first exchange between the two main characters in the series immediately displays the basis of the administrator's power as well as exemplifying the series' root joke. For in this passage the clash between the politician's and the administrator's frames of reference, on which 'Yes Minister' depends, is made evident to the viewer; and, at the same time, the administrator's greater awareness of this clash and his ability to employ that awareness for his own purposes is implied and used allusively to generate humour. In other words, in order to interpret 'I'm glad you *thought* so, Minister' as amusing, the viewer must find it to have a double meaning which indicates that the politician has failed to understand how the civil servant uses language and, hence, is in danger of being dominated by his subordinate.

If this account of the root joke of 'Yes Minister' is reasonably accurate, it follows that in this series the politician is depicted as the potential source of change but that, as a result of his own inadequacies and the skilled inertia of the Civil Service, his efforts can never be successful. As the scriptwriters themselves admit, it 'remains a slight puzzle . . . that Hacker, who was such a master of blurring and obfuscation in his own political dealings, should have found such difficulty in dealing with a group of civil servants whose techniques were essentially similar. Hacker's innocence, as revealed in these diaries, is quite touching' (Lynn and Jay, 1984, p. 9). However, what the authors describe here as Hacker's puzzling 'innocence', that is, his repeated failure to recognize Sir Humphrey's guileful dishonesty, is actually an essential feature of the series. For if Hacker had ever managed to find the key to Sir Humphrey's conduct and to take control of his own ministry, the comic formula would have ceased to work and the humorous duality of Sir Humphrey's 'Yes Minister' would have disappeared.

It seems that the narrative structure of this remarkably popular sitcom is inherently static, and that the power struggle between politician and civil servant is necessarily depicted as if there can never by any effective resolution. 'Yes Minister' appears to confirm my conclusion in the previous section that a stable contrast between opposing voices is an essential feature of any successful sitcom formula. Nevertheless, despite its static character, it is still possible in principle that 'Yes Minister' may have had a significant impact on viewers' understanding of British political life and possibly, thereby, have added to pressures for political change. For the social consequences of such a cultural product are not determined by its formal structure alone.

How a television programme relates to other currents in society will be only partially dependent on its formal qualities or narrative structures. Those matters will give a clue, but no more. The fact that 'Yes Minister' has a closed or circular narrative shape is not what makes it 'conservative': it is the articulation of that structure with the implicit political discourses it draws on from 'the real world'. (Oakley, 1982, p. 77)

Oakley argues that the cultural impact of 'Yes Minister' has in fact been conservative, and could only have been conservative, because its static picture of British political life contains nothing new and is indeed very close to the view of government bureaucracy and state action that was already being emphatically promulgated by the government of the day. Contrary to the critical plaudits quoted above, Oakley maintains that 'Yes Minister' has offered no penetrating new insights into British political life, but has merely recycled, in a skilfully humorous manner, certain longstanding stereotypes which were once more in vogue in political circles. Sir Humphrey, for example, is immediately recognizable as an incarnation of the 'bureaucratic machine'.

From the very beginning, the series made great play of this popular image of endless layers of paper-pushing bureaucracy . . . The strength and durability of this stereotype of the civil service bureaucrat has been of no little significance. When Winston Churchill and the Conservatives finally defeated the 1945–51 Labour Government there had been much Tory rhetoric about 'setting Britain free', both from nationalisation and the kind of austerity restrictions associated in the public mind with 'men from the ministry'. From then on, with the 1950s slogan 'Conservative freedom works', through to the 1970s when Margaret Thatcher (like Ronald Reagan) was promising to 'get the Government off our backs', our political culture has been deeply infused with these notions of Government as bureaucracy. (Oakley, 1982, p. 68)

Throughout the series, the only opposition to this popular stereotype and to the Thatcherite policy of reducing public expenditure on 'bureaucracy' comes from the civil servants themselves. Inevitably, the repeated, naturalistic representation of top-level administrators as resisting, by any and every devious means, the politicians' reasonable attempts to reduce the burden of state administration, serves to confirm what non-civil servants already 'know' about their inefficiency and political chicanery. This is well illustrated in the following extract from Hacker's supposed diary, where we, unlike the 'innocent' politician, are encouraged to draw on the popular stereotype in order to understand what is happening and to see its humorous meaning.

> The Doctrine of Ministerial Responsibility is a handy little device conceived by the Civil Service for dropping the Minister in it while enabling the mandarins to keep their noses clean. It means, in practice, that the Civil Service runs everything and takes all the decisions, but when something goes wrong then it's the Minister who takes the blame. 'No Humphrey, it won't do,' I interjected firmly before he could go any further. 'I prepared myself thoroughly for Question Time yesterday. I mugged up all the questions and literally dozens of supplementaries. I was up half Sunday night. I skipped lunch yesterday, I was thoroughly prepared.' I decided to say it again. '*Thoroughly prepared!*' I said. 'But nowhere in my brief was there the slightest indication that you'd been juggling the figures so that I would be giving misleading replies to the House.'
>
> 'Minister,' said Humphrey in his most injured tones, 'you said you wanted the administration figures reduced, didn't you?'
>
> 'Yes,' I agreed.
>
> 'So we reduced them.'
>
> Dimly I began to perceive what he was saying. 'But you only reduced the *figures*, not the actual number of administrators!'
>
> Sir Humphrey furrowed his brow. 'Of course.'
>
> 'Well,' I explained patiently, 'that was not what I meant.'
>
> Sir Humphrey was pained. 'Well really, Minister, we are not mind-readers. You said reduce the figures, so we reduced the figures.' (Lynn and Jay, 1984, pp. 177–8)

We do not, of course, have to take this as an accurate representation of the way that civil servants typically act. We are aware, after all, that this is meant to be a comedy and that humour is being contrived for our benefit. However, if we do take such passages to convey a serious critique, or even as having a kernel of truth, we find that we are encouraged to conclude that the popular image of the underworked and inefficient, but suave, evasive and manipulative bureaucrat is not far from the truth.

This stereotype of the civil servant, personified in Sir Humphrey, is balanced in 'Yes Minister' by that of the obtuse, ill-informed, hypocritical, yet surprisingly resilient politician. In most episodes, one or more of these largely negative attributes are displayed by Hacker and employed by Sir Humphrey to ensure the continuation of his own domination over the politician. These characteristic attributes are seldom identified explicitly in 'Yes Minister', largely because Hacker himself is on screen so much of the time (Klika, 1982). In the following passage, however, in which Sir Humphrey discusses the quality of Hacker's mind with the Master of his college, the civil servant reveals his own sense of intellectual superiority.

Master: Is he of the intellectual calibre to understand our case?
Sir Humphrey: Oh yes. Well, surely our case is intelligible to anyone
with the intellectual calibre of Winnie-the-Pooh.
Master: Quite. And Hacker is of the intellectual calibre of
Winnie-the-Pooh?
Sir Humphrey: Oh yes. On his day.
                    (Oakley, 1982, p. 74; see also Lynn and Jay, 1984, p. 230)

In this excerpt, Hacker's essential simplicity, without which his subjuga-
tion by Sir Humphrey could not be sustained, is clearly conveyed to the
audience. But despite his evident inadequacies and repeated failures,
Hacker cannot be allowed to become politically discredited. For if
Hacker's political authority were to be removed, the root joke would be
undermined. Hacker's political survival is assured in 'Yes Minister'
because Sir Humphrey always allows his Minister some way of saving face,
and because Hacker never refuses to say or do anything, no matter how
inconsistent with his previous pronouncements, in order to retain the
semblance of power. This image of the archetypal politician, bent on
furthering his own career no matter what the cost to others, is
fundamental to the series. It is, however, made fully explicit only when
Hacker and Sir Humphrey discuss a third party, Charlie Umtali, who is a
visiting African head of state with whom Hacker studied in London some
years before.

Humphrey was concerned about Charlie's political colour. 'When
you said he was red-hot, were you speaking politically?'
     In a way I was. 'The thing about Charlie is that you never quite
know where you are with him. He's the sort of chap who follows you
into a revolving door and comes out in front.'
     'No deeply held convictions?' asked Sir Humphrey.
     'No. The only thing Charlie was deeply committed to was
Charlie.'
     'Ah, I see. A politician, Minister.'
     This was definitely one of Humphrey's little jokes. He'd never be
so rude otherwise. (Lynn and Jay, 1984, p. 45)

This portrayal of politicians, like that of government bureaucrats, is
hardly novel. It is, rather, another well established stereotype which has
been employed for many years as a basis for humour. For example, Oakley
quotes the joke about ex-Prime Minister Harold Wilson, which was
current during his period of office:

How do you tell when he's lying?
When his lips move. (1982, p. 73)

This joke relies on our prior knowledge that this politician, and by implication other politicians, can never be trusted to speak honestly. Such a view of politicians is by no means confined to Britain (Galnoor and Lukes, 1985). The following Russian joke is less personal, but depends on the same implication that politicians have little regard for the truth.

What does two times two make?
Whatever the Party says. (Dolgopolova, 1982, p. 30)

Thus the portrayal of Jim Hacker in 'Yes Minister' tells us nothing particularly new about the conduct of politicians. The great achievement of the series is not that of exposing the realities of the political process to detailed scrutiny, but rather of combining quite traditional images of the 'bureaucrat' and the 'politician' to generate the contradictory discourses required as the basis for successful situation comedy.

It seems, then, that 'Yes Minister' is a naturalistic sitcom in the sense that it takes over and re-presents longstanding and easily recognizable political stereotypes which have been dressed up with elements from current political rhetoric. These resources can hardly be used to provide a biting exposé or a radical critique of political practice; and indeed, if 'Yes Minister' did attempt to do this, it is doubtful whether the mass audience would be able to decode the message or see the joke. Rather, in so far as it is taken to be true to life, this sitcom serves to confirm what the audience already knows: namely, that (some/many/all) politicians are selfish and untrustworthy, and that bureaucrats exercise too much power.

It cannot be denied that the images used to construct the narrative of 'Yes Minister' are strongly negative and, thereby, implicitly critical. But the defects that are displayed for our amusement are those with which we have long been familiar and which, as a result of the circular narrative structure of sitcom, come to appear regrettable, but unavoidable. Furthermore, the closed world of the sitcom draws our attention away from the serious consequences that may follow from political obfuscation and administrative inefficiency in the real world. In the realm of the political sitcom, what might in other contexts be taken to be real political issues appear only as plot devices. They arise in an unpredictable and fragmentary fashion from one episode to the next as temporary frameworks within which Hacker and Sir Humphrey can perform their unending, and inconsequential, dialogue.

In using the supposed defects of the state apparatus as the basis for comedy, political sitcom instructs its audience to find these defects amusing. In addition, because the audience is aware of the contrived nature of comic discourse, its members are unable to distinguish unambiguously between accurate reportage and humorous exaggeration.

In the following passage from the published 'diaries', the authors' added comment in brackets reveals a serious intent behind the comedy.

> Bernard was eager to tell me what I had to do in order to lighten the load of my correspondence. 'You just transfer every letter from your in-tray to your out-tray. You put a brief note in the margin if you want to see the reply. If you don't, you need never see or hear of it again.'
>
> I was stunned. My secretary was sitting there, seriously telling me that if I move a pile of unanswered letters from one side of my desk to the other, that is all I have to do? (*Crossman had a similar proposition offered, in his first weeks in office – Eds.*) (Lynn and Jay, 1984, p. 33)

In the editorial comment, Lynn and Jay communicate to the reader that the amusing proposal made by Bernard to Jim Hacker was based on an actual experience reported by the politician Richard Crossman. In the written text, the intention to depict a genuine incongruity in the practice of the Civil Service is made reasonably clear. But in the version which appeared on the television screen, the editorial comment would have been absent and the attempt at factual revelation would have been obscured by its necessarily allusive humorous form. In other words, the 'ludicrous' suggestion that the Minister's main task was to move unanswered letters from one side of his desk to the other could be taken to be, not accurate portrayal, but typical comic distortion. Thus, even when 'Yes Minister' is apparently intended to convey a serious message, the effectiveness of that message is likely to be undermined by its location in the humorous mode.

I have argued that 'Yes Minister' reaffirms longstanding political stereotypes in a way which makes them appear inevitable and without serious consequence. I have also suggested that genuine representations of incongruities in the administrative process will tend to be contradicted by the repeated signals of humorous intent that are required in the television sitcom. The sitcom audience is never allowed to forget that it is being entertained. Even when the performance is reasonably naturalistic, the audience is encouraged to laugh and to keep on laughing. In so far as laughter and amusement are substitutes for serious political action, it seeems likely that action designed to produce political change will be stunted rather than stimulated by the political sitcom:

> the historical trajectory of a series like 'Yes Minister' . . . has been to absorb these disquiets and render them harmless, as timeless inevitabilities. It does so by a kind of removal of history as a process. The characters in 'Yes Minister' have no real relationship to the past,

nor to the future. Each episode ends as it begins, at a moment of perpetual balance; no change has occurred and – it is implied – no change is really possible. (Oakley, 1982, p. 77)

The overall effect of this political sitcom seems to be that of confirming an existing negative image of the political process whilst, at the same time, discouraging recipients from undertaking remedial action.

If this is true of 'Yes Minister', which seemed on the surface to adopt an unusually critical approach to its subject matter, it is likely to be equally true of the great majority of television sitcoms. It seems reasonable to conclude, therefore, that if sitcom has any serious consequence, it is probably that of social conservation. This is in line with the general argument developed in the previous section that mass broadcasting tends to require a product which expresses and confirms those views that are most firmly established among the population at large. However, it can still be argued that this conclusion does not necessarily hold for all forms of mass produced humour. It may be, for instance, that television sitcom has little serious impact because it is too far removed from the social and political domains which it represents. It may be that the negative images of political life created in 'Yes Minister', for example, are politically impotent because the sitcom is merely entertainment and is not itself a part of the political realm. In order to explore this possibility, it is necessary to examine a form of mass humour which is actually embedded within the political process. In the next chapter, therefore, I will consider the relationship between serious political life and the political cartoon.

11

Humour and Political Action

Cartoons which appear as part of the public debate over current political issues in newspapers and satirical journals contribute directly to the world of real politics, and it is with such cartoons that I will be concerned in this chapter. Real politics, as opposed, say, to sitcom politics, is dominated by serious issues, serious actions and serious discourse. Political cartoons are, by their very nature, connected to those serious concerns. When a cartoon is presented or interpreted as political, its meaning is necessarily derived in part from the sphere of serious political conduct. Political cartoons acquire their meaning by taking elements from this sphere and by transforming them in accordance with the requirements of the humorous mode. This transformation can be modest or it can be radical. But it must always be possible for recipients to make some kind of serious reading by linking the cartoon to the wider political context of which it forms a part.

The message of the political cartoon

Political cartoons, then, necessarily allude to serious topics, and the political cartoon is, in this sense, a form of applied humour. Lawrence Streicher emphasizes this in his reflections on the need for a theory of political caricature, when he writes that political cartoons have 'claims to truth as do other forms of art which attempt to represent and reflect reality . . . Caricature *interprets* nations, figures and events and helps us to supplement the news presentation with statements of "meaning"' (1967, p. 438). Streicher's basic point here is, I think, correct. Yet if cartoons are a vehicle for political truth-claims, we must ask why these claims come to be presented in such a peculiar and ostensibly unrealistic way: that is, in the form of largely visual images which are not even subject to the usual conventions of naturalistic representation and are clearly intended to be amusing. In other words, why are 'political truths' so often communicated by means of a mainly visual and comic medium? And how far does this form of visual humour succeed in conveying serious political messages?

Let me begin to deal with these issues by asking one further question: namely, what kind of serious message is contained within the political cartoon? The answer is, at least in part, reasonably clear. For the message of the political cartoon is known to be overwhelmingly negative and critical (Streicher, 1967). In this formal respect, political cartoons resemble the political sitcom. However, the former are not commenting on the political process from outside, but are actually engaged in that process. Thus each political cartoon conveys its own 'truth' by humorously deconstructing a political claim seriously advocated by, or denouncing a political action undertaken by, some other party. The negative, oppositional character of the discourse of political cartoons has been widely recognized in the secondary, analytical literature, as well as in cartoonists' and other participants' descriptions of the genre. Streicher, for example, in the course of his theoretical review, maintains that political cartoons 'deal with the ridicule, debunking or exposure of persons, groups and organizations engaged in power struggles in society' (1967, p. 432). Participants in the political process frequently adopt a similar view of the critical, and serious, import of political cartoons. The following statement is taken from the British newspaper the *News Chronicle* in 1936, and refers to the work of the cartoonist David Low:

> The greatest cartoonist of our time, though sometimes playful, is rarely merciful. Politics is not a game. It is a serious business which, for good or evil, affects the daily life of every man, woman and child in the land; and for those who mismanage the business and stifle the hopes of the people there can be no quarter.
>
> That, it seems to me, is how Low approaches a task, which he accomplishes with a master's touch. (Streicher, 1965, p. 7)

Such opinions are echoed by the cartoonists themselves. The next example is from the American James Campbell Cory, who was active in the early part of this century.

> In dealing with political situations and with the men and forces involved, the cartoonist finds his greatest source of inspiration and usefulness. Satire is his strongest weapon, and if keenly directed, he can give his victim a more deadly thrust in one simple but deftly pointed and extensively circulated drawing than can the writer of a dozen articles. No one can portray in words the sinister hypocrisy of a politician as a cartoonist can blazen it in a well thought out and strongly executed picture. (1920, p. 12)

Most professional cartoonists have claimed, like Cory, to be using their visual talents to draw attention to the ills of society and to the errors and crimes of those in positions of political responsibility (Hess and Kaplan, 1968; Walker, 1978; Scarfe, 1982); and when we examine the actual cartoons, these characterizations are confirmed. For it is clear that they do, in the great majority of cases, debunk, ridicule and criticize in a fairly obvious way (see Hines, 1933; Alba, 1967; Coupe, 1967; Streicher, 1965, 1966). I cannot carry out an extensive empirical analysis here, but let me illustrate how political cartoons achieve this end by discussing the two examples reproduced below. The first of these, 'Reagun' by Scarfe (see below) refers to American political life; the second, 'Whoops' by Garland (p. 200) deals with politics in Britain.

We saw in previous chapters that standardized jokes are able to circulate widely because they are anonymous. They can be understood and appreciated by many unrelated people because they depict the actions of stereotyped social categories rather than those of individuals. The same is true of a political sitcom such as 'Yes Minister'. Hacker and Sir Humphrey become known to viewers as particular characters, but they do not openly depict any specific civil servant, politician or political party (Oakley, 1982, p. 76). Political cartoons, in contrast, although they too are distributed to a mass audience, tend to be highly personalized. Like the two examples here, they represent and focus upon the actions and statements of particular actors on the political scene. Cartoons constructed

"WHOOPS!"

in this way are accessible to a large, diverse audience because the views, actions and, today, physical appearance of these individuals are already widely known from their participation in serious politics.

Because political cartoons depend for their material on current political personalities and events, it is impossible for those who are not closely familiar with the relevant political culture to appreciate their humour or their serious significance. For example, I am sure that most non-British readers will have some difficulty in understanding 'Whoops'. In order to see the point of this joke, one has to realize, in the first instance, that the figures in the car represent the British Prime Minister at the time of publication, Mrs Thatcher, and a leading right- wing member of her cabinet. This is confirmed by the vehicle's number plate, which uses the common abbreviation 'HMG' to indicate that the car is equivalent to Her Majesty's Government. Secondly, the reader needs to know that the phrase 'No U turns' had been widely used to depict the government's supposedly unswerving commitment to a policy of vigorous reduction of public spending. Thirdly, the cartoon depends on the reader's prior knowledge that the government has just overturned its own procedures for distributing 'cold weather benefits', and had authorized payment from the public exchequer to certain categories of elderly people and other low-income groups of sums of money intended to help them buy fuel during a period of exceptionally bitter weather. Each of these elements was 'common knowledge' at the time. They were parts of a broader political scenario which were selected by the cartoonist and rearranged together to form the script for his humorous text (Raskin, 1985a). Finally, although no mention of forthcoming elections is made in the cartoon, it was generally assumed at the time of publication that the government would call a general election later in the year, and its unexpected concession to the needs of the poor was said, by some, to be no more than a cynical attempt to win the approval of the electorate.

Gerald Scarfe's cartoon 'Reagun' is equally difficult to interpret without background knowledge of President Reagan's views on private ownership of firearms in the USA. The representation of the President as a gun and the Reagun's advocacy of people's 'right to kill' are relatively unproblematic, if the reader is aware of the attempts made during Reagan's first presidential term to limit the sale and private ownership of such weapons, and of the President's involvement in the defeat of the anti-firearm campaign. However, Scarfe's treatment of this political issue is even more condensed and abstract than Garland's handling of 'cold weather benefits', and, as a result, the cartoon can also be read as a more general condemnation of Reagan's militaristic inclinations and of his support for the more aggressive tendencies in American Society. The cartoon can also, of course, be taken to allude to Reagan's having played 'gunslinger' parts during his film career. Whichever reading of 'Reagun' is chosen, it is clear that, as in the case of 'Whoops', the humour is constructed out of semantic resources taken from the serious domain and transformed into a humorous text that can be read as strongly critical.

There are at least three related ways in which cartoons such as these operate to criticize, undermine, challenge or devalue the actions of the politicians whom they represent. In the first place, they do this by means of visual distortion. In 'Reagun', for example, we are offered a likeness of the President. Yet, at the same time, the presidential image is grotesque and ludicrous. In (mis)representations of this kind, the respect and approbation which is often given to leading politicans, at least on official occasions and by members of their own party, are made to seem sadly out of place. By means of gross physical caricature, cartoons create political figures which are bound to act stupidly, venally and/or maliciously. Thus the Reagun image necessarily imples a president who, by his very nature, must behave in an aggressive, wantonly destructive manner. As the butt of the gun informs us, this is a president who is unthinkingly 'macho'. Similarly, the representation of the Prime Minister as a flustered, pop-eyed, panic-stricken 'woman driver' carries with it the necessary implication of political vacillation and incompetence. These observations help us to begin to understand why cartoons are used to convey political messages, and why political cartoons are so frequently highly personal in character. The reason is that the distorted visual representation of wellknown political figures is an effective technique for placing their actions and statements in an alternative, and inevitably unfavourable, context. Through his control over his subjects' physical appearance, the cartoonist is able to depict them in such a way that their failures, improprieties and sins are immediately understandable as the inevitable products of their most basic characteristics.

Political cartoons also devalue the actions and policies of the people they represent by removing them from the serious domain and by placing them in a realm inhabited by the fictional characters of mass humour. In cartoons, politicians take on some of the characteristics of creations such as Popeye and Donald Duck. Thus Scarfe, for example, in other cartoons has made Prime Minister Thatcher merge with the Tin Man and President Reagan with Mickey Mouse (Scarfe, 1982). In the political cartoon, however, the figures depicted can never become wholly fictitious or entirely humorous. For recognizable images of the powerful within the serious political sphere are an essential part of the text. The political cartoon blurs the boundary between serious politics and the realm of humour. It thereby enables and encourages its readers to 'see the funny side of' their rulers' activities. But there is always some implicit reference to their actions in the real world, and one effect of such cartoons is to question whether these actions are not more suited to the world of comedy. In the political cartoon, the conduct and policies of leading figures are reformulated and displayed so that they can be seen to be both real and ludicrous, both serious and laughable.

The political cartoon, like humour in general, always sets its reader a puzzle. The 'meaning' of the cartoon is never made fully explicit. Background knowledge of the political scene, of current affairs and of the conventions of cartoon humour, must be used to interpret the clues provided in the text. As in all humour, the components of political cartoons are organized bisociatively to create semantic oppositions which the reader must decode. These oppositions inevitably operate to undermine the position of one or more of the politicians involved and to reveal an alternative view which is implicitly advocated in the text of the cartoon. This process of semantic reversal is the third way in which political cartoons adopt a negative or critical stance in relation to their subjects.

The bisociations and semantic oppositions employed in 'Whoops' are fairly straightforward. In the first place, political action is represented visually by, or bisociated with, the act of driving a car. This representation is made particularly appropriate by the metaphor of 'No U turns'. Garland cleverly extends the bisociation by drawing a sheet of ice to represent the government's decision to pay 'cold weather benefits' when it was not formally required to do so. It is made clear, visually, that the sheet of ice threw the car out of control and that the Prime Minister and her colleague are now heading back the way they came. To put the message of the cartoon more succinctly, the government that says it is committed to 'No U turns' has in fact made a U turn. In other words, the semantic opposition at the heart of 'Whoops' reveals a contradiction between what the government says it is doing and what it has actually done.

As we saw above, politicians are regularly accused of lying, and Hacker's activities confirm this accusation in general terms. But in the political cartoon, unlike the political sitcom, the charge of intentional duplicity can be, and is routinely, levelled at specific political actors. Thus, the humorous incongruity of a cartoon like 'Whoops' can have serious implications in so far as it is taken to coincide with, and reveal, a genuine incongruity in the conduct of the government. As we saw in previous chapters, the discourse of speakers in the serious world is organized to avoid inconsistency and internal contradiction. In contrast, humorous discourse is designed to create these very features. Political cartoons are constructed in a way which bridges this divide. They are designed, like 'Whoops', as texts which display humorous incongruities and contradictions that directly parallel those to be found in the world of serious politics. The semantic contradictions which are correct and to be expected in the realm of humour have unavoidably negative implications when they are also taken to refer, as they necessarily are in the case of political cartoons, to particular actors in the serious domain.

The basic, visual bisociation in 'Reagun' is even more obvious than in 'Whoops'. For in Scarfe's cartoon, the President has actually become a gun without ceasing to be Mr Reagan. The semantic contrast, however, is much more subtle in this cartoon. Unlike 'Whoops', the text here does not offer the reader two evident and clearly opposed scripts. In 'Reagun', there is no glaring contradiction between the speaking gun and what the gun says. Indeed, one would surely expect a *gun* to insist on the primacy of the right to kill. Thus, if one treats the spoken component in 'Reagun' as being uttered by a gun, there is no humorous incongruity at all. However, because this is a bisociated text, the gun is also President Reagan who, the text implies, has never spoken *quite* like this – at least in public. In other words, the text of 'Reagun' is ironic. It implies the existence of some other serious text or texts which are to be reinterpreted in the light of the ironic text.

In order to read this text as humorous, as a cartoon, one has to contrast what is said here with the President's public pronouncements on the issue of firearm control. The reader is required to remember or to assume serious references by Mr Reagan to citizens' rights to self-defence, to freedom of choice, and so on, which can be, and which should be, translated into the more sinister and frightening utterance of the Reagun figure. The semantic contradiction of 'Reagun', then, lies in the implied opposition between what the President says in public and what his policy, and perhaps the man himself, really means. As in 'Whoops', and in political cartoons generally, 'Reagun' employs the semantic contrast required in humour to give voice to criticism of a major participant in the real world of politics, whose position is undermined by the counter-claim implicit in the organization of the text. Scarfe's cartoon suggests that *this* is what the President really means and what the President really means is ludicrous.

The discussion of these two cartoons has been brief and incomplete. My aim has been merely to illustrate how the oppositional and bisociative structure of humorous texts can be used to communicate to a mass audience serious attacks upon the activities of politicians. Now that I have shown how this is accomplished, I must consider why political cartoons take this particular form and what contribution they make to political life. In other contexts, humour can be pure and playful. Why is it that political cartoons are so uniformly and blatantly negative? My answer to this question stems from the previous observation that political cartoons are closely integrated into serious political discourse. It follows, I suggest, that they are oppositional and negative because political discourse generally is markedly adversarial in character.

Yah-boo politics and yah-boo humour

The phrase 'yah-boo politics' is taken from Max Atkinson's (1984) study of the rhetorical devices used in political speeches. It refers to a situation in which the 'leading parties continually throw insults at each other' (1984, p. 44). Atkinson shows that political life in Britain is organized around an asymmetrical distinction between 'us' and 'them' which is employed by all political parties; and that political discourse is overwhelmingly designed to express approval of and support for each speaker's 'us', whilst condemning and denouncing 'them'.

Atkinson's work has been confirmed and extended by Grady and Potter (1985) and by Heritage and Greatbatch (1986). The latter authors examined in detail the 476 speeches delivered at the three main British political party conferences in 1981. They extracted every statement which received collective applause at the conferences and allocated these statements to appropriate categories. They found that 'applause was reserved for a relatively narrow range of message types' (1986, p. 119). More specifically, three quarters of applauded political messages were either attacks upon an 'out-group', expressions of support for a group to which the speaker belonged, or some combination of the two. Furthermore, Heritage and Greatbatch report that critical statements were twice as likely to be applauded as supportive or constructive ones. They suggest that there is a marked tendency towards 'audience negativism' at such political rallies.

These empirical studies show very clearly that serious political discourse in Britain operates within 'the overarching "us and them" framework of national party politics' (Heritage and Greatbatch, 1986, p. 120) Approval of one's own political grouping combined with denigration of others' views and actions appears to be a basic structural principle within political language. These studies also establish that, even when politicians gather to confer with the members of their own party, the discourse is strongly negative in tone. It seems likely that in other important political contexts – for example, when politicians of rival parties debate together – this critical edge will be even sharper. Furthermore, although the studies cited above deal exclusively with Britain, there can be little doubt that political discourse is structured in a similarly oppositional fashion in the other 'democratic' societies of Western Europe and North America.

One way of making sense of this situation is to assume, as a first approximation, that members of different political groupings understand political events in significantly different ways. It is self-evident, I suggest, that people with different political commitments tend to employ divergent interpretative frameworks to formulate the character of the events in which they are involved. In this sense, the actors subscribe to different political realities; they inhabit divergent political worlds. For example, in relation to the issue of poverty, one set of actors may define the poor as responsible 'for their own plight and in need of control to compensate for their inadequacies, greed, lack of self-discipline and so on' (Edelman, 1977, p. 6). Alternatively, other actors may regard the poor 'as victims of exploitative economic, social, and political institutions' (Edelman, 1977, p. 6) and as in need of liberation rather than control. Of course, such background assumptions are never uniformly endorsed throughout any large political grouping. Indeed Edelman, in his study of political language, stresses that each individual is likely to make use of different assumptions in relation to a given issue on different occasions or in different circumstances. Participants' access to a range of divergent frameworks, he argues, 'makes possible a wide spectrum of ambivalent postures for each individual and a similarly large set of contradictions in political rhetoric and in public policy' (1977, p. 7). Thus each political grouping is characterized, not by a coherent interpretative consensus, but by a series of overlapping political vocabularies and, most of all, by a sense of common group membership.

Edelman is correct to draw attention to the range of variability within the discourse of specific political actors. But the last statement quoted in the previous paragraph is misleading if it is taken to imply that this variability necessarily gives rise, of itself, to 'ambivalent postures' or to 'contradictions in political rhetoric'. After all, each speaker typically insists that his own position is entirely consistent – as indeed he must do when subject to the requirements of the serious mode. Such 'ambivalences' or 'contradictions' in political discourse are, I suggest, almost always identified as such by some other speaker, and usually by a member of another political grouping where some opposing interpretative configuration is predominant. It is not that political discourse is characterized by certain specific and inherent inconsistencies. It is rather that the language of politics is uncertain and open-ended in such a way that participants' actions and claims, diagnoses and proposals can always be revised and challenged by a speaker employing an alternative arrangement of commonly available interpretative resources. 'Contradictions' and 'inconsistencies' constantly reappear within political discourse because one of the fundamental aims of those involved is to reveal the inadequacy of others' claims and the superiority of their own.

Language is an effective medium for political communication and action . . . not because it is neutral but because it is relatively uncontrollable and so hard to monopolize. Whatever biases I impart to the medium, it is hard for me to prevent others not merely from imparting their own biases but actually from using my imparted biases to construct and impart their own. (Pocock, 1984, p. 33)

It is impossible here to examine in detail the complexities of serious political language. The central point that I wish to make is that its interpretative diversity, combined with its adversarial character, leads to continual deconstruction of each grouping's discourse by its opponents, whose own discourse is then deconstructed in its turn. This process is documented copiously in Atkinson (1984), Grady and Potter (1985) and in Heritage and Greatbatch (1986). Fundamental to the process is the representation of some other speaker's version of the world as unreliable, illusory or not to be taken seriously. It is in the course of this kind of deconstructive display that serious political discourse often crosses into the humorous mode. The following example is taken from a speech at a party conference in Britain:

Conservative politician: The Labour Prime Minister and his colleagues are boasting in this election campaign that they have brought inflation down from the disastrous level of twenty-six per cent. But we are entitled to inquire who put it up to twenty-six per cent?

Audience: *(laughter and applause for 8 seconds)*

(Atkinson, 1984, p. 41)

In this passage, the Conservative politician elicits hearty laughter as well as enthusiastic applause from his audience by, first, formulating a self-congratulatory claim supposedly made by the opposing party and then suddenly transforming the interpretative context of the claim and, thereby, its meaning. The sudden change of context is the source of the humour. At the same time, however, it operates to reveal the 'true character' of that claim – that is, as the kind of one-sided misrepresentation that Conservatives have come to expect from their opponents. Because the interpretative configurations employed by the members of different parties are systematically discrepant, not only are participants constantly forced to reinterpret each other's assertions, but they often have great difficulty in accepting that their opponents are acting and speaking honestly and without conscious intent to deceive.

This recurrent doubt about others' good faith underlies much political humour and can sometimes give rise to humorous texts in which one's adversaries are depicted as cynically inventing politically potent stories. The following example of this form of humour is taken from the satirical journal *Private Eye*. It purports to represent a lead story in a strongly Conservative and anti-Labour daily paper.

MAGGIE SAVES CHILD'S LIFE
by Lunchtime O'Booze

'Its all in a days work,' said Mrs Thatcher today after rescuing a small child from the path of an oncoming Inter-City train yesterday.

The incident took place in the imagination of a *Daily Mail* journalist earlier today when he had been instructed by his Editor to 'come up with something good' for the early edition. (*Private Eye*, no. 560, 1983)

In the next column of the '*Daily Mail*', in contrast, an ex-leader of the Labour party is reported to have savagely assaulted a ninety-one-year-old woman as he went on a walk-about. The humour here is particularly significant because it is directed at the basic interpretative practices by means of which the asymmetrical representation of 'us' and 'them' is reproduced in the media of mass communication. Through radical exaggeration and the use of various humorous cues and semantic reversals, the very process of political reportage is made to appear laughable.

The serious assumption behind the joke from *Private Eye* is that the newspaper being parodied is utterly committed to supporting the Conservative Party and to undermining support for the Labour Party by means of systematic misrepresentation. In Britain, virtually every daily and weekly paper is wedded to a political party – in most cases to the Conservative Party. It is in this context that British political cartoonists perform their craft. In other countries, the link between the press and political parties may be less direct. But, in general, the task of the modern political cartoonist is to give expression, in graphic, humorous form, to the political views of his employer.

> In rare cases (e.g. Nast in *Harper's Weekly*) cartoonists have played an important role in deciding editorial policy, occasionally they have enjoyed a sort of 'fool's freedom' – one thinks of Low with his anti-Establishment outlook on the conservative Beaverbrook's *Evening Standard*. More commonly, however, they have probably gravitated to newspapers which roughly corresponded to their own outlook and there more or less toed the editorial line, or like the unfortunate Will Dyson of the *Daily Herald*, paid dearly for their freedom: few editors can afford to lose favour or circulation in the interests of a cartoonist's freedom of expression. (Coupe, 1969, p. 82)

It has been argued that the frequency and impact of political caricature varies from one era to another in accordance with the degree of political conflict (Streicher, 1967). This may have been the case in the past, when cartoons were printed and distributed individually, and when cartoonists were relatively independent agents. But today cartoonists are, in most cases, contractually committed to producing a given number of cartoons per annum in accordance with the political line adopted by their newspaper (Coupe, 1969; Walker, 1978). Thus the products of present-day cartoonists are firmly embedded within the institutionalized discourse of the political realm. It is for this reason that they reproduce so closely the asymmetrical, adversarial structure of the wider domain of political discourse. On the surface, the political cartoon appears to be part of the rhetoric of persuasion employed by mass journalism. For each cartoon seems to reformulate some aspect of serious political life so as to reveal its 'real' meaning. Yet there is considerable doubt among analysts and participants about the persuasive effect of political cartoons. Thus Coupe, having noted the apparent impact on practical affairs of Thomas Nast in America and Sir David Low in Britain, concludes: 'We never really know exactly what the impact of a given cartoon was on a given reader or group of readers' (1969, p. 83).

Although this cautious conclusion is doubtless correct, it is possible to offer a less tentative account of the contribution made by cartoons in general to political life. It is reasonably clear, in the first place, that the primary audience for political cartoons is the audience for the newspaper of which they form a part. This audience, we know, will be strongly inclined in favour of the political stance normally adopted by that newspaper and endorsed by its cartoonist. As Walker writes, in his *Daily Sketches: A Cartoon History of British Twentieth-century Politics*: 'Cartoonists today tend to work for one main newspaper, with a clearly defined readership and a clearly defined political line' (1978, p. 24). It seems to follow that the message conveyed by political cartoons will tend to coincide with and to confirm the political presuppositions of their initial audience. They may also, of course, give their readers a certain mild amusement, and sometimes perhaps a sense of delight, by depicting their political opponents in unflattering terms. They will also, in order perhaps to avoid becoming too predictable, occasionally make fun of the political grouping to which they owe allegiance. But on the whole, political cartoons, like the speeches at party conferences, are addressed to the converted and are designed to strengthen, and reaffirm, recipients' political commitment rather than to change it.

It is true, of course, that the mass audience for political cartoons is far from uniform, and that cartoons will sometimes be read by people with quite different political views and commitments. But such readers are unlikely to be persuaded against their will by interpretative work carried out in the humorous mode. For the serious import attributed to any cartoon will depend on the frame of reference within which its political meaning is construed. Consequently, cartoons can be easily deconstructed and their apparent message transformed or disregarded. For example, it is possible for recipients to give a positive value to elements which must be taken critically if the humour is to work. In the case of 'Reagun', this could be done by endorsing the right to kill and by treating the President's machismo as a quality to be admired. On this reading, the text would involve no internal contradiction and would, indeed, cease to be funny. Similarly, Mrs Thatcher's apparent change of political direction in 'Whoops' could be taken as a genuine response to the special problems faced by the poor and elderly during exceptionally cold weather, arising out of her natural generosity of spirit, and as being in no way incompatible with her overall commitment to the reduction of public spending.

Read in this way, the two cartoons would still be recognizable as jokes. But they would be seen to be mere humorous contrivances with no serious significance (Gruner, 1976). Such a response to humorously coded messages is always possible. Thus use of the humorous mode is unlikely to be persuasive because its content is heavily dependent on such interpretative work and because, by its very nature, it can always be defined as unworthy of serious consideration. Unlike the political sitcom, the serious intent of the political cartoon can hardly be missed. Nevertheless, the use of the humorous mode enables recipients to reject any critical message on the grounds that the text relies unduly on the distortions typical of humour; or, more colloquially, that it is just a 'cheap joke'. It is perhaps for this reason that most cartoonists make very modest claims for the persuasive power of their own products. Thus Gerald Scarfe, who is generally acknowledged to be one of the most powerful of modern cartoonists (Coupe, 1969, p. 90), confesses sadly: 'I have no feeling that any cartoon has ever changed the course of events' (1982, p. 13).

In the course of this discussion, we have seen that the semantic structure of the political cartoon appears at first sight to be designed to challenge, question and change the conduct of affairs in the serious political realm. On closer inspection, however, this has come to seem an illusion. Institutionalized political humour is derived from, and dependent for its meaning upon, the established pattern of serious political discourse. It seems likely that political cartoons serve to confirm existing views and to strengthen the established political structure rather than to undermine it. Indeed, it may be that such organized, repetitive political humour contributes to a sense of political apathy which actually makes it easier for our rulers to continue to exercise political domination in the customary manner.

Far from tearing the deceitful mask from public figures and holding up a warning finger to the reader, the tendency is to represent serious political problems in humorous allegorical guise and to invite us to laugh at our political predicaments, thereby in a way robbing them of their reality, or at least cocooning us from the horror in a web of gallows humour. (Coupe, 1969, p. 90)

In the last two chapters, I have chosen to combine an investigation of the mass production of humour with an examination of two forms of political humour. I have approached mass humour by way of its political variants because I wished to make an assessment of the social impact of mass humour and because it seemed that political humour would be most likely to have such an impact. Broadly speaking, I have come to the conclusion that both political sitcom and political cartoons, in so far as they have any significant political consequences, tend to conserve rather than to subvert the existing patterns of political life. My appraisal of mass produced humour has undoubtedly been selective and incomplete. It seems, nevertheless, to establish a prima facie case in favour of the conclusion that mass humour in general, even when its surface content may appear to be critical, tends to maintain and preserve the structures of serious discourse and conduct within which it is embedded.

In our inspection of political sitcom we saw that this conservative impetus is due to the creation of a humorous form designed to provide regular light entertainment suitable for a mass audience. Because political sitcom employs fictitious characters and is only indirectly related to the serious political arena, it generates its humour by constructing a balanced interplay of stereotyped figures which tends to imply the inevitability of the present system, despite its defects. Political cartoons are more centrally involved in the real political process. But the result of this direct political participation is that they come to reflect the asymmetrical structure of serious political discourse and to give expression to the views of established political groupings.

As we saw in chapter 9, the more closely is humour incorporated into existing social structures, the more it comes to maintain those structures. We have seen in the present chapter that this is as true of mass humour as it is of humour in situations involving direct interaction. Political cartoons seem more likely to strengthen than to undermine participants' political commitments, and they appear to reinforce the entrenched divisions within the political community. It seems unlikely that they work in any significant way to alter prevailing political practices.

These conclusions tend to confirm the impression that has been emerging during the last three chapters that humour is predominantly a conservative, rather than a liberating or constructive, force in society. Consequently, we are faced with another 'paradox of the humorous mode'. For although humour appears to be a radical alternative to serious discourse in the sense that it is socially separated from the serious mode and is organized in terms of contrary discursive principles, it seems in practice overwhelmingly to support and reaffirm the established patterns of orderly, serious conduct. In the course of the last chapter, I will consider why this is so.

12

The Mute Voice of Humour

Why is there such a thing as humour? Why does it occur in all known societies? Could humour take a different form? In this chapter, I will offer some broad speculations that bear upon such questions. It is clear that I cannot proceed by discussing humour in isolation. For the existence of the comic can be understood only by looking first elsewhere, that is, at the nature of our serious social world. For humour is, in its purest form, an inverted image of that serious world, and it arises as a response to the difficulties that inevitably occur in the course of the socially coordinated production of the serious domain.

Humour and multiple realities

As we saw in chapter 2, people's ordinary, everyday discourse is organized around principles of coherence and uniformity. By attending to these principles, participants are able to sustain the sense of living in a unitary world that is shared by all. But coherence and uniformity are not inherent characteristics of the social world. They are, rather, the precarious outcome of our use of the serious mode and are constantly under threat from the dynamic processes of social interaction. In the last chapter, for example, we saw how the members of different political groupings endorse strikingly divergent views of the social world in which they live. In such circumstances, each participant maintains the assumption that he inhabits the same world as others by denouncing those who disagree with him as mistaken and incompetent (Gilbert and Mulkay, 1984; Heritage, 1984). He speaks as though others inhabit *his* world without realizing it. Of course those others, committed by the use of the serious mode to the same assumption that there is only one reality even though there are many contradictory accounts of it, respond in a like manner and recurrently deconstruct his understanding of that supposed reality.

The existence of multiple formulations of the one shared-in- common world is not confined to the realm of politics. It occurs wherever there are differences of social position and of social experience. Mothers formulate the world differently from their daughters, wives from their husbands, men differently from women, judges from defendants, hosts differently from guests, nurses from their patients and Nobel laureates differently from non- laureates. Furthermore, each person moves frequently from one social position to another and from one social context to another. On each occasion, their use of the serious mode and their formulation of the social world are likely to change, sometimes dramatically (Halliday, 1978). In other words, the basic structures of social differentiation that occur in all societies generate a potential babble of discrepant voices, each of which speaks as if its particular version of the world is the real world within which all other voices have their being (Gilbert and Mulkay, 1984).

I will not attempt here to substantiate this view of social life as a complex of opposing realities (see Goffman, 1974; Gilbert and Mulkay, 1984; Mulkay, 1985; Potter and Wetherell, 1987). Nor will I describe how many of the problems caused by the interpretative multiplicity of social life are resolved by participants without departure from the serious mode (see Pollner, 1975; Heritage, 1984). The point I wish to emphasize is that, if this view is accepted, it appears that ordinary social activities depend overwhelmingly on a mode of discourse which is critically flawed, in the sense that it denies the multiplicity of social life and is consequently in constant need of repair (Garfinkel, 1967). It is, I suggest, this discrepancy between the basic assumptions of the serious mode and the multiple realities of social life that makes the maintenance of mundane interaction such a demanding and skilful accomplishment (see Atkinson and Heritage, 1984). One of the skills which we all acquire, to varying degrees, is that of employing humour to help deal with the problems of multiplicity and contradiction, incongruity and incoherence which are built into our organized patterns of social action and which persistently threaten to disrupt the course of our serious social activities (see chapter 9). It is this basic flaw or contradiction in the serious mode of discourse that is, in my view, the ultimate source of humour. Humour occurs because mundane, serious discourse simply cannot cope with its own interpretative multiplicity.

In the domain of humour, the multiplicity of the social world does not have to be denied. The contradictions, incongruities and deviations implicit in the serious realm are the very basis for its existence. In this alternative mode, these problematic features are humorously exaggerated, creatively contrived and celebrated enthusiastically. When we adopt the humorous mode, we are able to give voice to the deficiencies of serious social life and of our serious procedures of language-use, whilst at the same time disregarding them. By signalling that we are abandoning the serious mode, we indicate that there is a legitimate region of the social world in which the requirements of that mode are inapplicable. Having signalled our departure, we are not obliged to take seriously whatever follows; that is, we no longer have to employ a unitary, internally coherent speech. In the world of humour, what before were problems to be overcome are now resources to be exploited, added to and enjoyed. The implicit multiplicity of social life is transformed from a threat into a potentiality to be realized and explored with others.

As we saw in chapter 10, participants sometimes maintain that humour helps us to recuperate from the tensions of the serious world. There seems no doubt that humour is often a source of relaxed enjoyment from which we emerge refreshed (see chapter 6). But, as participants, this observation seldom leads us to consider why being 'non-humorous' is such a strain. My suggestion is that speaking and acting in the serious mode is a continual problem for us all because the unitary principles of serious discourse conflict with the underlying multiplicity of social life, and because each social actor's serious discourse is in recurrent danger of being deconstructed by those with whom he deals, and undermined by his own interpretative variability (Gilbert and Mulkay, 1984; Potter and Wetherell, 1987).

Humour furnishes a realm of safety and release from these problems. The existence of the humorous mode enables participants periodically to enter a domain in which the features suppressed with difficulty under normal circumstances are allowed free rein. Thus when we set out to enjoy ourselves, to be convivial, as at a Thanksgiving dinner, we are inclined to suspend the requirements of the serious mode and to engage frequently in what I have called 'pure humour'. Continual activity of this kind is pleasurable, and participants often become increasingly animated when humorous interaction is prolonged (see chapters 3 and 9). This is presumably because some of the constraints of serious interaction have been removed, and because a whole range of new interpretative possibilities has been made briefly accessible. When viewed from outside, the world of humour is a world of discursive privilege. It is no accident that entry into the humorous mode is often represented as requiring a transformative passage: for example, through a door, a hole or a looking glass (Nash, 1985, p. 108). This is symbolically appropriate because, on the other side, the onerous duty of maintaining a unitary world-view has been replaced by the joyous creation of multiple realities.

The social origins of laughter

We can never know for certain how humour came into existence or why it is so closely linked with laughter. But there is nothing to prevent us from speculating about such issues in the light of the detailed discussion carried out in previous chapters. It seems likely that laughter, or something like laughter, was once employed by our ancestors as a sign of deference and submission in the course of serious interaction (see chapter 6). This leads us to consider what connection there might have been between deference and submission and what we now call humour. As we have seen, the characteristic features of humorous language tend to create conflict and misunderstanding when encountered unexpectedly in the course of serious interaction. It seems likely that when such difficulties arose during the early evolution of ordinary, everyday language, they were experienced as disturbing and as potentially threatening by those involved.

If this is so, it is possible that, when contradictions, ambiguities, incongruities, and so on occurred inadvertently, and when the serious mode seemed to be in danger of breaking down, participants made use of the customary sign of non-aggression to indicate that no offence was meant and that the apparent breech of the unitary mode should be accepted as having no serious consequences. In other words, it may be that laughter and smiling came to be employed to mark off such discourse as being not intended in the usual way and, in this sense, as non-serious. With the passage of time, we may suppose, participants came to realize that this subordinate, derivative mode of discourse was permanently available and could be adopted more or less at will; and that it made possible a form of sustained interaction which employed regulative principles radically opposed to, and much less restricting than, those operative in the ordinary world.

This line of argument provides an alternative to Koestler's account of the function of laughter and humour; that is, laughter comes to be seen, not as a physical mechanism whereby aggressive energies are released, but as a signal which accompanies and facilitates adoption of an alternative form of discourse. This alternative mode is functional in the sense that it provides participants with an enjoyable release from the restrictions of serious discourse, and also in the sense that it helps them to deal effectively with certain kinds of recurrent interactional difficulty. The fact that laughter appears, on occasion, to burst forth in an involuntary manner does not mean that it is essentially different from other forms of social interchange or that it can only be understood and explained at the physiological level. As we saw in chapter 6, laughter has to be seen as a critical part of the symbolic domain. It is an essential sign which we use skilfully to register, and to coordinate, our movements into and out of radically different modes of interaction.

Once adoption of the humorous mode has become a matter of choice, it is essential that participants are able to distinguish humour from serious discourse. If participants' entry into this mode is not properly communicated, the ensuing interaction is put in jeopardy and recipients are likely to be bewildered and to respond with irritation. As we saw in chapter 3, an elaborate repertoire of cues has evolved for this purpose. With their help, we are able to sustain a form of interaction that is distinct from the serious domain and to create contradictions and incongruities which can be taken to be separate from that domain. In this alternative world, we can engage in humour that is pure in the sense that it is generated in playful pursuit of the semantic multiplicity which becomes available once the restraints of serious discourse are removed. As we noted in chapter 4, much humour seems to be accepted by participants as having no serious consequences. Humour of this kind is enjoyed or, minimally, acknowledged as a form of non-serious discourse that is legitimate in its own right.

Nevertheless, we have seen time and again that the boundary between the serious and humorous modes is highly ambiguous and that participants make use of this ambiguity for serious purposes. Because the language of humour is necessarily implicit and allusive, and because its signals mean that serious intent can be easily denied, social actors regularly use the humorous mode, not as a self-contained alternative to serious discourse, but as a useful resource for accomplishing serious tasks. In many situations, participants make use of the discursive licence of the humorous mode to perform various kinds of serious interactional work. When this happens, humour becomes directly subordinated to the demands of the serious domain, despite its symbolic separation.

Humour as a subordinate mode

We have seen in several chapters that the more integrated the two modes of discourse become, the more completely is humour shaped by the established patterns of the serious domain. This is the case, I suggest, because there is a fundamental imbalance between the two modes. This is revealed linguistically in a variety of ways. For instance, genuinely humorous utterances, participants say, do not have to be 'taken seriously' because the speaker was 'only joking'. But there are no equivalent phrases to express the humorous irrelevance of serious talk. It simply makes no sense to point out that serious remarks do not have to be 'taken humorously' because the speaker was 'only being serious'. The reason for this is that our basic perspective on the world is couched in the unitary terms characteristic of ordinary, serious interaction. It is this perspective that defines for each of us 'the real world' – a world which, we assume, we share with those around us. The realm of humour, in contrast, has no such substance, no countervailing reality. Humorous discourse is fundamentally derivative. It is created by means of playful reinterpretation of resources taken from the serious domain. Consequently, when bartenders, cartoonists, politicians, and the rest of us, make use of humour in the course of our serious activities, or even in our sustained attempts to create humour for pure enjoyment, our humorous formulations inevitably reflect to a considerable degree the substantive social assumptions built into our primary form of discourse.

Another factor in the subordination of the humorous mode is the apparent unsuitability of its discourse as a basis for practical action. It is our serious discourse that appears to be designed to facilitate action and control. When we employ the serious mode, although we may accept that the world is diverse and complex in many respects, we assume that behind its superficial disarray there is a single, coherent and organized reality. This reality poses puzzles, difficulties and dangers. Within the framework of assumptions of the serious mode, however, it is taken for granted that we can understand how this world works and that its puzzles can, at least in principle, be solved by systematic manipulation of our symbolic and practical resources. In our everyday, serious language-use and also in such specialized discourses as those of politics, economic activity and science, we presume that there is one real world which is independent of our language, but which is open to representation and control by means of language. Because the world created by use of the serious mode is taken to be unitary, organized and predictable, it is this mode which we use to identify appropriate courses of action and which we adopt when we choose to act upon the world and to attempt to control it.

In contrast the humorous mode, as we know it, is essentially a marginal discourse of withdrawal and multiplicity. Within the realm of humour, it is accepted that 'reality' is constantly changing, that various contradictory 'worlds' can coexist, and that it is through our active use of language that these 'realities' are created and made to alter. When seen from the outside, however, these 'worlds' and 'realities' come to seem unreal, and they have to be signalled as such by, for instance, the use of quotation marks. In our everyday world, humour is a form of play rather than an engagement with the practical realities of life.

Because serious discourse is geared to action and control, and humour to inaction and withdrawal, the serious mode necessarily comes to dominate when the two discourses are brought together. As we saw, for example, in the examination of sexual and political humour, the resources of humour are regularly taken over and used in the pursuit of serious objectives. It is, of course, equally true that the symbolic resources of the serious world are absorbed within the humorous domain and used there for humorous purposes. But in the borderland between the two modes, it is inevitable that the language designed for action and control will come to dominate. That language will necessarily express the established system of social relationships operative within the serious world, and will be employed in ways which reflect the patterns of social control to be found there.

The paradox of serious discourse

We have seen in previous chapters that the operation of the humorous mode generates a series of inconsistencies or, as I have loosely termed them, paradoxes. It is important to understand that these paradoxes appear to be problematic only in so far as we insist on judging the humorous domain by the criteria of serious discourse. Within the frame of reference of the humorous mode itself, it would be inconsistent or paradoxical only if inconsistencies and paradoxes were entirely lacking. Ultimately, therefore, it seems that the existence of these inconsistencies makes the humorous mode internally 'consistent'. Given that we are dealing here with humour, it should not surprise us that this ultimate consistency is itself inconsistent with the requirements of humorous discourse, and that we have arrived at yet one more paradox of the humorous mode.

Put in these terms, my reasoning seems to lead towards an infinite regress. But this can easily be avoided if I step back and summarize with the conclusion that the humorous mode is formally adequate in the sense that my appraisal displays the kind of interpretative duality that is essential to humour; that is, depending on where we stop, humour is found to be either consistently inconsistent or inconsistently consistent. The reader may think that this is mere sophistry, no more than playing with words. But this is to be expected when we try to assess the coherence and formal adequacy of the humorous mode within its own terms.

I also suggest, however, that humour is satisfactory in a more substantive, and a more sociologically significant, way: namely, in the sense that the interpretative openness of humour seems more accurately to reflect or reproduce or allow for the multiple realities of the social world. In this important respect, humour seems to be superior to ordinary, serious discourse, which is premised on an implicit denial of the fact that we live in a world of multiple meanings and multiple realities. It seems, therefore, that the serious mode is seriously defective. Its fundamental presupposition appears to be wrong and to be inconsistent with the demonstration of social multiplicity which its very use has made possible.

I realize that not everyone will be willing to accept that we inhabit, not one shared-in-common world, but a diversity of ever-changing worlds. Furthermore, I have to admit that my claim does give rise to major interpretative difficulties. For instance, my proposal that reality is manifold, given my use of the serious mode, is inevitably a unitary claim. It seems to deny the validity of alternative versions of the world and thereby, implicitly, to deny the viability of other realities. Like other serious speakers, I seem to be asserting that social life is the way I say it is. My very act of speaking seriously seems to presume the existence of a unitary world independent of my speech (Mulkay, 1985). I seem to be involved in a self-contradiction whereby my claim regarding the existence of multiple realities denies the validity of other contrary claims and thus implies the existence of but one reality – namely, mine.

This contradiction can, of course, be taken to undermine my claim. This is certainly the customary response to what is sometimes described as 'sociological relativism' (Doyal and Harris, 1986). However, I want to suggest an alternative view: that the lack of consistency arises, not from the falsity of the claim, but from the inadequacy of the mode of discourse within which it is formulated. The underlying problem is, I suggest, that the serious mode is not a neutral medium for making sense of the world. It involves positive assumptions about the world, the most fundamental of which is that there is one, real, unitary world that can be described without paradox and inconsistency. Given that the discourse of the serious mode is organized around this premise, any serious claim which challenges it will inevitably encounter problems of consistency – particularly when the claim is turned upon itself and its own necessarily unitary character is revealed. These problems, however, do not necessarily mean that the claim is wrong. They are, rather, built into the very structure of our serious discourse and are a sign of its inherent limitations.

I wish to argue, therefore, that the serious mode itself is subject to a basic and unavoidable inconsistency. Moreover, within this mode, such a defect cannot easily be ignored. Given the demand for consistency, it is difficult to feel comfortable with a mode of serious discourse which leads to conclusions about the world that contradict its own taken for granted assumptions. Consequently, it is a matter of some concern that this fundamentally flawed form of discourse and action should be so dominant within our culture. The danger is that we have become almost completely blind to the limitations of the serious mode, and that we have come to mistake what are only the tacit assumptions of our discursive practice for real features of an independent world. Furthermore, because the serious mode provides our 'discourse of reality', its use has inescapable consequences in our world.

The most important of these, in my view, is that it generates a language of domination and opposition rather than, let us say, a language of collaboration and accepted diversity. The fact that each speaker assumes that the real world speaks through *his* voice means that the legitimacy of alternative versions of events is continually denied. This is not only the case in everyday life, but is also characteristic of powerful specialized forms of discourse such as those of politics and science. In short, our language and our culture are pervaded by a form of language-use that requires us all, including our rulers and our purveyors of knowledge, to assert our own privileged access to reality, whilst placing us in a social world where that privilege must, to varying degrees, be constantly challenged and undermined.

Humour and the world of paradox

This brief account of the 'paradox of the serious mode' is meant as no more than a sketch. I have tried merely to hint at what I see as the fundamental danger of undue reliance on our serious mode of discourse. The major weakness of my warning is, of course, that there seems to be no *practical* alternative. As I have pointed out, the serious mode as we know it seems to be designed to enable us to relate to, and to control, the world in an organized manner. If we were to relinquish the assumption that we are able correctly to formulate *the* pattern of events around us, if we were to abandon ourselves to the recognition that other contradictory formulations are equally viable, it might appear that we would be permanently confused and utterly unable to act upon the world. Furthermore, even the consolation of laughter, it seems, would be denied us. For in a social world where multiplicity, contradiction and incongruity were normal and built into the dominant mode of discourse, the interpretative accomplishments of humour would no longer strike us as unexpected or amusing.

It may, at first, seem inconceivable that social life could continue if the characteristics of serious and humorous discourse were fundamentally different. Yet this almost self-evident conclusion may seem so obvious only because we have failed to think imaginatively enough – that is, we have not tried hard enough to envisage what could happen if we were to change the basic presuppositions of our discourse. For instance, if what we now call the humorous mode *were* dominant, it would have become the *serious* mode. In this new world, the criteria of semantic adequacy would be radically different. In particular, genuine claims about the nature of that world would not be acceptable *unless* they generated inconsistency, incongruity or paradox, or in some way revealed or acknowledged the multiplicity of the world. Moreover, a mode of humorous discourse would still exist. It would occur, for example, when people inadvertently or consciously implied that some event or action had a unitary meaning. When this happened, people would signal their recognition that the remark was not to be taken 'seriously' by responding with smiles and laughter.

Such a world, of course, seems bizarre to us. It may read like the germ of an idea for a sitcom – with very restricted appeal. But there seems to me to be nothing inherently impossible about such a form of social life. It is inevitable that *we* find it difficult to imagine how participants could choose and act within that world. It is difficult for *us* to understand how they could decide to do one thing rather than another. But this very formulation of the problem is couched in our typically unitary terms. For these actors, acting seriously would necessarily involve them in recognizing the multiple character of their actions, in accepting that those actions were necessarily open to diverse, opposing construals. Our objections would seem to them a somewhat ludicrous misrepresentation. They would be inclined, being themselves 'serious folk', to ask whether we were trying to be funny.

It is particularly difficult for us to imagine how the members of such a 'relativist culture' would deal with the practical side of human affairs. How, for example, could they cope with the task of repairing a defective motor car or curing a dangerous illness? It seems to me unlikely that in a fully fledged culture of multiplicity the technologies of transport or medicine would at all resemble those with which we are familiar. It does seem likely, however, that the practical side of life would have to be treated with what participants themselves would regard as levity. In other words, they would approach practical activity by means of their humorous mode; that is, they would employ a coherent, organized, unitary discourse. This use of a unitary humorous mode to perform practical action would be analogous to our use of a multiple humorous mode to accomplish certain kinds of awkward interactional tasks. In this mirror-image culture, the comparatively organized, orderly and predictable realm of practical action would not be taken very seriously.

It may appear that I am teetering on the edge of *our* humorous mode. If so, I am making use of it for serious purposes. I am trying to suggest that the humorous mode as we know it, despite its subordinate position in our culture, should not be regarded as an inherently inferior form of discourse. In its purest form, it constitutes a radical alternative to the way in which we create our ordinary social world. As this world is organized at present, what we know as humour is unavoidably subordinate to the dominant mode of discourse. It operates, as we have seen, to buttress and support the established patterns of social life. But its existence serves as a constant sign of the failures, inadequacies and limitations of our serious world and of the pattern of language-use by means of which we produce that world. The multiplicity of the humorous domain, even though it is restricted by its surrounding context, reminds us that the world in which we live is not exhausted by any one set of meanings; and certainly not by those which happen to be dominant in our own society. Understood in *this* serious way, humour can be seen to be a potentially liberating force.

As you will have come to expect, my text ends in yet more paradox. For my final claim has been that, although humour is moulded by the serious mode and shaped in accordance with the established patterns of social life, it nevertheless stands as a perpetual reminder of the inadequacies of our social world and as an indication of our limited understanding of it. This 'paradox' could be taken to reveal a serious weakness in my analysis. However, I prefer to regard it, more comfortably, as showing that I have not sought analytical mastery over the realm of humour; that I have tried, not only to reveal something *about* humour, but to learn something *from* humour as well.

One important lesson I have learned is not to be unduly cowed by paradox and inconsistency. These features are not always the result of our own mistakes. On some occasions, they may even be due to the basic features of our common modes of discourse. Furthermore, if our serious attempts to understand the world inevitably end in inconsistency and paradox, if in this sense the world *is* paradoxical and inconsistent, it may be foolish to insist too emphatically on a form of knowledge that seeks to avoid these characteristics. If we come to the conclusion that the world is fundamentally contradictory and in this sense comic, we may be well advised to try to create a form of serious discourse which is suited to that idea. It may be, therefore, that if we are to deal successfully with the multiple realities of the social world, we will have to devise a new kind of analytical language which resembles in certain critical respects what I have called the 'humorous mode' (Ashmore, 1985; Mulkay, 1985; Pinch and Pinch, 1988; Woolgar, 1988). The aim of developing an alternative form of discourse designed to achieve a more accurate representation of the social world would of course be, from the multiple perspective of the new discourse itself, essentially paradoxical. For this reason, we may be reasonably confident that it would improve our ability to understand the paradoxical world in which we live. Such a discourse might help to establish a serious context in which we could, at last, begin to respond appropriately to what is at present the mute voice of humour. In the words of the quotation with which this text began, perhaps the crucial task for those of us in search of truth is to create a way of communicating which will enable us 'to make people laugh at truth, *to make truth laugh*'.

References

Alba, Victor 1967: The Mexican revolution and the cartoon. *Comparative Studies in Society and History*, 9: 121–36.

Alvarado, Manuel and Buscombe, Edward 1978: *Hazell: The Making of a TV Series*. London: British Film Institute.

Apte, Mahadev L. 1985: *Humor and Laughter*. Ithaca and London: Cornell University Press.

Ashmore, Malcolm 1985: *A Question of Reflexivity*. D.Phil. thesis. University of York, England.

Atkinson, Max 1984: *Our Masters' Voices: The Language and Body Language of Politics*. London and New York: Methuen.

Atkinson, J. Maxwell and Heritage, John 1984: *Structures of Social Action*. Cambridge and New York: Cambridge University Press.

Austin, J.L. 1962: *How to Do things with Words*. Oxford: Clarendon Press.

Bamforth's Saucy Postcard Annual 1977. London: Pan Books.

Bartlett, Rachel (ed.) 1982: *Off the Wall: A Collection of Feminist Graffiti*. London and New York: Proteus Books.

Bateson, Gregory 1955: A theory of play and fantasy. *Psychiatric Research Reports*, 2: 39–51.

Bergson, Henri 1911: *Laughter: An Essay on the Meaning of the Comic*. New York: Macmillan.

British Broadcasting Corporation Handbook 1980. London: British Broadcasting Corporation.

British Film Institute 1982: *Television Sitcom*. London: British Film Institute.

Brittan, Arthur and Maynard, Mary 1984: *Sexism, Racism and Oppression*. Oxford: Basil Blackwell.

Bruner, Edward M. and Kelso, Jane Paige 1980: Gender differences in graffiti: a semiotic perspective. *Women's Studies International Quarterly*, 3: 239–52.

Cantor, Joanne R. 1976: Humor on television: a content analysis. *Journal of Broadcasting*, 20: 501–10.

Chapman, Antony J. 1976: Social aspects of humorous laughter. In Antony J. Chapman and Hugh C. Foot (eds), *Humour and Laughter: Theory, Research and Applications*, London and New York: Wiley, 155–85.

—— 1983: Humor and laughter in social interaction and some implications for humor research. In Paul E. McGhee and Jeffrey H. Goldstein (eds), *Handbook of Humor Research*, New York: Springer-Verlag, 135–57.

Cook, Jim, 1982: Narrative, comedy, character and performance. In *Television Sitcom*, London: British Film Institute, 13–18.

Cory, James Campbell 1920: *The Cartoonist's Art*. Chicago: Prang Publishing Co.

Coser, Rose Laub 1960: Laughter among colleagues: a study of the functions of humor among the staff of a mental hospital. *Psychiatry*, 23: 81–95.

Coupe, W.A. 1967: The German cartoon and the revolution of 1848. *Comparative Studies in Society and History*, 9: 137–67.

—— 1969: Observations on a theory of political caricature. *Comparative Studies in Society and History*, 11: 79–95.

Curtis, Barry 1982: Aspects of sitcom. In *Television Sitcom*, London: British Film Institute, 4–12.

Davies, Christie 1982: Ethnic jokes, moral values and social boundaries. *British Journal of Sociology*, 33: 383–403.

—— 1987: Language, identity, and ethnic jokes about stupidity. *International Journal of the Sociology of Language*, 65: 39- 52.

—— 1988: *Jokes are about Peoples*. Indiana: Indiana University Press.

Dolgopolova, Z. (ed.) 1982: *Russia Dies Laughing: Jokes from Soviet Russia*. London: André Deutsch.

Douglas, Mary 1968: The social control of cognition: some factors in joke perception. *Man*, 3: 361–76.

—— 1975: *Implicit Meanings*. London: Routledge & Kegan Paul.

Doyal, Len and Harris, Roger 1986: *Empiricism, Explanation and Rationality*. London: Routledge & Kegan Paul.

Drew, Paul 1986: Po-faced receipts of teases. Unpublished paper, University of York, England. *Linguistics* (1987), 25: 219–53. (Page references in the text are to the unpublished manuscript.)

Eaton, Mick 1981: Television situation comedy. In Tony Bennett, Susan Boyd-Bowman, Colin Mercer and Janet Woollacott (eds), *Popular Television and Film*, London: The Open University Press, 26–52.

Eco, Umberto 1984: *The Name of the Rose*. London: Pan Books.

Edelman, Murray 1977: *Political Language: Words that Succeed and Policies that Fail*. London and New York: Academic Press.

Emerson, Joan, P. 1973: Negotiating the serious import of humor. In A. Birenbaum and E. Sagarin (eds), *People in Places: The Sociology of the Familiar*, London: Nelson, 269–80.

Fine, Gary Alan 1983: Sociological approaches to the study of humor. In Paul E. McGhee and Jeffrey H. Goldstein (eds), *Handbook of Humor Research*, New York: Springer-Verlag, 159–81.

—— 1984: Humorous interaction and the social construction of meaning: making sense in a jocular vein. In *Studies in Symbolic Interaction*. New York: JAI Press, 83–101.

Flaherty, Michael G. 1984: A formal approach to the study of amusement in social interaction. In *Studies in Symbolic Interaction*, New York: JAI Press, 71–82.

Freud, Sigmund [1905] 1966: *Jokes and their Relation to the Unconscious*. London: Routledge & Kegan Paul.

Fry, William F. 1963: *Sweet Madness: A Study of Humor.* Palo Alto: Pacific Books.

Galnoor, Itzhak and Lukes, Steven (eds) 1985: *No Laughing Matter: A Collection of Political Jokes.* London: Routledge & Kegan Paul.

Garfinkel, Harold 1967: *Studies in Ethnomethodology.* Englewood Cliffs, NJ: Prentice-Hall.

Gilbert, G. Nigel and Mulkay, Michael 1984: *Opening Pandora's Box: A Sociological Analysis of Scientists' Discourse.* Cambridge and New York: Cambridge University Press.

Goffman, Erving 1961: *Encounters.* New York: Bobbs Merrill.

—— 1974: *Frame Analysis.* New York: Harper & Row.

Golding, Peter and Murdock, Graham 1977: Capitalism, communications and class relations. In James Curran, Michael Gurevitch and Carrie Roberts (eds), *Mass Communication and Society*, London: Edward Arnold, 12–43.

Grady, Kevin and Potter, Jonathan 1985: Speaking and clapping: a comparison of Foot and Thatcher's oratory. *Language and Communication*, 5: 173–83.

Grice, H.P. 1967: Logic and Conversation. Unpublished MS of the William James Lectures, Harvard University.

Gruner, Charles R. 1976: Wit and humour in mass communication. In Antony J. Chapman and Hugh C. Foot (eds), *Humour and Laughter: Theory, Research and Applications*, London and New York: Wiley, chapter 13.

Hall, Frank 1974: Conversational joking: a look at applied humor. *Folklore Annual of the University Student Association*, 6: 26–45.

Halliday, M.A.K. 1978: *Language as Social Semiotic.* London: Edward Arnold.

Hancher, M. 1980: How to play games with words: speech-act jokes. *Semantics*, 9: 20–9.

Heritage, John 1984: *Garfinkel and Ethnomethodology.* Cambridge: Polity Press.

Heritage, John and Greatbatch, David 1986: Generating applause: a study of rhetoric and response at party political conferences. *American Journal of Sociology.* 92: 110–57.

Hertzler, Joyce O. 1970: *Laughter: A Socio-scientific Analysis.* New York: Exposition Press.

Hess, Stephen and Kaplan, Milton 1968: *The Ungentlemanly Art: A History of American Political Cartoons.* New York: Macmillan.

Hines, Edna 1933: Cartoons as a means of social control. *Sociology and Social Control*, 17: 454–64.

Hobbes, Thomas [1651] 1914: *Leviathan.* London: Dent.

Independent Broadcasting Authority Annual Report, 1983–4. London: Independent Broadcasting Authority.

James, William 1950: *Principles of Psychology*, vol. 2. New York: Dover.

Jefferson, Gail 1979: A technique for inviting laughter and its subsequent acceptance declination. In George Psathas (ed.), *Everyday Language: Studies in Ethnomethodology*, New York: Irvington Publishers, 74–96.

—— 1985: An exercise in the transcription and analysis of laughter. In T. van Dijk (ed.) *Handbook of Discourse Analysis*, London: Academic Press, vol. 3, 25–34.

Johnson, Robbie Davis 1973: Folklore and women: a social interactional analysis of the folklore of a Texas madam. *Journal of American Folklore*, 86: 211–24.

Klika, Deborah 1982: A note on textual analysis. In *Television Sitcom*, London: British Film Institute, 80–6.

Knott, Blanche 1985: *Outrageously Tasteless Jokes*. London: Arrow Books.

Koestler, Arthur 1964: *The Act of Creation*. London: Hutchinson. Page references are to the 1966 edition, London: Pan Books.

Kramarae, Cheris (ed.) 1980: *The Voices and Words of Women and Men*. Oxford: Pergamon Press.

—— 1981: *Women and Men Speaking*. Rowley, Mass.: Newbury House.

Leacock, Stephen 1937: *Humour and Humanity: An Introduction to the Study of Humour*. London: Thornton & Butterworth.

Legman, Gershon 1968: *Rationale of the Dirty Joke: An Analysis of Sexual Humor*. New York: Grove Press.

—— 1975: *No Laughing Matter: Rationale of the Dirty Joke*, (second series). New York: Breaking Point.

Leonard, Diana 1980: *Sex and Generation: A Study of Courtship and Weddings*. London and New York: Tavistock.

Lovell, Terry 1982: A genre of social disruption? In *Television Sitcom*, London: British Film Institute, 19–31.

—— 1986: Television situation comedy. In David Punter (ed.) *Introduction to Contemporary Cultural Studies*, London and New York: Longman, 149–67.

Lynn, Jonathan and Jay, Antony 1984: *The Complete Yes Minister*. London: BBC Publications.

Malinowski, Bronislaw 1929: *The Sexual Life of Savages*. London: Routledge & Kegan Paul.

Martinich, A.P. 1981: A theory of communication and the depth of humor. *Journal of Literary Semantics*, 10: 20–32.

McGhee, Paul E. and Goldstein, Jeffrey H. (eds), 1983: *Handbook of Humor Research*. New York: Springer-Verlag.

Middleton, Russell and Moland, John 1959: Humor in Negro and White subcultures: a study of jokes among university students. *American Sociological Review*, 24: 61–9.

Milner, G.B. 1972: Homo Ridens: towards a semiotic theory of humour and laughter. *Semiotica*, 6: 1–30.

Morreall, John 1983: *Taking Laughter Seriously*. Albany, NY: State University of New York Press.

Mulkay, Michael 1984: The ultimate compliment: a sociological analysis of ceremonial discourse. *Sociology*, 18: 531–49.

—— 1985: *The Word and the World: Explorations in the Form of Sociological Analysis*. London: Allen & Unwin.

—— 1987: Humour and social structure. In William Outhwaite and Michael Mulkay (eds), *Social Theory and Social Criticism*, Oxford: Basil Blackwell, 243–63.

Mulkay, Michael and Gilbert, G. Nigel 1982: Joking apart: recommendations concerning the analysis of scientific culture. *Social Studies of Science*, 12: 585–613.

Nash, Walter 1985: *The Language of Humour: Style and Technique in Comic Discourse*. London and New York: Longman.

Nobel, Les Prix 1979 (Published annually). Stockholm: Almquist & Wiksell.

Oakley, Giles 1982: Yes Minister. In *Television Sitcom*, London: British Film Institute, 66–79.

Obrdlik, Antonin J. 1942: 'Gallows Humor' – a sociological phenomenon. *American Journal of Sociology*, 47: 709–16.

Osborne, K.A. and Chapman, A.J. 1977: Suppression of adult laughter: an experimental approach. In Antony J. Chapman and Hugh C. Foot (eds), *It's a Funny thing, Humour*, Oxford: Pergamon Press, 429–31.

Paulos, John Allen 1980: *Mathematics and Humor*. Chicago and London: University of Chicago Press.

Pinch, Trevor and Pinch, Trevor 1988: Reservations about reflexivity and new literary forms: or why let the Devil have all the good tunes? In Steve Woolgar (ed.), *Knowledge and Reflexivity*, London and Beverly Hills: Sage.

Pocock, J.G.A. 1984: Verbalizing a political act: toward a politics of speech. In Michael J. Shapiro (ed.), *Language and Politics*, Oxford: Basil Blackwell, 25–43.

Pollner, Melvin 1974: Mundane reasoning. *Philosophy of the Social Sciences*, 4: 35–54.

—— 1975: 'The very coinage of your brain': the anatomy of reality disjunctures. *Philosophy of the Social Sciences*, 5: 411–30.

Pomerantz, Anita 1984: Agreeing and disagreeing with assessments. In J.M. Atkinson and J. Heritage (eds), *Structures of Social Action*, Cambridge and New York: Cambridge University Press, 57–101.

Potter, Jonathan and Wetherell, Margaret 1987: *Discourse and Social Psychology*. London and Beverly Hills: Sage.

Private Eye, 1983, No. 560.

Radcliffe-Brown, A.R. 1940: *Structure and Function in Primitive Society*. London: Cohen & West. Reprinted 1952.

Raskin, Victor 1985a: *Semantic Mechanisms of Humor*. Dordrecht and Boston: Reidel.

—— 1985b: Jokes. *Psychology Today*, October, 34–9.

Redfern, Walter 1984: *Puns*. Oxford: Basil Blackwell.

Rees, Nigel 1979: *Graffiti 1*; *Graffiti 2* 1980; *Graffiti 3* 1981; *Graffiti 4* 1983; *Graffiti 5* 1986. London: Unwin Paperbacks.

Rigby, Peter 1968: Joking relationships, kin categories, and clanship among the Gogo. *Africa*, 38: 133–55.

Rivers, Joan 1985: *The Life and Hard Times of Heidi Abromowitz*. London: W.H. Allen.

Roche, Christine 1985: *I'm Not a Feminist but . . .* London: Virago Press.

Roy, Alice Myers 1978: Irony in conversation. Unpublished Ph.D. dissertation. University of Michigan.

Sacks, H. 1978: Some technical considerations of a dirty joke. In J. Schenkein (ed.), *Studies in the Organization of Conversational Interaction*, New York: Academic Press, 249–70.

Scarfe, Gerald 1982: *Gerald Scarfe*. London: Thames & Hudson.

Schieffelin, Bambi B. and Ochs, Elinor 1986: *Language Socialization across Cultures*. Cambridge and New York: Cambridge University Press.

Schenkein, James N. 1972: Towards an analysis of natural conversation and the sense of *Heheh*. *Semiotica*, 6: 344–77.

Schutz, Alfred 1967: *Collected Papers: The Problem of Social Reality*, vol. 1. The Hague: Nijhoff.

Sharman, Anne 1969: 'Joking' in Padhola: categorical relationships, choice and social control. *Man*, 4: 103–17.

Sherzer, Joel 1978: Oh! That's a pun and I didn't mean it. *Semiotica*, 22: 335–50.

Spradley, James P. and Mann, Brenda J. 1975: *The Cocktail Waitress*. London and New York: Wiley.

Streicher, Lawrence H. 1965: David Low and the sociology of caricature. *Comparative Studies in Society and History*. 8: 1–23.

—— 1966: David Low and the mass press. *Journalism Quarterly*, 43: 211–20.

—— 1967: On a theory of political caricature. *Comparative Studies in Society and History*, 9: 427–45.

Stubbs, Michael 1983: *Discourse Analysis: The Sociolinguistic Analysis of Natural Language*. Oxford: Basil Blackwell.

Suls, J.M. 1972: A two-stage model for the appreciation of jokes and cartoons. In J.H. Goldstein and P.E. McGhee (eds), *The Psychology of Humor*, New York and London: Academic Press, 81- 100.

Sykes, A.J.M. 1966: Joking relationships in an industrial setting. *American Anthropologist*, 68: 188–93.

Tannen, Deborah 1984: *Conversational Style: Analyzing Talk among Friends*. Norwood, N.J.: Ablex Publishing Corporation.

Thompson, John B. 1984: *Studies in the Theory of Ideology*. Cambridge: Polity Press.

Walker, Martin 1978: *Daily Sketches: A Cartoon History of British Twentieth-century Politics*. London: Granada.

Walle, Alf H. 1976: Getting picked up without being put down: jokes and the bar rush. *Journal of the Folklore Institute*, 13: 201–17.

Ward, J.P. 1979: The poem's defiance of sociology. *Sociology*, 13: 89–102.

Whyte, William Foote 1973: The social structure of the restaurant. In A. Birenbaum and E. Sagarin (eds), *People and Places: The Sociology of the Familiar*, London: Nelson, 244–56.

Williams, Raymond 1974: *Television: Technology and Cultural Form*. London: Fontana.

Wilson, C.P. 1979: *Jokes: form, content, use and function*. London: Academic Press.

Winick, Charles 1963: A content analysis of orally communicated jokes. *The American Imago*, 20: 271–91.

Woolgar, Steve 1988 (ed.): *Knowledge and Reflexivity*. London and Beverly Hills: Sage.

Wright, Edmond 1978: Sociology and the irony model. *Sociology*, 12: 523–43.

Zijderveld, Anton C. 1983: The sociology of humour and laughter. *Current Sociology*, 31: 1–103.

Index